Foreword by Kelly "SkyyFlower" Beech

100 Poems & Possibilities *for* Healing

Volume 2

I0569021

Laura Di Franco

Featuring: Melanie Barnes · M. Princess Best · Trish Brewer · Thais Conte
Jacqueline Diaz · Lyn Veneziano Fry · Stacey M. Gayer · Korinna Zoya Hunter
KaNikki Jakarta · Yantra-ji · K.J. Kaschula · Michol Mae · Pauline McGuirk-Penedo
David D McLeod · Dr. Pamela J. Pine · Jen Potter · Dr. Oliver T. Reid
Rev. Dr. Karen Schuder · Simply Sherri · Tanya Stokes · Nydia Laysa Stone
Dinahsta "Miss Kiane" Thomas · Lulu Trevena · Emily Atlantis Wolf

Foreword by **Kelly "SkyyFlower" Beech**

100 **Poems** *&*
Possibilities
for **Healing**

Volume 2

Laura Di Franco

Featuring: Melanie Barnes · M. Princess Best · Trish Brewer · Thais Conte
Jacqueline Diaz · Lyn Veneziano Fry · Stacey M. Gayer · Korinna Zoya Hunter
KaNikki Jakarta · Yantra-ji · K.J. Kaschula · Michol Mae · Pauline McGuirk-Penedo
David D McLeod · Dr. Pamela J. Pine · Jen Potter · Dr. Oliver T. Reid
Rev. Dr. Karen Schuder · Simply Sherri · Tanya Stokes · Nydia Laysa Stone
Dinahsta "Miss Kiane" Thomas · Lulu Trevena · Emily Adantis Wolf

The Brave Healer Resources Vault
Get access to free writing and business resources for author entrepreneurs:
https://lauradifranco.com/resources-vault/

DEDICATION

To my poetry family:
I love you. Keep loving. Keep writing. Keep healing the world.

FOREWORD
by Kelly "SkyyFlower" Beech

I am beyond honored to have been invited to write this foreword for such a yummy experience. Yes, a *yummy* experience. I use the word yummy because it's the word I use when my heart smiles, and I feel the giggles bubbling up on the inside and goosebumps all over my body like the warm, cozy feeling of deep satisfaction of warm pie and ice cream. I wish I could use emojis!

I'm in the energy of *100 Poems and Possibilities for Healing Volume 2.* The author poets in this book are incredible to me because they're brave in using their words to heal the world! Laura Di Franco is a special special being of light. So yummy! My heart smiles so often because she has created platforms for Brave Healers all over the world. She gives from the depths of her soul to pour out words into the world with such bravery. Laura says, "Your words change the world when you are brave enough to share them." Trust me, being a Brave Healer poet, I know without a doubt a mass healing is taking place—right now. I know it and feel it!

What you will experience in this book will encourage you to keep going, heal, and become brave yourself. I remember at a poetry open mic, a poet saying, "Poetry found me then I found me." That was profound to me.

This book is full of pure unconditional love and hope shared through intentional words of poetry and storytelling for the purpose of healing.

You'll be soulfully encouraged. You'll be engaged with the poet authors as they share their poems and stories then invite you to write with a prompt at the end of each chapter. So enjoy reading and healing through poetry.

I'm so happy for you! Be well. Be brave as your soul is "Waking up to what's possible!" It's absolutely possible to heal, live freely, and be whole. Peace and wellness be upon you and all that you love and care about.

Dear Poetry,

I unconditionally love you!

I am wholeheartedly grateful for beautiful you!

Intertwined. . .interwoven into the fabric of my very being

Catharsis. . .Metamorphosis

Healing. . .Renewal. . .Restorative

I inhale poetry. . .I exhale poetry

Dear Poetry, I so enjoy our Soul-tie, which transcends time and space.

We've always been connected it's such a yummy feeling. All the giggles and goosebumps!

Poetry with you, I am free

Poetry with you, I embrace self-care

Poetry with you, I embody self-love

Poetry with you, I heal

Poetry with you, I give and receive unconditional love.

Poetry, I love you so very dearly. Thank you for being who you are and all that you give.

What letter would you write to poetry?

Gratefully yours,

Kelly "SkyyFlower" Beech

TABLE OF CONTENTS

Introduction

Introduction

A community of poets is one of the best things in life. When you get soul-driven, passionate, heart-centered, hippie warriors of love together to share brave words, it's heaven.

Start basking now. Because you just landed here.

In this, our second volume of this gorgeous series, the poets that raised their hands (some returning and some new) came together in the spirit of healing and poured their hearts and souls onto the pages for you.

Getting this second volume of authors together completely solidified something in me: I was born to write and share my poems and be the catalyst for others to do the same. I also realized that so many of my friends were so quickly turned off by poetry because of early experiences in school. I'm here to help those who need a gentle guide back to it, to their heart and soul—to that soul speak.

The poems here aren't meant to have to be analyzed. There's no right answer. There's no test. We want you to feel something. We especially want you to feel the spark of awareness, healing, and transformation when something resonates, and maybe, for the first time in a while, you feel hope.

One line can change your life.

We've included 100 beautiful poems to explore and 25 prompts to inspire self-discovery. This is also way more than a book. It's a generous community waiting for you to reach out.

We can't wait to get to know you!

With warrior love,

Laura

Awakening

By Laura Di Franco

This fear isn't mine.

I looked seven generations behind.
The lightbulb blinded me.
Confusion disappeared.
The very straight line pointed to me.

Fear was stuck
thick-crusted and glued to my heart.
I pried away pieces for years
pulling off huge chunks of flesh
to save myself from the pain.

I discovered octopus powers.
Something brand new grew
whenever the sharks dismembered me.

All I needed was time to heal
awareness to feel
wisdom to recognize the deal
I made with God.
And I knew.

I'll be the one to alchemize the fear
into fuel.
I'll be the one to clear the line.
I'll be the one who alters time.

I floated and breathed.
I noticed crow's wings
illuminated gold on sunrise beams.
I stared into a circle of rainbow spears
shimmering in the sky.

I touched my third eye
and remembered to listen—closely.

It's time to be brave.

Chapter 1

Coming Fully Alive with Brave Words
Laura Di Franco, MPT, Publisher

My Story

Vulnerability hangover is real. Repeatedly surviving and overcoming that feeling is the path to success as a performer.

Me: *Do the Brave Healing poem for the group.*

The voice is strong. And also, I'm tired.

The other voice: *What if you fuck it up?*

I want two things—to give my author group the full-on, unapologetic, sexy, badass hippie warrior of love that I am when that poem comes through me. And I want to hide. I haven't practiced.

The voice: *You know it's a crap shoot whether you'll miss a line or not. This has to be perfect.*

Because when it's perfect, man, it's good. I fall in love with myself when that poem comes out like it's supposed to.

This is what it means to come alive with brave words. The expression is raw, authentic, and soul-driven. It's like Maya Angelou, Mary Oliver, and Tony Robbins had a baby, and I'm possessed. My posture and voice change. I'm in my body and also out. Afterward, I can't remember what happened. Sounds like drugs, huh?

I feel like more of me—my body recognizes it's what my soul came here to do. I don't care how I look, sound, or feel. I love her. I watch in awe. I'm not exactly sure who that is. I haven't spent too many years being her.

When I come down from that high, my mind sabotages it all to Hell and gone.

Imagine the area around your heart being suffocated in shrink wrap and this weird feeling of shame flushing your face and creating a shriveling pull on your solar plexus so that all there is left to do is literally cower a little in your seat: *I hope they can't see me bleeding.*

Ugh, I know. But it's that bad.

I remember sitting in the audience at an open mic. A young man took the stage and began his (very long but awesome) spoken-word poem, but then he totally forgot it and had to stop.

I palmed my chest.

When it happens to them, I feel it.

"Whoo hoo! You got it! Let's go!" The crowd lifted him up, and he finished what he could, accompanied by the clapping, snaps, hoots, and hollers. He wasn't a rookie, either. The look of disappointment on his face tugged on my heart—hard. He chose to stop, not start again.

I remember a night with my poet peers—a fundraiser.

"Oh shoot, I'm just going to start again y'all."

And I did. The second go, while a bit speedier than it should've been, worked. But it felt like a failure.

Why are we so hard on ourselves?

"You know it's okay to read, right?"

That one line KaNikki Jakarta (go read Chapter 5) shared in a poetry workshop changed my poetry life—permission to take the pressure off and read my awesome words instead of trying to memorize them.

You know what?

People clapped and snapped and loved those brave words.

And I came alive again.

Poetry helps me come alive.

The Poems

Battle Cry

a little girl
screaming in silence
the vibrations stick
and reverberate
against my heart walls
ping off my soul
dent my worth

inhibited forever
small as a habit
told I should
and made to believe
I navigate
in a much wiser body now
question things a lot

a grown woman
screaming in silence
the vibrations rip
and tear
until I pry open a path
for release
and paint it with courage

a warrior goddess
perfecting my battle cry
the vibrations soar
and spread
from my gut to the sky
from my heart to the world
from my soul to yours

The Center Of The Ring

I am gonna wake up
to the stuff of my life
I won't play small
I'm gonna do it right.

I'll feel what it's like
in the center of the ring
get my ass kicked
and show up again.

Cuz it's no real fun
to watch from the crowd
wishing I was there
shouting out loud to the world.

I am gonna play big
hear my roar
I will shine out my light
and give a little more.

I'll save seats for those
who aren't ready to play
realize their fear
gets in their way.

I will walk to the center
of that great big arena
feel what it's like
to really be seen.

I'll fight my best fight
speak my full truth
write my deep thoughts
and connect with you.

Cuz when I play large
I win the prize
a life full and rich
among the bright stars.

The best part is when
you catch my starlight
meet me in the center
help me to fight.

Alongside each other
we shine so much brighter
what we had alone
multiplies infinitely together.

A powerful force
of Warrior Love
now let's build our team
from those seats above.

Wave to your friends
and critics alike
they all want to play
they all want to fight.

Help them wake up
help them play large
help them show up
even when it's hard.

If they can't take the heat
and you are alone
show up again
show them how it's done.

I want to play
I rather stand tall
I will play large
even if I fall.

Because if there is one thing
I have learned to trust
being seen, playing big
for me is a must.

The center of the ring
waits for the warrior
come, take my hand
we'll get our asses kicked together.

Say It Out Loud

Before they vibrate
from my mouth,
the words are just thoughts
into symbols,
smushed together into sentences,
wished into meanings,
with hope for healing.

I speak them out loud
from a place deep inside
and they are sounds,
melted into rhythm,
connected with tones,
wished into a song or story,
with a hope for connection.

When they are spoken out loud
I step into my power and passion.
I feel-speak them out
and they are alive,
wished into memories
with hope of a lingering touch
on your heart.

Feel it out loud
for others who can't.
Spread your wings
for those who can't fly.
Just by trying
you will succeed
in helping.

Say it out loud
and find your voice
from the heart
to the tongue
you will speak
the language of spirit
and there will be healing.

My Performance

I love the feel
of cool dawn air in my lungs
and the promise of a poem
in a birdsong.

She tip-toes down the hall
and peeks around the corner of my heart
looking to see if the coast is clear.

With no clutter of fear to navigate
she's free
and dives onto the slip-n-slide to my soul
head first.

They dance, wriggle, and shake
bump booties
and wait for me to hear the music,
which shivers me awake
with a careful word or two.

Then, a smile.

Then a shimmy, disco-style. . .
. . . as lines flow through my pen
pouring out onto the deserted street
waking up the paper at 2 am
again.

It's party time motherfuckers!
Can't you see?
Life is meant to be loved
with everything you have
so get your ass out here
and dance!

I party a little too hard
as notes spill over the sides
onto the second and third pages;
me trying to convince my neighbors
not to be a grumpy pants
and come and dance, too.

But not everyone hears the music.

It's not our job to tune their dial.

It's our job to enjoy
what our own souls do
with the beat of that cosmic bass.
Understand the rhythm inside our own space first,
completely.
See what moves our hips and pens make
when the spotlight beams through
and we find ourselves in the middle
of the stage
unafraid, for once.

The question is. . .will you dance?

And never mind everyone else's trance.

Will you dance because you can;
take the bigger risk
that someone else is watching
and might just hear the music, too
by hearing it through you?

Oh yes,
I love to feel the promise
of a poem.

My dance.

My performance.

And the gift of the magnificence of life
pumping through my veins, waking the neighbors
again.

I wonder if they'll dance with me this time?

Dear reader, now it's your turn to write! Use the blank space below. Try not to censor yourself.

What burns to be expressed out loud? Can you start by writing a few lines here?

Laura Di Franco is the CEO of Brave Healer Productions (including Brave Kids Books and Brave Business Books), an award-winning publisher for holistic health and wellness professionals with over 89 Amazon bestselling titles.

She's a retired physical therapist, 14-time author, and third-degree black belt. More than an inspirational spoken-word poet and speaker, Laura's enthusiasm is contagious and will inspire you to bust through your purpose-driven fears. She has a mission to help you experience what's possible when you share your brave words with the world in a bigger way. The Brave Healer community is 3000+ authors strong and growing.

If she's not writing, you'll find Laura bouncing to the beat at a rave, most often with something made of dark chocolate in her mouth. Feathers are her sign.

Author-entrepreneurs will enjoy free access to The Brave Healer Resources Vault with thousands in training and master classes at BraveHealer.com

Chapter 2

Poetry, a Prescription for Life's Pain

Dinahsta "Miss Kiane" Thomas,
Poet, Performer, Safe Space Facilitator

My Story

The amplified sound of my grandmother's breathing echoed through the house, and it both comforted and petrified me. The sound reassured me that we were still doing life together, but if there was a pause, my chest would freeze as if she was falling but still holding my heart in her hand.

God, I know this is inevitable, but I don't know if I am strong enough for this.

During and after my grandmother's transition, I processed her loss through poetry. Poetry has always been medicinal for me. A self-proclaimed healer, I wrote my own scripts, adjusted the dosages, and filled my own refills. What I did not know is that my poetry would serve as a dual-action pill—helping to relieve my pain and the pain of others.

I landed like a glove into the indentations on the chaise of my sectional.

"Wait Jelly! Give me a minute. I need a minute."

My silver-haired chihuahua looked at me with her jelly bean eyes, snorted, and retreated to my feet instead of my lap, so I scrolled.

"My timeline is filled with so much happiness."

Then why do I feel so sad?

I turned to Jelly with earnest anticipation. She simply jumped into my lap as if to say, "Rub my belly and everything will be okay." She closed her eyes in bliss. I closed my eyes to barricade tears.

Am I really making a difference?

Zzzz Zzzz—That's my sister-friend calling.

"Hey, lady!" I said with all the glee I could muster.

"Hey, Kiane. How are you?"

"I'm alright. How *you* feelin' is the question?"

She took a breath, and I could hear in her voice a slight hesitation, something "The Affirmation Queen" rarely demonstrated.

"I had a moment today, Sis. Did I show you a picture of the Proton Machine? It's like something out of a sci-fi."

My heart sank at the thought of my sister-friend facing this monstrous metal machine alone, and I felt powerless to make her pain go away.

"You know, my five-foot-three self is always down for a fight, but today—today all I could think was, 'I am not strong enough for this.'"

I searched my brain and my heart for a scripture, an emotionally soothing response, or something, but a listening ear was all I had to offer. Then, to my surprise, she thanked me. My eyebrows furled in the middle of my forehead.

Thank me? For what?

"Laying on that proton table with tears in my eyes, I could hear the words of your poem in my head;

'You have no idea how strong you are.

Your legs are made of titanium…'"

At that moment, I realized that the same poetry that served as a prescription for my pain was also activated to encourage others through theirs. While poetry does not cure cancer or bring loved ones back to life, it certainly possesses the ability to assuage the pain of a weary soul and provide a gentle reminder: You are strong enough.

The Poems

Dear You

Dear You,
You have no idea how strong you are.
Your spine is made of flexi-steel,
Agile,
Shock absorbing,
never broken.
I have never spoken
of this strength before.
Not because it doesn't exist,
but because you have always closed the door
to this belief...
Your reality
laden with grief
Blinded by the insanity
that your humanity
was vanity.
Life served you up on styrofoam plates,
warmed over leftovers,
and plastic cutlery.
Fine china seemed imaginary,
but tell me,
What good is a fancy bowl
if the content is old?
You have no idea how strong you are,
how bold you are,
how unlikely to fold you are.

And while others drop and break
like those china plates,
you bend and lean,
And if at first you don't succeed

You try,
Try,
Try again
Stand up again
And Hope
Again.
Your strength is strong
like God's light on a Sunday morning.
Incredibly, you keep rising
like God's light on a Sunday morning.

You have no idea how strong you are.
Your legs are made of titanium
Bionic like an alien,
Corrosion-resistant
Fully competent
to stand
even when
you don't
understand.
Don't you get it?
I'm your biggest fan.
Not in an infatuated kind of way,
but in an everything I made was good kind of way
See, it pains me
every time you question your tenacity.
The audacity of your doubt
re-nails me to a cross of limitation.
When will you walk out
the liberation
I bled out for you
in my crucifixion?
When will you wear
the victory I gave you
in my resurrection?
When will you learn
I'm a mathematician?
Your weakness plus *My* strength

Equals perfection.
Stop saying you can't do the math
Because I'm the teacher, the tutor, and the equation.
Everything you need
you have
if you would just grasp.
Stop bowing in obeisance
to social media's meritocracy.
Better yet, bend your knee at Calvary.

Has anyone ever told you how strong you are?
That your spirit is irrepressible,
And your wins are non-refundable.
Has anyone ever told you?
That your heart is made of unbreakable feathers
And though it weathers
nearly unbearable measures,
it keeps thumping and pumping and
BEATING the charges held against it.
I know what I say is true
'cuz, Baby, I made you!

I made you with imported metal
from the invisible kettle
that the Big Dipper rested on.
I made you with the periodic table's finest.
Creating elements just for you,
defying gravity just for you.
So, when I tell you
your strength is strong,
don't dismiss me
and tell me I'm wrong.
Better yet stand up in this truth
and say it with me:

I AM STRONG!
I AM STRONG!
I am strong.

Silent Noise

(Poem first published in chapbook Syncopated Hearts ©2015)

On the bedside, I sit with her in silence.
Who knew there was so much noise in the silence?
Whispering questions,
Heartfelt I love you's
And even soul-stirring confessions –
All in the silence.

I sit with her on the side of the bed in silence.
Holding her hand
In the silence.
I can feel the undercurrent of blood flowing in her veins.
I can hear the weak metronome beat of her heart
In the silence.
I'm aware of every breath-
Hers and mine
In the silence.
At her bedside, I sit in the silence quietly screaming
In a schizophrenic frenzy;
> *Go..... Don't Go.... Go.... Don't Go.......*
> *you have to go.....*
Out of breath from this intense emotional tug-of-war,
My heart clangs against the hospital bed rails.
Who knew there was so much noise in the silence?

And when the plague lifted...

Pale, wrinkly flesh wrapped loosely
Around stiff bones
Began to unfold
Stretching tautly
As those bones stirred
Slowly from the ashes
Of social isolation
Like zombies, they stirred
Resurrecting from their
Masked graves
Peeking from latex-covered caves
They stirred
Squinting at the ball of fire in the sky
Burning their weak frames but
With welcomed dis-ease
They stood
At ease
Jangling like skeletons
Absorbing the heat from the Fire god
It was time-lapse in real time
Colorless skin turns rainbow
While empty pores fill
With memories from their yester-lives
and questions for their tomorrow-days.
Eyelids flutter uncontrollably
attempting to re-calibrate
but the only option is to calculate
this new destination
esoteric equations
trudge through mushy craniums
but who cares
because all that really matters
is the feeling of alive
the sound of the heart knocking at the chest's door

all that really matters
is the taste of fresh air on the tongue
the residual scent of a welcomed hug
all that really matters
is the glimpse of hope in the eyes of the one staring back at you
When the plague lifted.....

Stay Awhile

To the person whose heart is slipping face down in an ocean of mud
whose eyes no longer conjure movies of themselves leaping over the finish line but
rather leaping to their finished line outlined on the sidewalk below.

To the young person whose boo-boos won't go away
with mommy's kisses no matter how many times she kisses
the blood keeps dripping from wrists and inner thighs.

To the person whose imagination machine is broken
Whose ability to see life without pain ever again is choking
Coughing up their future while swallowing their will to live

To the person whose rainbows have become colorless
Whose pot of gold is diminished to a pot of coal

To the person whose peripheral vision is shot
and you can no longer see hope coming up on you

To the person whose laugh was stolen in broad daylight
To the person whose self-reported price tag is zero

To the invisible person standing center stage
with spotlight bright and eyes glued on you,

I beg your attention.
I have something to tell you.
Please listen closely and
lean in.

You were never an accident.
You were always created with purpose in mind.
The intense intention behind your creation
still brings tears to the eyes of God.
Despite what they told you
and what you told yourself,
God has a plan for you
and no tragedy,
No trauma
No travesty
can defeat the victory
That is YOU.

You are worth more than the numbers can count.
More than all the stars in the galaxy.
You matter.
You are special
not because you have a gift,
Or because of your last name,
Or who you know,
Or even the number of 0's in your account.
But because you were custom-made,
Divinely crafted,
Uniquely engineered,
One of a kind.
You are The Designer's Original.

So. . .take off your coat;
Stay awhile.

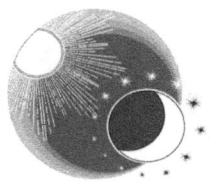

Dear Reader, now it's your turn to write! Use the blank space below. Try not to censor yourself.

Think about a time you almost threw in the towel and said, "I don't think I am strong enough for this," but you found yourself on the other side of the very thing you thought you couldn't do. Reflect and write about the who, what, when, where, and how you found strength.

As an author, performer, and safe space facilitator, Miss Kiane's first love is poetry. Published as young as seven years old, she has shared her poetry before several audiences across the United States. Miss Kiane is the Administrator of a Facebook Group called *Words on Wednesday with Miss Kiane* where she creates a virtual safe space for creatives to imagine, write, and connect. Miss Kiane's work can be found in several anthologies. The latest being *100 Poems and Possibilities for Healing*. Miss Kiane uses her skills as a poet and facilitator to inspire hope, healing, and change through her non-profit, The InkWELL.

In her words, "Poetry is my friend, my catharsis…my gift to the world."

Connect with Miss Kiane: https://linktr.ee/misskiane

Chapter 3

The Day Time Stopped

A Mother's Story of Loss and Unbreakable Love

Tanya Stokes

My Story

April 7th is a date forever etched into my mind. It's the day everything changed.

That morning, I woke up with a strange heaviness in my chest. It wasn't pain, exactly, but a discomfort, as if my heart knew something my mind couldn't grasp yet. I brushed it off, thinking it was just stress or fatigue. After all, life had been overwhelming, and my thoughts were cluttered with endless worries. Then the phone rang. I answered, "Hello?"

"Hello, beautiful! Let's go to church!" The familiar voice was cheerful, but I hesitated. *I really don't want to get out of bed,* I thought. But something inside me nudged me to go. "Sure, I'll meet you there."

I hadn't been to church in months, and my faith was shaky. I felt disconnected from God, as if He had turned away from me. Still, I felt compelled to go that morning.

When I walked into the church, I was hit with an overwhelming sense of exhaustion. I was drained physically, emotionally, and spiritually. I hoped that the service might lift the weight I carried. As the pastor began to speak, something strange happened. My eyes grew heavy, and before I knew it, I fell asleep.

I woke up startled, confused by how much time had passed. I glanced at my watch: 10:30 a.m. The service was still going, but I felt a deep sense of urgency. Something inside me said it was time to leave. I gathered my things and slipped out of the church. There was a strange pull, as though my soul was trying to catch up with something I couldn't quite understand. I didn't know why I had to go, but I knew I had to. I stepped outside, still feeling that nagging ache in my chest, still feeling not fully myself.

At 10:36 a.m., my son's life was taken from him.

I would later learn that 10:36 a.m. was the exact time of his motorcycle accident. The moment his life ended, my world stopped spinning. Six minutes after I left the church, while I was trying to make sense of my strange feelings, my son was breathing his last breath.

The timing haunts me—that I sat in church, falling in and out of sleep, while my son fought for his life. And that in those final moments, as my chest tightened and my body was overwhelmed with exhaustion, he lived his last moments. The connection is both profound and unbearable.

Why did I leave church that morning? I can only live with the knowledge that while I searched for peace, my son was taken from me. And that haunts me every single day.

April 7th was the last day I was the person I used to be, and the day everything changed. In those six minutes, my world shattered. Now, I'm left to pick up the pieces, one broken shard at a time.

The Poems

Writing has been my refuge through grief, helping me navigate the depths of loss and uncover hidden truths within myself. It's a brave endeavor to explore the recesses of one's own heart and mind. I hope you find comfort in my words.

When I Am Gone

When I am gone, don't strive to live without me.
Instead, live with my love that lingers in every breath you take.
Feel it in the wind that kisses your cheek, in the softness of a quiet dawn.
If ever you miss me, close your eyes and I'll be there,
Or find me in your shadow, dancing beside you when the sun bathes the Earth.
I am not far—never far.

Sit with me in the stillness of your heart.
Listen, and you will hear the echo of my soul entwined with yours.
I did not leave—how could I, when love has woven us together,
When our spirits have become one, inseparable?

There is no departure in love like this,
No end to what we have shared.
When I am gone, don't search for my absence—search for my presence,
In the rustling leaves, in the laughter of the breeze, in the spaces between your thoughts.
I'll be there, always, woven into the fabric of your days,
Whispering in the quiet moments, loving you from every corner of existence.

I Miss You

I miss you asking me for money,
To fix that car that never quite ran right,
I miss the way you didn't pick up after yourself,
Leaving little pieces of you scattered around my life.

I miss Vador, though I said no cats allowed,
His quiet shadow still slips through the door.
I miss you stealing my alcohol,
Though I knew, and I let it go,
Like a secret only we could share.

I miss that loud motorcycle,
Even though I cursed it under my breath,
Now, when the rumble of one rolls by,
I look for you, as if you're on your way home.

I miss the chaos you brought,
The moments, the mess, the sound.
Now, in the quiet, I hear you louder than ever.
I miss you.

777: A Path to Light

Upon my skin, the numbers rest,
A sacred mark, a silent crest.
Three sevens etched, not just for show,
But signs of change, of seeds to grow.

Through shadows dark and trials long,
I find the strength to carry on.
Each line a journey, each curve a guide,
To where the truest self resides.

777, the call of soul,
A path that leads to being whole.
With every step, I shed the past,
And in this light, I'm free at last.

A journey inward, through and through,
To find the me I never knew.
In growth, in change, I find my flight,
777, my beacon bright.

ANT 777:
Wheels of Safety, Winds of Care

In the hum of engines, where freedom rides,
A mission born, a cause that never hides.
Not just for those on two wheels that glide,
But for every soul on the road, side by side.

You planted a seed, a vision so clear,
A world where safety rides without fear.
For the rider, the driver, all who steer,
In the name of Ant, forever near.

The roar of the road is no longer wild,
It's tamed with wisdom, cautious yet mild.
With every turn, with every mile,
Your foundation stands—strong, reconciled.

In every helmet, in every light,
A reminder of the roads made right.
For in your name, through day and night,
Safety shines—bold, bright, and tight.

So let the winds carry the tale afar,
Of a legacy written on every tar.
For Ant's dream, a guiding star,
In the heart of riders, near and far.

Dear reader, it's your turn to write! Use the blank space below. Try not to censor yourself.

I feel your pain. Grief often shows up physically, as heaviness, tightness, or pain. This prompt invites you to reflect on how sadness feels in your body and how you try to soothe it.

Think about a day when grief was especially strong—what helped you cope, and what made it harder?

Tanya Stokes found her true passion in the world of graphic design. Specializing in bringing her clients' dreams to life, she excels in crafting logos, designing business cards, and creating striking book covers and websites. In 2018, she took a bold step forward, founding Compassionate Designs LLC. The choice of the company name "Compassionate Designs" reflects her unwavering commitment to delving deep into her clients' vision, understanding their needs on a profound level, and creating designs that truly resonate.

Connect with Tanya: https://compassionate-designs.com/

Chapter 4

True Rest—Deeper than an Act of Self-Care

Yantra-ji, Therapist, Artist, Author, Spiritual Teacher

Words of truth scattered
Like breadcrumbs in the forest
Show the pathway home

My Story

There can be an aversion to rest, even when our body refuses to take another step.

As a child, rest was for illness and recovery, not being able to do, get up, or join in. Rest was sleep at bedtime, preparation for an outing or late night, and sometimes rest or quiet time was a punishment.

I was taught, as a girl, teen, woman, wife, and mother, to keep going, push through, push past, endure, and encouraged to hide or disguise the monthly female cycle and need for rest. Rest was seen as weak, unattractive, unproductive, lazy, and not fun by a masculine society, ads on TV, friends, family, and partners.

It's no wonder, then, as an adult, that I had such an aversion to rest.

Maybe, like me, you too have experienced the crash and burn cycles of exhaustion and illness, forced rest, forced recovery, only to get up again and push through until there was no other option, a need to reassess and release what was keeping this unhealthy cycle in place.

What, then, really is true rest?

At first, slowing momentum to wind down, a pause, reflection, meditation, a cup of tea, a good book, some scrolling, but is this really the rest that is needed?

There is a need to pause, a total stopping, without worrying if I'll get up or do anything again.

In the process of pausing and stopping, I discover rest is deeper than an act of self-care; it's a journey home. I pause right here to discover this moment.

What is right here and now if I don't move, don't follow a thought, don't fantasize about the future, or reminisce about the past?

Here, I meet the deep center of myself, this that is still and quiet, happiness, sweet simplicity.

Ah yes, the discovery of stillness, quiet, peace, a total stopping, the incredible beauty of not-doing, a deepening in my love affair with stillness, silence, with God, and the longing of my soul to simply BE at rest.

Then the question arises—can I remain at rest, in the simple activity of life, in the turmoil of life's storm?

I'll try it and see.

Taking a breath, pausing right here, I'm deeply at rest in this moment, as I get out of this chair, walk across the room, make a cup of tea, talk with another, moving about freely in life.

Yes, this is the willingness to be here and now, deeply at rest in this moment. It builds what I call the *spiritual habits muscle*. Each moment here, allows deep rest in the simple activity of life and the ability to be at rest in the turmoil of life's storm.

There is something so simple, beautiful, and precious about the choicelessness of this—that surrender, deep rest, is the only option.

Let's discover true rest is both the pathway home and who we are.

The Poems

True Life - Freedom, Love and Joy - If ...

If ....

If you want the truth, be here

If you are willing, really listen

If you are awake, see the incredible beauty of the moment

If you love, your heart will break again and again

If you want to know the depths of love, you will let it

If you could allow this, and open, you will be held by the endless mystery of love

If you are willing, you will discover, you and love and God and all - are one

It's up to you - 'if' ...

If you really want to awaken all of humanity, are you willing awaken all of yourself?

If you want to end the pain, hurt and suffering of the world, are you willing to end all the negativity, pain and projection in yourself?

Our hearts can lead us if we are willing, this is the greatest offering

When we heal the mistake of separation and brokenness, when we awaken to our true divinity, this that is our true self our true nature

Then this is the biggest gift we can give to ourselves, each other and the world

Is it time to share who you really are and heal?

To live a life of freedom, love and joy, this is transformative - this is true life

If ....

If you want the truth, be here

If you are willing, really listen

If you are awake, see the incredible beauty of the moment

If you love, your heart will break again and again

If you want to know the depths of love, you will let it

If you could allow this, and open, you will be held by the endless mystery of love

If you are willing, you will discover, you and love and God and all - are one

It's up to you - 'if' ...

God's Endless Embrace

God's grace

is the unseen hand

that has held me

through all of life's journey

God's endless embrace

Stillness in the madness of the world

Remaining here

There is no want or need to 'take in' any more

Let me be in Silence

Let me remain in sweet surrender

The world of form obsessed with x and y and z

Endless chatter, endless motion like a ship at sea

Let me be shipwrecked here

Let me drown in the depths of love

Let me not return to the world of madness

But remain here as I am

The sweet joy of silence

In God's endless embrace

Yes, God's grace

the unseen hand

that has held us

through all of life's journey

Awakening

is the simplicity and realization

Of That

Home - Simplicity and Surrender

Am I this one
this life

How can one know

How do we look
with the mind
the heart
the body
the senses

With knowing
feeling
sensing

With what we call the life
past memory
present experiences
future projections

What about with nothing

What then can be seen
felt, heard, known
what can be relied upon

Can I look with nothing
from nothing
to nothing

Yes nothing
No nothing

Silence

Simplicity

God

Grace

This is the simplicity
The ultimate surrender
this is life
the one

To not know
and to know nothing
just this

Quiet mind, open heart
surrendered life

Nothing other than this

Home
forever here

How could I
have overlooked
this grace

The face of love
in everything

Not as thought
or as believed

Not an idea
feeling
or event

Love as all

Without moving
or grasping
or clinging

Love is discovered
not as a thing
but as being

Yes – Home

Sit Quietly Beloved

Sit quietly beloved
And notice

Sit quietly beloved
Notice where your mind goes
As you are quiet, notice the mind is not
as it moves here and there
towards enjoyment or suffering
following experiences of past and fantasies of future

Sit quietly beloved
Notice where your mind moves
and bring it back here
Attention here, awareness here, resting here
in this present moment
there is nothing to control or repress
no movement, no following, no suffering

Sit quietly beloved
Notice this moment
There is no inner dialogue
no internal conversation
The mind silent
the heart and life at peace
stillness, silence
open, aware, presence and love

Sit quietly beloved
And notice

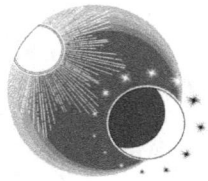

Dear reader, now it's your turn to write! Use the blank space below. Try not to censor yourself.

No matter where you are or what you are doing, you can take a micro-moment, to pause, to stop right now. Close your eyes for a moment, let your awareness rest here, breathe deeply, without all of the external engagement, and notice the beauty, the stillness, the silence that is here.

Now, as you open your eyes, notice the same beauty, stillness, and silence that remains, even as the senses are activated again. Allow the grace of silence to be the impulse that moves you, as the writing of this discovery flows out onto the page now.

Yantra-ji is the founder of Living Alignment, an in-person and online center for living a truth-filled life of freedom, love, and joy. She is a facilitator of Self-Inquiry, The Enneagram, and The Myth of Fixation Enneagram Retreat, a senior practitioner of The Journey Method, spiritual teacher, therapist, speaker, artist, illustrator, and author of 11 published books.

I support you in discovering the truth of who you are—regardless of gender, form, identity, life, or circumstances—this that you are, is always here, fresh, present, and free in every moment. In meeting together in stillness there is an opportunity to ask deeper questions, to know the truth—that we are totally free in this very moment now.

Take advantage of free resources and gifts on the website, and I encourage you to schedule a complimentary call to meet with me. Together, we will discover how I may be of true support for you.

Connect with Yantra-ji: https://livingalignment.com/

Chapter 5

Whatever You Say You Are, You're Right!

KaNikki Jakarta,
The First Black Poet Laureate of Alexandria, Virginia

You are manifesting with two words: **I** and **am.** Whatever you say after *I am* is the truth. Have you ever awakened and said, "I am going to have a bad day?" Yes? Me too!

My Story

It was March, cold, and snowing during rush hour. When you work for the hospital and are an "essential" worker, you're still expected to make it work on time, even if you live twenty-seven miles away. If you've ever driven in the DC Metro Area, you know that "rush" is not relevant, but "Hour" is the relevant word. As soon as my eyes opened and I realized it was snowing, I said immediately, "I am going to be late, and I am going to have a bad day." My usual thirty-minute drive took eight seven minutes.

I clocked in five minutes after eight. "I am so tired of coming to this place." My supervisor, Dottie, was difficult, a micromanager, and eagerly awaiting the chance to write me up.

I was cold and ready to get to my cubicle to warm up. I rolled my eyes at the ringing of my desk phone as soon as I saw Dottie's extension. There is only a three-minute grace period, even on snow days.

"Can you come to my office?"

I didn't have a choice. "Sure." I sighed. I wore a sweater with the word "Love" on the front. In healthcare, you cannot wear clothing with words on it. "See, it says it right here in our employee handbook," Dottie reminded me. "You can turn it inside out, cover it, or go home to change." She provided my options.

"I will cover it," I said, walking out before she said anything further.

I was steaming by the time I got back to my cubicle, so I immediately started to pack my personal things. *Who hates on love?*

"Sit. Down!" Ashanti demanded peering over her cubicle into mine. She is not my mother, but she sounded like her. My body reverted to childhood and responded accordingly. I quickly sat with my purse strap on my right shoulder, my car keys in my left hand, and a frown of frustration on my face

"I don't have to take this," I said in a loud whisper. "I can go home to my mama in ALABAMA!"

"Do you *really* want to go back to Alabama?" She didn't wait for an answer as she sat down at her desk.

"I am going to apply for jobs right now!"

"I am hired by another employee" was my affirmation.

"Are you okay now?" She asked.

I was better than okay; I was motivated.

At the end of the week, I had an interview. Two weeks later, I unpacked my belongings at a new job. I looked down at the sleeve on my shirt that read the word "Love" and smiled. I was in a place where no one was hating on love.

The Poems

I Am!

I am self-assertive
When I know I am right
I am love
I am light
I am shinning
Lighting the way
I am careful with the words that I say
I follow my purpose path
I know the way
I am loquacious
I am motivated
Audacious: surprisingly taking bold risks
I am adult; Not to be played with
Able to admit
When I am wrong
I am confident
I am strong
My past does not define me
I define myself
Not afraid to ask for help
Successful at birth
I've been healed, I've been hurt
And still able to know my worth
I am confident in the life that I choose
I am destined to keep win
I will not lose

Posed and Poised

I Stood…
As I watched the pieces of my life shatter and fall down at my feet
I did not cry in response
Instead, I marveled at the fact that I was still standing
I smirked at the devil and his helper's countless attempts
I watched in astonishment
Folded my arms in confidence
Inhaled
Exhaled
Waited
Until it all crashed completely
Then immediately
Stepped over what I didn't need anymore
Gathered up the pieces of learned lessons
And decided
To rebuild
Again

Mirror Talk

See something nice
See something beautiful
Don't see things that need improving
Notice the good things first
See my self-worth
Tell me I'm priceless
Don't sell me short
Don't sell me at all
Remember that I don't have to stay down
Even when I fall
Put me first
See what God meant for good
Explain myself again
When I'm misunderstood
See my dreams become reality
See it with anticipation
Make these words a manifestation
Love your self
Do it today
Say what you mean
Mean what you say
Be a good person
Be a good friend
Even if you fail at these tasks
Live tomorrow to try it again
Don't be ashamed to laugh aloud
Don't be ashamed to cry
Remember that nothing beats a failure
But a person willing to try
Remember that even in darkness
That you already know the way
Don't wait for tomorrow
Do it today
Remember to not be selfish

But do something for yourself
Put your needs ahead of everyone else
Now this may sound selfish
But remember this to be true
You can't do anything for anyone
If there is no you

Patience, Poet

Dear Poet:

When things aren't right
and you can't write
hold on tight
to your poet title
knowing that writing will return in time
when you've cleared your mind
Poetry will be near
Poetry is not impatient
When you've lost your patience or become the patient
When there is a weight on you
Poetry WILL wait for you
Like children waits on parents
when it is apparent
that you need to step away to regroup
Poetry will wait for you
Like a groom waits for his bride
Take it all in stride
Poetry will sit in a period of delay
So even if you do not write today
Poetry will wait
And wait
And wait
While you're starting a family
Starting a new job

When life is hectic
When life is hard
Through broken heartedness
To "getting over this"
Poetry WILL WAIT FOR YOU
For goodness' sake
While you're sleep and awake
When you've had all, you can take
Poetry will wait
Like a hope-ful romantic
When you're at ease or panicked
When you're taking care of yourself
When you're caregiving for someone else
Poetry will never give up on you
So, hold all of this to be true
You
Are the best thing that happened to poetry
No matter how long it has been
You will still be a poet
As soon as you pick up your pen

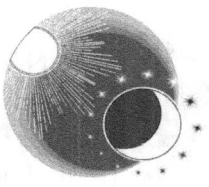

Dear reader, now it's your turn to write! Use the blank space below. Try not to censor yourself.

What are you doing right now that your older self will thank you for? Write a letter from your older self to your younger self in gratitude.

KaNikki Jakarta has been featured on NBC, WUSA9, and Comcast. She is the First Black Poet Laureate of Alexandria, Virginia. She's a Teaching Artist, Human Resource Specialist, and an Award-Winning Performance Poet. As an internationally known professional performance poet, she has toured the US and the UK. KaNikki is the Inaugural Poet in Residence for the Northern Virginia Fine Arts Association, the author of three novels, two poetry collections, a memoir, a short story poetry collection entitled *Alabama Girl, Virginia Woman* and the co-author of *The Ultimate Guide to Self-Healing, Volume II*. She facilitates a quarterly workshop entitled *Write Like a Woman* in Alexandria, Virginia, a virtual, bi-monthly workshop entitled *Prep to Publish,* and offers *Marketing and Manuscripts,* a virtual workshop for authors. She is a wife and a mother to three daughters: Trinity (Angel Daughter), Taliyah, and Selah. She can be found on social media platforms @kanikkiJ

Connect with KaNikki: https://linktr.ee/kanikkij

Chapter 6

What If. . .You're the One You've Been Waiting For?
Lulu Trevena, Artist, Soulful Living Coach, Retreat Leader

My Story

You can't simply love and light your way through the ending of a 30-year marriage. And divorce.

New, beachfront city. 60. Alone!

Long stretches of white sand and an array of blues swirled in the ocean's skirt. Unmistakably, I needed to be barefoot, sand gently exfoliating my hardened heels. My heart might have smoothed from some exfoliation had lightning not already shattered it, splintering fragments to the wind.

The vast sky, my canopy. Daily, I wandered, listening to nature's ebb and flow, rhythmic on the shore, sustaining life like a regulated breath.

The last few months were abrasively full of activity: packing, stuffing stained memories, and tarnished dreams in boxes. Grief takes hostages, and it must for a time.

When a nightmare visits, it will take you down—down to the Underworld. Outside the hour of soothing respite, during my sandy sunrise strolls, I resided in that dark place. The rest of the 23/7—misplaced and disjointed.

The Underworld is not a mythical place. It's genuine and visceral, a cold, dark, damp, barren pit void of coziness or care. Likened to Hell. Its purpose is to wake us from our deepest slumber. Face our demons. If we dare. We must dare, boldly.

I am no Persephone. No mother was searching for me.

My chest was an eternity hollow, my heart squishy yet guarded vigilantly. I resolved to stay in that hellish place or die! I did not kick and scream; I camped out there! Or in there! Time moved forward while I cocooned.

I was companioned by a mantra, an ancient chant that arose from within me and rocked me: *Tender, Tender, Beloved.*

Parts dying, rebirth biding her time. Ceremoniously, I stood, firm-footed.

No more harsh internal blackness okay, Lulu? You potent, audacious feminine you.

Brightness arrived each afternoon, rainbow light arched across my ceiling, beauty and magic intertwined.

I felt the Earth's steady hum, my lifelong faith, unwavering and true.

Eventually, an inner churning arose, an unsettling roller coaster feeling, and an equally invigorating rhythmic vibration embodied me—revealing that I was, indeed, the one I was waiting for!

And now my life was. . . all about ME! Divine timing.

I had no idea what day or week it was or when I last ate. I dozily shuffled to the fridge. Opening it, the cool air leaped at my skin, beckoning me and reminding me that I have a body; I am alive. It was a simple, pleasurable moment. *Ah, so good.*

Spying the yogurt, I declared nonchalantly to nobody, "My yogurt."

With the fridge light illuminating my face, I removed the lid from the yogurt, dipped my fingers in, and served myself a divine, sensual serving. With total presence and delight, I licked each finger and nodded with gratitude—*my yogurt.*

I laughed giddily. Confirming joyously to my heart that simple pleasures are abundant.

The Poems

I wrote over 100 poems during the dawn of my 'new life'—yes, right through my own Dark Night of the Soul. And trust me, we all go through more than one of those transformative journeys in this lifetime! Writing is my sacred outlet, my way of marking each little metamorphosis and every moment of emerging into the light.

I can't recommend it enough! Writing through major transitions is like creating your own personal timeline of growth. It's a sacred balm, soothing every crack, and let's be real—it's also our biggest cheerleader, shaking those pom-poms with joy for every tiny, magnificent step we take forward.

Because each step (or word) is a celebration, and we deserve to celebrate every single moment of our unfolding and our life. Come, meander with me for a brief glimpse along the winding path of my poetry timeline, so that you can find your own treasure.

Cocooned Abyss

knowing yourself
on a razor's edge
balancing on a nailhead
crossing a collapsed bridge
barefoot
at the foot of the cliff
with bloodied hands
and raw knees
you crawl through the midnight hours-
when the world is silent
but your mind spins
like an untamable storm
no anchor
no harbor

just the crashing waves of truth
the lies you once wore
unraveling
thread by thread
your breath slows
each inhale a tremor
each exhale a release
quietly
like the softest feather
gliding
open
open your heart
wide enough to let your thoughts loosen
let then escape
rising like balloons
trailing the broken strings of your past
naked, you lay
on the cold floor of the Underworld
cocooned
in the creeping black void, in stasis
time dulled-
you begin to dissolve
disintegrating into the unknown
becoming something unrecognizable
a form not yet realized
when the constrictions come
tight like the fist of rebirth
know this:
you are emerging
and with all your might
with all the fire you've gathered
you will rise
leaving behind ashes

Grace

Deep, Deep, Deeper I go-
Is it friend, or is it foe?
I explore the sharp emotions that arise,
Tugging me down to unearth the lies.

The visceral weight of each thought and bend,
Screaming for my focus- no room for Zen.
I sort, I sieve, I untangle, I face,
From chaos to clarity, I get a taste of grace.

There's no judge or jury waiting to receive,
Contrary to what I've been led to believe.
Just me, with dull pieces strewn at my feet-
If I stomped on them, would they know defeat?

Or I could whisper soft lullabies to each shard,
Let the lies lift off, no longer scarred.
And in their place, what's left becomes clear-
Lessons of growth that draw me near.

The alchemy begins with truth revealed,
Where broken pieces are transmuted and healed.
With elements combined, their form refined,
A brand-new essence, beautifully aligned.

Fragments of truth in darkness unfold,
In the warmth of my heart, courage grows bold.
Love's quiet power guides me through,
While life's mystery reminds me to continue.

Grace flows.

What If!

what if…
you're the one you've been waiting for, all along?
you have a body-
a life woven with the love of family and friends
perhaps a passionate lover whispering your name
work which fuels your fire
activities that light up your soul
dreams manifesting… just on the horizon

you think maybe, just maybe
having or getting, any of these things
will fix it all-
solve your problems
ease your burdens
heal the broken pieces
make you happy!

it's often said
healing is the path
self-love, the key
what if…
all the striving, all the searching
all the "out there" pursuits
were simply guiding you gently
turning you inward
leading you back to the softest
most tender part of yourself?
the place you've always belonged

what if, nothing, nothing compares to you?
yes, you!
not in some song or someone else's arms
but in the quiet melody
of your own heart
what if, you reframed every love song

and sang it sweetly, softly
to yourself?
and every love letter you've ever written-
each word, each tender syllable-
was always meant for you
a devotion scribed by your soul
waiting to be fully received

for all the mistakes, the twists and turns
the glorious mess of it all
for every moment you have over managed
mismanaged
fumbled through the pain
numbed yourself just to survive
or to keep going
took detours
walked uneven terrain-
it was all part of this wild, beautiful journey
back to you

Loving Yourself

yes, with all caps on-
not a Hallmark card version
not a quick fix
not a mantra you say three times fast and forget
L O V I N G   Y O U R S E L F -
expanded in every way
like it truly, deeply matters
because... it...
truly
deeply
matters

LOVING YOURSELF
like that's what the whole crazy journey
on Earth has been about all along

more than any goal or destination-
there's nothing more important
than this tender, pure love
this potent, refined love
resting, waiting
circulating within you

and what if…
all of this-
the pain, the detours and unmarked roads-
the distractions, the busyness-
was like a game of hide and seek?

And you are it!

and finding yourself
this sweet, wild delight
wasn't just the destination
but the journey itself?
what if all along
you were never truly lost
but circling closer and closer
to the truth already inside you?

you are the one-
the one you've been seeking
all along
the light that guides you
the sanctuary that soothes you
the answer that has been quietly waiting
wrapped closer than close
you, love, it's always been you

Pleasure Invitation

We think of pleasure,
as a broad, bold brushstroke-
colorful, electric, magical,
like fireworks bursting in the night,
launched rockets,
an orgasmic celebration through sexuality.
But what if pleasure,
was more?
So much more?

An invitation, a soft unfolding-
not a crescendo peak, but a way of BEING.

Simple pleasures,
abundant pleasures,
falling like petals all around us,
meant for our sweet delight.
Pleasure, as simple goodness,
pleasure, as a gentle hum'
that kind that whispers,
"this feels right, this feels real."
Pleasure, as a felt expression,
rising delicately through the senses,
a sacred waltz,
here to guide us back to ourselves.

Yes, it might be a leap-
but darling, it's one so worth taking.
Follow the thread,
trust yourself,
and when it tugs, let it carry you forward,
with your whole being open and ready,
because slowly... oh so slowly,
is the sweetest way to savor.
Gently set aside any comparison-
of what pleasure should be or look like,

for there is no need to look beyond yourself.
You, and only you,
are the tender vessel of your pleasure,
fully communicating and receiving,
perfect union.
Let your exploration guide you,
as your whole being receives its own wholeness, pleasurably.

Breathe.
Right here, in this moment.
Feel the gentle weight of your body,
grounded, held in the softness of now.
Let yourself sink into the simple delight of being cradled,
your body wrapped in the reassuring embrace,
of the chair beneath you,
as if it were molded just for you.
Notice how it supports every curve,
how it meets you,
inviting you to rest, to release,
like a pair of nurturing arms,
offering comfort and safety.
Soften in.
Let it be a reminder that, even in stillness,
you are held, cherished, and at home within yourself.

Breathe deep,
slow and aware.
Imagine now, the scent of your favorite flower-
how it lingers in the air, delicate and sweet,
awakening something deep within.
Let it bloom inside you,
its petals unfolding in your chest,
a quiet reminder of beauty,
even when it's not there.
Breathe it in,
feel it weaving through you,
its fragrance gently filling you, with its botanical presence.

Breathe again,
slow and soft,
and let your nose wiggle-
just a little, like a joyful secret.
Feel the delight in that simple, silly gesture,
as if your nose is laughing quietly with you.
Let the pleasure dance-
light and carefree,
in that playful movement.
In this moment,
feel the innocence, like a child at play.

Feel the breath arrive again,
run your fingertips lightly across your forehead,
like silk on your skin,
find the sweetness in that tender touch.
Slowly, slowly.
Follow the breath as it leaves,
like the lingering warmth of a sunset's glow.
Let pleasure envelop you,
gently reorienting you to quiet joy,
this delicious goodness,
that's been waiting at your fingertips all along.

Be curious, love,
you are fully resourced,
right here, right now,
with humility,
for pleasure-
and isn't that the loveliest thing?

Remember, slowly... oh so slowly,
is the deepest way to savor.
Yes, it might be a leap-
and
darling, it's one so worth taking.

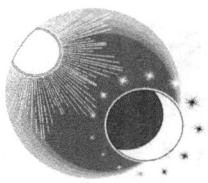

Dear Reader, now it's your turn to write! Use the blank space below. Try not to censor yourself.

Love letter: Make it divine, soulful, and filled with adoration that makes you glow from within. Write it to yourself unabashedly. Read it often. Out loud. Let the words sink in, truly listen, and take them to heart. Claim your pleasure; claim your treasure. So, my beloved, Write On!

Lulu Trevena is a multi-award-winning author, artist, women's workshop and retreat leader, mother, and Soulful Living Coach dedicated to changing the societal narrative about women and aging.

Her beautiful hardcover book, *Soul Blessings,* won the 2018 Silver Nautilus Book Award. Becoming a published author after the age of 55, she also created the card deck *Moments of Transformation* and the *Epiphany Journal and Playbook.* Lulu is the founder of Live Life with *Wonder and the lead author of Wholehearted Wonder Women 50 Plus,* as well as a contributing author in several healing-focused titles.

A passionate world traveler, Lulu enjoys her time at home with her cats and sunrises at the beach, she believes in the power of personal tenderness. She encourages others to stay present to meaningful moments and find beauty within and all around as a daily practice.

Connect with Lulu: https://livelifewithwonder.com/

Chapter 7

MUD Between the Lines

Dr. Oliver T. Reid, "The Writing Coach"

My Story

Mud lines trace my feet,
Blind hands mold where sight has failed,
Fire shapes what's formed.

Mud. You can feel it, can't you? That thick, clinging weight pulling you down, caking around your feet, inching up your legs. The texture, rough and gritty, binds you to the ground. The air smells damp—heavy with sorrow. You try shaking it off, but the harder you struggle, the deeper you sink. You know this mud. We all do.

The MUD of misery—you've been there. Maybe you're there now. It smells like fear, like the stale breath of unspoken words. It's that crushing darkness of depression where every breath feels unbearable. The cold, unforgiving mud silences your screams, the kind that echo in the emptiest corners of your mind. But there, in that pit of despair, is where the Potter begins His work. His hands find you, even in the mud, shaping you when you've lost all shape.

Then there's the MUD of undone. Bitter, sharp, it's the taste left in your mouth after divorce, when what you thought was forever falls apart. You watch the pieces of your life break away, but the mud clings tighter. It wraps around your soul, leaving you shattered. You think it's over, but the Potter isn't done. His hands press into the cracks, reshaping what you thought was beyond repair.

And the MUD of defeat? The heaviest of all. It's the mud weighing on your heart when your children are taken, custody slipping through your fingers like sand. The loss burns in your throat like acid. You feel inadequacy like a cloak, heavy and suffocating, and you're blind to everything except failure. But even when you can't see Him, the Potter's hands are still at work, shaping you through the pain.

Life doesn't spare you the mud of emotional inadequacies either. It's like blindness, but deeper. You lose sight not only of the world but of yourself. What does it feel like to lose hope, to have your vision clouded with doubts and fears? It feels like sinking in mud that covers your eyes, your heart, your soul. But even when you lose sight, the Potter does not. His hands are steady, molding you in the fires of life, making something new from the mess you've become.

Can you smell it? "I thought that everything good smelled sweet and everything bad reeked, but found out it was the polar opposite." The mud is changing. It no longer reeks of despair. There's a warmth now, a subtle aroma of renewal, like the Earth after rain. You begin to feel the shift—the weight lightens, and suddenly, the mud isn't holding you back anymore. It's becoming something more, something refined.

In the Potter's hands, you're not broken. You're becoming. What was once mud is now a masterpiece—pain turned into purpose, molded by divine hands into strength. You are the clay.

The Poems

Muddy Eyes

I used to think the mud meant my vision was gone,
Blind in one eye, felt like I couldn't see the dawn.
Everything's a blur, the lines ain't crisp,
But I learned in that struggle, the mud ain't a miss.
It's a mess-age, a metaphor, thick and slow,
Like life sometimes, it's hard to know where to go.

Have you ever had mud in your eyes? Not just the physical ones.
From the inside—your spiritual, emotional lens—
Where the mess blurs your vision, time and again?
It's a fight to see clear, a battle to find,
That vision ain't lost—it's just confined.

See, the mud covers, hides what's beneath,
But beneath that cover, there's always belief.
In the dark, in the mess, in the thick of the fight,
Vision ain't lost, it's just learning to find light.

I wrestled with blindness, couldn't see clear,
One eye open, but still full of fear.
Now my left eye's blurry too—what's left to see?
The office scene of going blind haunts me.
Life's like that, yeah, it gets gritty,
Blurry at best, man, it's far from pretty.
But mud ain't the enemy; it's the ground I stand,
It shapes the vision, molds the man.

Every day I wonder if I'll see straight,
If the haze in my soul will dissipate.
But you know what's real? The blur ain't defeat,
It's just the pathway for a new kind of heat.
A fire inside that won't dim or fade,
'Cause vision ain't about what's made or displayed.

See, we think clarity's found in the crystal clear,
But the mud's where real vision appears.
In the grit, in the grime, that's where you see,
Not with the eyes, but with the soul that's free.
The mud makes you humble, makes you dig deep,
Makes you face the nights when you can't sleep.

I used to curse the mud, curse the blur,
But now I realize it's the only thing that's sure.
It's in that mess I found my truth,
Vision ain't always about seeing proof.
It's about feeling, about knowing what's real,
About touching the world with what you can't steal.

Blind in one eye, but my sight's sharper now,
Though my left eye's fading, I'll find the how.
How to see what others might miss,
How to embrace the world with every twist.
The dirt, the grime, the tears I've cried,
All part of the journey, no reason to hide.

The mud showed me that life's not a straight line,
It's a twist, a turn, a struggle with time.
And the clearer you want it, the more you fight,
But sometimes, the blur gives you true sight.

And as I write this, I write blurry,
Muddy between the lines, in no hurry.
Vision ain't about seeing clean and bright,
It's about embracing the blur and finding your light.

Mud and Mirrors

The mirror in front of me is caked in mud,
Smudged reflections, stained by my father's flood—
A flood of rejection, thick like clay,
Thrown at me in anger, leaving marks that won't sway.
Each muddy pile stacked high, layer on layer,
But I stand here now, no longer in prayer for repair.

What's a reflection but a truth that's bent?
Through a muddy lens, I see where my life went.
Homeless as a child, living in a car,
The smell of damp upholstery, the rain's bitter scar.
It tasted like despair, cold metal, and grime,
Where the mud of neglect buried my rights, my time.
My stepfather's hand wasn't just rough; it was mud,
Thick with abuse, drawing rivers of blood.

He beat and battered me, a twisted craft,
Like mud in the hands of a demented potter, I was cast.
Each strike was a splash, each bruise a design,
A masterpiece formed from pain so divine.
The dirt under my nails told stories untold,
Of a childhood shattered, of innocence sold.
Every mark on my skin, like mud on the glass,
Reflected the struggles that shadowed my past.

I looked in the mirror, wondering who I was—
Is this reflection a man or merely a pause?
What did I see? A warrior, a fool?
A broken boy clinging to hope's rusty tool.
"Why me?" I'd ask as a child in the rain,
Where was my worth in a world full of pain?
The mud of divorce left streaks down the glass,
Losing my children, my job—all part of the mess-age.
The taste of that loss, bitter like ash,
And the smell of despair—like fire in a crash.
The mud piled higher with every failed try,
But still, I kept looking, still asking why.

My father threw mud; my stepfather too,
But that mud is the soil where something new grew.
It stained my mirror, but I began to see—
The mud didn't define me; it set me free.
For in that mess, I found my own way,
Not washed clean, but molded like clay.

At 19, I stood on the brink of the end,
Mud caked my mind; I couldn't pretend.
A suicide attempt, the mud weighed me down,
But in that moment, I refused to drown.
Each pile of mud was a scar, a stain,
But I began to embrace it; I began to gain.
The more the mud, the more I'd rise,
Seeing beauty now in the mud-caked skies.

Diabetes, losing jobs, losing my place—
All part of the mud that splashed on my face.
But in that mirror, through the filth and grime,
I saw a reflection that transcended time.
"Embrace the mud," my soul began to say,
For mud isn't a curse; it's a new kind of way.
It molds, it shapes, it leaves its trace,
But it's in that mess I found my grace.

The mirror still shows me the piles of my past,
But now I see clearly, at long last.
For in the mud, I've learned to thrive,
To find beauty where pain used to hide.
I'm not spotless; I'm not pristine,
But this mud, this dirt—it's where I've been seen.

Each muddy stain is an imprint, a mark,
But it's in the mud where I've ignited my spark.
I write my way out; I own my own land,
In the mud and mirrors, I finally stand.
No longer buried; I'm learning to soar,
For in every reflection, I discover more.

Mudbound Memories

In the stillness of the night, a mental boxing match,
Imagining the ring where shadows clash.
I'm both the giver and receiver of blows,
In this fight against myself, where the tension grows.
Thoughts ricochet, like fists in the air,
Silent screams echo, a burden to bear.

Every punch I throw is steeped in my past,
A barrage of memories that grip me fast.
I issue the blows of regret and despair,
Each jab a reminder of wounds laid bare.
Am I worthy of healing? I ponder and sway,
In this gritty arena, I wrestle and fray.

I step into the mud, thick with neglect,
Each clump tells a story, a wound to dissect.
Childhood whispers float through this mire,
Fueling my struggle, igniting my fire.
A shadowy figure dances in the ring,
My inner demon, my most relentless fling.

Frustration brews like a storm deep inside,
With every breath I take, I feel myself slide.
These memories, mud bound, cling like wet clay,
Pulling me down, making me feel frayed.
The past is a boxer, relentless and mean,
With every round fought, I know what I've seen.

The symmetry of my black face reflects this mud,
Not just a memory, but a thickening flood.
These stains are not limits; they won't seal my fate,
No bars can define me, no walls can dictate.
I won't be the label or the script I rehearsed,
Not confined to a life where my potential is cursed.

Can I just be free? Can I rise from the earth,
Not chained by expectations, but claiming my worth?
Can I be more than what they taught me to be,
A mudman, a dark man, just yearning to see?
I refuse to be shackled by what they say I lack,
No, I'm breaking the chains, I'm taking it back.

I sift through this dirt, I feel every grain,
Acknowledging hurt while learning to gain.
But I also embrace the beauty that grows,
For from the mud, a wildflower knows.
It rises from darkness, from deep within ground,
A testament to healing where love can be found.

In this journey of healing, I find my own way,
For I am not what I touch but what I hold at bay.
As I clear out the mud, let the sunlight unfold,
I embrace my true self, a story retold.
Remember this truth as you navigate through:
You are not what you touch, but you are imprinted by what you hold on to.

Mudprints on My Soul

Step into the canvas of my existence,
where mud prints linger, etching stories beneath my feet.
Each step taken, a testament to the journey,
each print an echo of where I've been,
the will to rise, the mind to think,
the emotions that swell like tides.

MUD—
Make peace with the past,
Unlock the doors of perception,
Discover the strength within.

In the morning light, I wake,
feet planted in the soft earth,
a reminder of all I carry.
The mud beneath me holds the weight
of silent screams and whispered dreams.
It absorbs my fears, my hopes,
the echoes of laughter, the shadows of pain.

Each print tells a story:
the first steps of a child in a world unknown,
navigating puddles of doubt,
leaping over streams of despair.
The squelch of the mud beneath my shoes,
the sound of resilience,
the rhythm of survival.

The intellect weighs heavy on my mind,
searching for answers in a fog of uncertainty.
Questions swirl like dust in the air:
Who am I beneath these layers?
What does it mean to be whole?
With every answer, another question arises,
but the mud—
it grounds me,
reminds me that I'm here.

In this journey of healing, I trace the prints,
the pathway forward unfolding like a map.
Steps lead to purpose,
each footprint a marker of growth.
I embrace the stains, the smudges of experience,
they form the tapestry of my being,
and though I may stumble,
I leave my mark on the world,
beautifully imperfect.

Oftentimes, we must take baths in the mud,
embrace the mud,
walk through the mud,

become one with the mud.
Feel the heaviness of the past dissolve,
as I learn to walk with intention,
to dance with the shadows,
to welcome the light.
With every step, I'm shedding
the burdens that weigh me down,
releasing the past,
making room for the new.

The prints on my soul are not just remnants,
they are the foundation of my strength,
the stepping stones to my destiny.
I learn to navigate the mud,
to find beauty in the struggle,
to see the reflections of possibility
in the puddles of my past.

As I continue this journey,
I gather the mud,
the earth from which I rise.
With every step, a declaration:
I am alive,
I am transforming,
I am creating a masterpiece.

In the end, mud is not just dirt;
it is the essence of life,
the grit that shapes us,
the prints we leave behind.
With every print, I embrace my truth,
and carry the essence of my journey
as I step boldly into tomorrow,
reminded that every imprint
is a part of my story,
and my soul's journey.

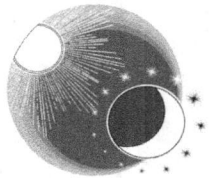

Dear reader, now it's your turn to write! Use the blank space below. Try not to censor yourself.

Envision yourself walking through the thick mud of your past—what discoveries arise with each step? Jot down three actions you can take to transform the weight of your experiences into fuel for your journey ahead.

Dr. Oliver T. Reid is an international bestselling author, award-winning speaker, and the founder of I Am a Solution Consulting Firm, LLC. His firm offers specialized services in relationship and business consulting, coaching, and counseling. Known as "The Writing Coach," Dr. Reid uses innovative techniques to help entrepreneurs, speakers, and coaches maximize their potential. He also created The InnerView™, an interactive card game for singles and couples.

Over the past ten years, Dr. Reid has published 30 bestselling books, contributed to 17 anthologies, and earned awards like the IALA Distinction of Excellence Legendary Honoree and the NAACP Black Men Image Award. His work has reached global audiences, and he has coached clients across four continents.

Connect with Dr. Oliver Reid: https://drolivertreid.com

Chapter 8

Unfolding Through Breath and Verse – Sharing the Unsharable

Trish Brewer

My Story

There was a time when my voice felt like it didn't belong to me. It lay hidden, tangled in fear and old stories about who I should be. Unspoken words became heavy, and my truth sank deeper into silence. Then one day, a breathwork teacher asked a question, and everything changed: "Have you ever considered writing poetry?"

The simple question began to unfold something within me—my voice.

It went something like this:

Teacher: "To connect with your audience, you need to share your stories. Especially the ones that broke you and how you healed."

Me: "I can't possibly tell some of my stories! What if my mom reads them? Or my family? I have kids! Someone could get hurt. Nope, I can't do it."

Teacher: "Your stories could help others. Poetry is a softer approach."

Wait... I don't have to do it their way? The thought hit me like a slow exhale, releasing tension I hadn't realized I'd been holding. *I don't need to write long, raw posts.* Poetry felt safer, like a whisper instead of a shout. *Yes, poetry can hold my truth.*

And so, I began writing alongside my breathwork healing journey. Poetry became a way to bring my deepest darkest thoughts into the light, sharing in a way that felt true to me, yet gentler for others to digest. It became a gift—a form of freedom, even anonymity. In a noisy world, it became a way to be heard.

Breathwork was the catalyst for my unfolding, and poetry gave shape to my voice.

Finding my voice has been a journey—far from easy. From childhood through adolescence, I was told so many stories about myself. I was too loud, too sensitive, too opinionated. I needed to be a "good girl" and not talk back. Growing up with a parent who was larger than life, my voice felt small, dismissed, and unworthy. No wonder it took me until 50 to reclaim it.

But when I did, I reclaimed parts of myself that had been buried for years. My voice, once stifled, became my most powerful tool for self-expression and empowerment.

So, what helped this once-shy Italian girl speak out and stand tall? Therapy, journaling, meditation, and Reiki all played a role. But it was breathwork that cleared the path back to myself.

I settle in and begin the rhythm: two inhales—first into my belly, then my chest—followed by an exhale. Each breath peels back layers of fear and old stories. With each cycle—inhale, inhale, exhale—the weight lifts and space opens. In the stillness, I feel something stir: my voice. Faint, but there. Words begin to form, not in loud declarations, but in soft whispers. Stories I thought I could never share surface, woven into verses carried on the breath. Each exhale brings me closer to sharing the unsharable.

My hope is by witnessing my journey, you too may find a path to healing—and perhaps, discover your voice.

The Poems

Shedding and Grieving

the process of shedding
permeated by layers of what once served us
forcing us deep into the shadows of our stories
grieving the old
rebirthed on the other side

with every tear I shed
it is a release
it is a cleansing
it is freedom
it is forgiveness

on the other side
there is an exhale
there is light
there is peace
there is home
there is something brighter
there is growth

with each breath, I surrender
to the grief
to the tears
to the pain
to the peace
to the light
to whatever it is that emerges on the other side

Look for Softness

Inspired by a conversation with my dear friend Quinn and these words she spoke to me, "look for softness."

in the moment of unyielding harshness,
when it all seems to be crumbling around you,
when the laughter and the joy have temporarily departed,
when you are hanging on by your bootstraps,
be gentle with yourself, and
look for softness

in the moment of feeling most lost,
when all seems forlorn,
when you are apprehensive,
when you want to run,
look for softness

Unfolding into the Unknown

I am unfolding into something not yet defined.

What is being burned away will be missed by many, including me, but it has served its purpose.

The transformation causes turmoil. This I acknowledge. And, yet, I cannot stop it, nor do I want to.

I feel a fervor of excitement at the possibility of what is expanding simultaneously feeling the contraction in my heart.

I feel it all. I let it all flow through me.

Expanding.

Contracting.

Breathing through it all.

Moving into the unknown.

Trusting in the unfolding.

Trusting in what will be born out of the ashes.

Love it All

I am learning to love it all.

Love for imperfect perfections, for it is those characteristics that make one special.

Love for the failures, for it is in those where we find the lessons of growth.

Love for the scars, for they each have a story to tell.

Love for the darkness of the shadow, without it the light would not shine so brightly on the other side.

Love for the tears flushing away the toxins and stress hormones.

Love for the vulnerability that shows us strength and courage.

Love for the anger and resentment that leads to a path of discovery and healing.

Love for the fears and doubts, in their place building acceptance and conviction.

Love for the betrayals and heartaches foraging a path to forgiveness and peace.

Love for the shame as it sheds light on the desire to hide and why.

Love for community, for this is where we find support to get us through some of the hardest of times.

Love for joy and laughter when you're not feeling it but knowing it's always there.

Love for the process and expansion when the journey feels grueling.

Love for Mother Earth, for she nurtures and supports us.

Love for the Universe, for she always provides.

Love for Faith, even in the darkest hours.

Love for yourself. Always, love for yourself.

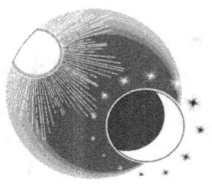

Dear reader, now it's your turn to write! Use the blank space below. Try not to censor yourself.

But before you do, place one hand over your heart and the other over your belly, close your eyes, and take a few deep diaphragmatic breaths.

Ask yourself, what part of yourself have you hidden, and how might your life change if you allowed it to be seen?

Trish Brewer is a certified trauma-informed breathwork coach, Reiki Master Teacher, and Practitioner. She helps individuals committed to deep inner healing transform their lives by releasing trauma, reducing stress, and reconnecting with their authentic selves.

As an intuitive guide, Trish employs a trauma-aware approach, utilizing the transformative elements of breathwork, processing work, and Reiki to guide individuals back to their complete selves. Her sessions are sensitively designed to anticipate the messy and unexpected aspects of the healing process, acknowledging both the light and the dark and witnessing the beauty along the way.

She's a co-author of *Hot Mess to Hot Mom: Transformational Tools for Thriving After Childbirth and Beyond,* and *We Lead Vol. 2, Building Connection, Community, and Collaboration for Women in Business.*

Connect with Trish: https://www.trishbrewer.com/

Chapter 9

Use Metaphors to Help
Your Inner Beauty Shine Brighter

Rev. Dr. Karen Schuder, EdD, MDiv, MAM

My Story

People's expectations can be crushing when we don't fit neatly into their categories. Pressures to conform have made it difficult to reflect who I feel called to be, especially when gender discrimination, harassment, and abuse are present. One early professional experience illustrates such challenges.

Beautiful pine walls and freshly brewed coffee couldn't bring warmth to the small rural church where I spent a year offering care as their pastor. Six people sat around the table to discuss my contract. Several had their arms crossed and stared with frowns creasing their brows. Two looked silently at the table with hands in their laps. My husband and three children, including a three-month-old, seemed a world away.

"I don't like how you make us listen to different readings."

"I can't believe you had maternity leave during our busy time."

"You don't deserve a contract renewal. Women shouldn't be pastors."

Why didn't you say anything about what you liked? I wasn't aware of a busy time and I remember you saying, "Karen is the best speaker I ever heard."

"It just wasn't right that we had to pay when you weren't working."

"Her husband has a good job, so we shouldn't have to pay her as much."

"You just had a baby and shouldn't be working."

I can't believe this! You pay me below minimum wage, and it isn't my husband working. Why do you think you have a right to decide what I do?

My chest tightened and my hands trembled. Criticisms slammed into my perception of how things were going. I looked at Thelma hoping for some common sense. She mumbled, "This isn't right," and resumed looking at the table. Harsh voices continued but faded into the background of my mind.

Later at home I fell to my knees and wept. My husband, Steve, held me saying, "You don't deserve this. I love you." During worship the next few Sundays I spoke about love while facing scowls and frowns. One day, as I soaked up rare winter sunshine, I was flooded with peace and a message from the Divine said: *You can let go.*

That was not the first nor the last time I experienced such treatment. Discrimination and harsh judgment have reared their heads whether I was a pastor, non-profit leader, or baseball coach, and I'm certain it won't stop anytime soon. I have endured discrimination, harassment, and abuse. Unfair treatment continually presents challenges, but I refuse to let it define me.

I am a strong woman driven to make the world a better place. Seeing and promoting my inner beauty is an ongoing struggle with constant challenges trying to dull who I am. I've learned to love myself and embrace others who help me so I don't get confined by destructive limitations.

I hope my poems inspire you to step beyond repressive and oppressive barriers. To see and delight in your inner beauty. Let's help each other shine and make the world a brighter place.

"My Story" contains excerpts from *Resilient and Sustainable Caring: Your Guide to Thrive While Helping Others* published by Whole Person Associates.

The Poems

I Think I Saw a Butterfly

See inner beauty in a judgmental world

For the briefest of moments on a very ordinary day,
Wings with blue, yellow, orange, and rose fluttered before my eyes.
I whispered, "I think I saw a butterfly."

My husband looked at me with brown, soulful eyes,
His face creased with an impish grin as he said,
"Every day I see that beautiful butterfly."

A stranger walking by paused to look,
And with a frown proclaimed, "Butterflies are only orange and green."
"You did not see a butterfly."

In that moment my child danced over with laughter on her lips,
She threw her arms around me and sang,
"Mama, I love your butterfly."

In response to such childish words a critic's scowl deepened,
As he shook his head and shouted,
"You are imagining it. You did not see a butterfly."

A friend stepped forward, not afraid to enter the fray.
Squinting as if to see more clearly while saying,
"Why yes. I think you see a butterfly."

I shut my ears and stopped to look on this very ordinary day,
When wings of blue, yellow, orange, and rose fluttered to a steady beat.
I know I saw a butterfly.

Searching for Hope
Let go of limiting notions

Puffy white clouds reflected on the still blue lake
while leaves whispered among the trees behind me
in my search for hope.

I hoped to see a black bear rumbling through the brush,
but instead a doe glanced and flicked her tail before leaping as if saying,
"Do you see it?"

I longed to hear the wolf's plaintiff cry,
but instead the loon spread his wings and laughed as if calling,
"Do you hear it?"

I wanted to smell the wild roses rising above their thorns,
but instead the breeze carried the scent of fresh pine as if murmuring,
"Do you smell it?"

I desired to touch the soft green moss nourished by dew,
but instead the speckled boulder stood firm beneath my feet as if
shouting,
"Do you feel it?"

I dreamed of tasting a sweet red raspberry bursting in my mouth,
but instead cold water splashed upon my lips as if challenging,
"Do you taste it?"

I sighed and shook my head before walking away
from the doe, loon, pine, boulder, and water
as I continued searching for hope.

I Will Lend You Courage

Face the difficult together

I will lend you courage.
I too have stood before the abyss
And experienced the dilemma -
Turn back
Or jump to a new way.

I will lend you courage.
I also was shaken by grabbing hands
And struggled to respond -
Give in
Or say "No. Not today."

I will lend you courage.
I have seen scowls shouting judgment
And faltered on my path to question -
Stop moving
Or believe I'm going the right way?

I will lend you courage.
I too have heard people's disparaging views
And stopped seeing true while asking -
Accept their cynicism
Or create a better day?

I will lend you courage.
To leap the abyss
Shake off grabbing hands
Ignore destructive sneers and shouts
To see your truth
And follow your own lovely way.

I will lend you courage,
With kind, affirming words
And a vision of hope
For going beyond imposed limitations
To embrace possibilities of today.

Will you lend me courage?
When I again stand at the abyss
Try to escape grabbing hands
Face distracting scowls
Or hear shouts diminishing hope.

I will lend you courage.
Will you offer me the same?

Square Peg in a Round Hole

Go beyond the status quo

The board is square and filled with round holes.
Circular pegs align the best and find an easy place to sit.
Being not so round, I've sadly shaved off pieces to try to fit.

Take a closer look, you'll see many strangely shaped pegs.
Some lay aside, while most contort like a phony horde.
And I wonder if maybe … we should change the board.

Dear reader, now it's your turn to write! Use the blank space below. Try not to censor yourself.

You carry an inner beauty filled with possibilities. This is true despite what the world has told you. We can find much strength and meaning when we promote the goodness we carry within. To help your inner beauty shine brighter, write down or illustrate metaphors that lead you to:

- See the beauty you carry within your less-than-perfect humanness.

- Reflect your inner beauty while making decisions and dealing with challenges.

- Find grace to let go of past hurts and embrace hope.

- Increase courage to get beyond unfair criticisms or restrictive social norms.

Karen Schuder, EdD, MDiv, MAM, speaker, and best-selling author, has extensive experience promoting resilience and role sustainability. Years of helping people during traumatic times, leading organizations, and working globally inform her work with people in personal and professional helping roles. Karen offers life-changing concepts and practical strategies with an enjoyable, interactive approach. Check out her book *Resilient and Sustainable Caring: Your Guide to Thrive While Helping Others* and chapter in *The Caregiver's Advocate: A Complete Guide to Support and Resources*. Learn more about how to promote resilience, increase healthy life balance, and decrease anxiety on her website.

Connect with Karen: https://www.karenschuder.com/

Chapter 10

Firewalks and Dragon Songs

Tantric Vision Quest for Ecstatic Abundance
Beyond Menopause

Nydia Laysa Stone, Somatic Therapist, ReWilding Coach

Your wild is free
Lilith laughs through broken chains.

My Story

"YOU AGAIN! You can't do this in a church, girl!"

These dragon songs always poured out of me,
whirling and twisting my nine-year-old body in wild arcs and spirals.
My heart heavy because they hurt them.

Though I knew they weren't dead.
Just like they hurt me—and I wasn't dead.

"You've got no right to harm the dragons!
You priests and this Saint George are *vicious*!"

My voice still echoing, I spiral up the 365 narrow stairs to the church tower; breathless, ninety meters above my 'City of 10 Million Diamonds', a dragon wing tenderly wraps around my shoulders...

MAIDEN TO MEDICINE WOMAN—DANCING WITH SPIRIT

I was born in the crater of a meteorite. My sleepy medieval Bavarian town, built from micro-diamonds and crystals, is shadowed by its horrifying history of witch trials.

Climbing around these Witches' Rocks in forbidden forests, singing my channeled dragon light healings to the injured, to animals, trees, a sad old lady—my inner Maiden had already been claimed by Spirit and the Wild Woman.

VISION QUEST—DAKINIS AND YONI FLOWERS

By 17, I escaped. I studied therapy, Yoga, and Tantra in India, thirsty for wisdom.

They offered me droplets—though my soul craved oceans!

Exploring the world, ancient rites, and healing rituals, I ran without a pack, following the wild compass of my body, my senses, and my desires—sacred and raw.

Pleasure became my prayer, joy my guiding force.

Bare feet, hips swaying to foreign drumbeats, I devoured sweet nectars, the bitter, tender, and savage alike.

My heart knew no fear—except missing out on life's adventures!

Through my shadows—ancestral wounds, abuse, toxic relationships—I faced my demons.

Every labyrinth, a space of expansion, piercing illusion; every moment of ecstasy, another gateway back to primal forces stored in my womb, my bones.

My sacred rebel—fierce, untamable.

Stripping bare.

So I'd remember.

Who I am.

RITES OF PASSAGE

I danced through life, rising, falling, each phase calling me to shed outworn skins and reset my visions.

While menopause snuck in on silent paws—storms of change raged within, demanding deeper surrender, offering yet another passage to ecstatic abundance and freedom.

SECOND AWAKENING

Violent years of fighting free from narcissist bondage. . .

How could I've fallen into this?

Me!

Jaguar Woman, Priestess!

My passion for creation turned into award-winning projects, a million-dollar business, a castle in the Pyrenees. . .

Cost me only my soul.

Reclaiming my soul almost cost me my life.

FIREWALKS AND RADICAL MIND-SHIFTING

Pleasure was my savior again.

Living in Fiji with my new Indian partner—spiritual, a natural Tantric—seemed a dream come true!

But when the very same abusive patterns re-emerged, I realized I was still available for being violated.

My Dragon Songs burst out at a fire ceremony on Beqa Island, where an elder of this ancient Fijian fire-tribe recognized my medicine—and my struggles.

She made me walk the fire.
A new healing portal opened!

INVITATION

I've danced the flames countless times.

Like you.

Are you ready to ignite your ecstatic abundance?

COME - LET'S MEET AT THE FIRE!

The Poems

Passage Rites

Throughout life, in every culture, there are moments when we stand at the edge of what we are familiar with.

Alone on the mountain, facing the unknown and the wild within ourselves.

Welcome to circle, beautiful—the fire's lit. . .

Munay Ki
Jaguar's Path of Luminous Heart

I tore open the night with my own hands
And the stars bled into my soul

Born from the fires of ancient Songlines
We all walk through Rites of Change

Through water and flames, in circles of stone
Unseen paths open new visions

Munay Ki - each Rite a luminous thread
Their seeds rooted deeply in me
Like a river finding its course

JAGUAR meets me at the edge of my fears
She walks me through the shadows
Teaching me to face the unknown with grace
A mirror to my own wild heart

SERPENT, Sachamama - who sheds her skin
Show me the art to release
The illusions - and who I thought I was

HUMMINGBIRD, voyager!
Remind me to seek the sweet nectars of life
How to fly beyond the impossible!

ANCIENT ONES! Lineage and Blood
Your wisdom sings deep in my womb
I stand taller, knowing I'm not alone

CONDOR! EAGLE!
Elevate my vision beyond my horizons
To rise above the storm
See life with clarity

Crimson threads through labyrinths
The Mysteries of womanhood
Circles of laughter, tears, shadow and light
Rebirthing Realities

These Rites are not mere rituals
They're how I breathe
And walk through life

The Journey I have chosen.

AHO

Wildflower

Do you think desire fades
as the scarlet songs of my moons
grow quiet?
Do I not still thirst for life
as my blood no longer answers
the calling of the tides?

Ay, no!
I rise, I bloom, I burn.

My Yoni, still my temple of joy
My sacred portal
More alive! Deeper and savage
Unbound by time

I flow through streams of Amrita.
Curious, joyful, daring
Each riverbed a lover's secret
Each side stream a forgotten pleasure
Waiting to be explored

Some flow profound and slow, wide as my hips
Others frolic, teasing like mountain creeks
Where ecstasy leaps from rock to rock
Like a child's laughter in the spring

This is my wilderness
My sovereign territory
Where I roam free
Where the ancient Goddesses still dance
to their violent drumbeats 'round our fires

Can you hear them?

Their songs echoing in my bones
In the nectar dripping from my petals
In the roaring of my throat
As I sing my liberation

I melt into pools of my own creation
Giggling like bubbles of pink champagne
Flowing down my breasts, my thighs
Drenched in the scents of roses and musk

Trading the highways of quick eruptions
for long and lazy afternoons
and mornings out of time and space
Where Ecstasy is not a destination
but a journey

A wild excursion through jungles untouched
A dragon ride of dancing fire
And breathless full-body release

No guilt, no shyness
Only the pulse of pleasure
the truth of the moment
the raw, untamed joy of this flesh
of this body I call home

No longer bound by fear nor chains
I unlocked the chastity belts
they tried to shackle me with
Their sermons of shame
Their cold little gods!

While my Goddesses sit with Lilith
Sipping tea, waiting for me
to remember
To return to the Knowing

My body, my world, in liquid motion
each breath a ripple
each touch a spark, delicious storm
causing my cosmos to tremble

Spellbound, I rise
My lips burn with the kiss of life itself
Do you hear it hissing?

The sound of joy on flaming tongues
hungry, thirsty
for life
for love
for all that I am

Firewalk Your Mindset

I stand at the edge of the flames
where fear and courage merge into one
becoming palpable

The coals beneath my feet

ALIVE

sacred, primal, undeniable

This first step is not of the foot
But of the Spirit

Kali - fierce in her thirst for truth
her fiery tongues licking my ankles

Pele - red glowing gown of liquid stone,
stirring the lava of my blood
Reminds me to ignite the fires of my womb

This bed of flames—my path of challenge
My Passage Rite
Fiercely inviting me
to cross
the untamed edges
of my soul's wild longings

My Dragons
watching
over me
from the other side
of fear

My Goddesses, seducing me, encouraging
"We'll walk with you!"

The first step though
is mine to do

Step in and burn
Myself
Alive
TO LIFE!

Wild Woman howls, her laughter growls
with the spirits of the flames

I feel my trembling heart, the pulse of Earth
flickering through sparkling coals

Throughout all ages and all times
Women like us have offered
their fears and hopes to churning flames

In darker days, also their bodies burned
A sacrifice to man's blind faith

Now I'm the one to CHOOSE the fire!
My privilege!

I'm tuned into the songs of all
who walked this path before

"Listen closely!" they crackle
"It's your turn now!" they blaze
"Its time, it's time..." they whisper

"You're the one!" they sing
Who can shatter the line!
Who knows the way
To change the course...

All our wisdom has been poured into your soul.
Now use it wisely!

Add your courage, your sacred rage
Ignite your full potential
Fulfill your vow!

Remember, Child!
Fear is a Portal!
And you're the key...

Step forward now
And walk!

Dance through this Gate
To burn away illusions
The pain and grief of our lineage!

A passage opens on the flaming path
This is my invitation!

NOW!

Sekhmet, my fiery desert queen
Blows laughing winds across the flames
Across my heart, my soul

"What's your intention, your demand?
Your loudest wish of heart?
Your shyest, hidden one?

What needs to burn, my daughter?"

Another step, the coals beneath
Becoming friends now
Allies of my journey

Heart pounding hard against my chest
My throat is dry, but clear

My song rising from deep within
My Dragon Healing can begin!

My voice flows loud and strong:

"I'm not your toy to play with as you please!
To pour your grief and pain upon

Your vicious words and mind
Your violent hands and heart

The chains of jealousy, mistrust
Your punishments and threats
Insidious Manipulations!

All this - and more
Will Change!

I cannot bear your wounds, your scars. . .

So I will rise
and lock my gate
To let you know:

I'm not available
For this HELL
Any
More!

Your stage will crumble, and
Your audience won't cheer for you forever!"

The masks are off - the Play is over
The King stands naked
In his ugly truth!

The heat, the flames, like open arms
wrapping their fiery love around me
Taking my breath away

My soul ignites
Holding me tight

Forming a Sacred Chalice
A glowing, glimmering cauldron

To drop my sufferings
My oh! so human weaknesses

My doubts
and insecurities

My need to please
Be loved and honored

Each tread becomes a declaration

I won't be ruled by Fear!
Nor by what seeks to bind me

My Dragon heart
My Phoenix wings
Rising from the ash

Reclaiming my throne
My Sovereignty

With each step I shed
Old wounds—not mine to carry

Old names, old faces, words and gestures
now dissolve
and burn away like fragile parchment

I am Undone.

The Shift comes suddenly
Causes my spine to straighten

My breath expands beyond my skin
Beyond my limitations
I'm growing, claim my space!

It seems, the fire's sounding softer
The crackling picks a melody

There's room to breathe
And move

My Dragons
Smile at me
Blinking their eyes

Each further footfall now
branding not the skin
But Soul

With agency, authority
Carving resilience in my bones

I dance my fiery path with dignity
and pride

While I'm emerging

Light-footed now, with freedom in my heart
the flames no longer bear the fear, consuming me

But they adorn me
Crown me with their radiance!

Another gate, another Rite

Farewell
until next time around

I'll sing my song of Bliss!

Bliss of an Untamed Morning

The sky opens in a blaze
fluorescent gold, red fires streaked with tangerine and rose
some amber feathers in between
a moment's pleasure
flowing from the paintbrush of the gods...

The scent of salt and mango
Sweet as sin

Can you taste it?

Juice running down my chin, my fingers
As life itself, sticky and wild

Doesn't pleasure always come with a mess?

My tongue licking, savoring it all...

LIFE!

Untamed as the Caribbean breeze that tangles in my hair
The sun, her growing glow
warming my skin

I feel alive!
Present
More than a moment's spark
More than just flesh

Bare toes dig into powders of white sands
Still cool beneath the surface, moist
Remembering
The birth of stars, first breath
Times when the ocean worlds were virgin

Turquoise waters rolling in
Each crest a piece of art
A dance of shimmering blues and jades
swirling 'round my ankles

A lover's caress
that asks nothing
But me being here

You are beside me now
Or is this just an illusion of you?

I feel your hand tracing the length of my spine
a touch as soft as sunlight slipping through the sway of palm leaves
tension blooming, expanding...
a slow stream of desire
No need to rush it

Bliss

The way the world tilts just before the kiss
Like fruit swollen on the vine

ripe and waiting
We linger
Letting the space between us crackle

Your skin on mine, tangled with the smell of seaweed and surf
drifting between us like forgotten dreams

I taste you in the salt on my lips
Feel you in the rhythm of the ocean's sighs

I smile, I laugh aloud!
Not because there's joy to find

But because joy
has just found me

Horses leap and bound along the beach
Manes wild, hooves churning the sand
An untamed freedom we once knew
before we learned to cage our ecstasy

Is this Bliss?
Or just the moment before?

I kneel in the sand, soft grains between my fingers
And listen to the tides, their songs in ancient tongues

The sea does not apologize
for its endlessness
its force, its glorious, majestic powers!

Nor for the way it keeps its secrets
hidden within the depths of emerald eternity
The tales of thousands of forgotten lovers
of ships lost to the night

The sea foam bubbling with mischief
And mermaids
dancing, swaying, chanting
Teasing me
to come and play

Hummingbirds flutter
Their tiny wings burst in a blur of light
as they sip from vibrant flowers
Feeding only on the sweet nectars of life

Bliss is not just a moment
It's not a fleeting wave
Nor sudden rush
of pleasure, touch
from sun or sea

Bliss is not a destination
It's our decision

A constant choice
To deliberately focus
On the beauty
Amidst chaos

The grace we choose to see
Even in the shadows
And all the in-betweens

Do you ever feel like gazing deeper?
For the hidden treasures buried beneath?

It's in the way we guide our vision
Not by blinding ourselves
to the ugly, sorrow, pain

But by letting our light
reach into the abyss
Illuminating all that is...

By standing firm within our values
while still acting from a place of love

I sit by the shore
Each wave lapping against my feet
the rhythm pulsing in my blood

A reminder
of what's possible

when I allow to just surrender

Life is not perfect
But isn't it marvelous?!

Counting my blessings
Small wonders of my world
The sun, spilling shades of copper on my skin
The gentle breeze, drawing dragons in the clouds

The stars, dancing in the waves
Sparkling like jewels
Fallen off the skies

Bliss is in these simple acts
My fingers walking labyrinths in the sand
Your lips pressed softly to my neck
light as air
Yet grounding me, anchoring me
in this moment
of infinite Yes

It's in the sweetness of connection
The glance between us
through the windows of our soul

The way the world narrows
to the space between our hearts

The capacity to feel
To allow joy
flooding every corner of my being

To open myself fully
to the abundance of sensation
emotion, and desire

It's in my daily gratitude
The childlike curiosity
To be enchanted, mesmerized
by the beauty all around
In others, and the beauty within me

My body
Awake, healthy, strong
Graced with creative mind, heart, soul
Holding such depth
such glee and passion

Bliss is the Yes I offer to the world
My Yes to love
To ecstasy, that's not just physical
but transcendent
Breaking through the boundaries of skin and bone
Into spirit

Bliss is not the seeking
It's the Being

Bliss is my YES to Life!

Dear Reader, now it's your turn to write! Use the blank space below. Try not to censor yourself.

In my global retreats and sessions, I love to work with myriad tools of expression—tantric embodiment, somatic dance, art, the power of word.

MIRACLES ARE SIMPLY A SHIFT IN PERCEPTION

We all seek wonders—but are you ready for them?

Have you prepared your landing place? A cozy chair with joyful patterns, flowers, and scents, inviting the extraordinary?

Or can these blessings only glimmer through the curtains of your tears, cutting their feet on shards of broken dreams left scattered on the dance floor of your life—for centuries?

Pick up the broom! Dust off your wings! Speak your deepest heart's desire.

YES! I'm ready for miracles to land in my life!

My heart's growing dragon wings!

These are the shards and limiting beliefs I'll sweep off my floor right now! I'm calling in these blessings to dance life in ecstatic abundance and joy!

Nydia Laysa Stone is a Somatic Therapist, ReWilding and Life Transition Coach, international bestselling author and artist, blending neuroscience with ancient shamanic practices since over 35 years.

Master teacher of multiple Energy Healing modalities, Yoga, Dynamic Mediations, Tantra, dance, and art expression, she integrates Egyptian Sekhem, Violet Flame, dragon light language, Soul Retrieval, and the Rites of the Munay Ki.

A global nomad, Nydia lives mostly between the Islands of the Caribbean, Fiji, Bali, Greece, and India, where she facilitates her Signature ReWilding Retreats: cultural and spiritual immersions in the world's highest frequency locations.

Rooted in Tantric embodiment and passionate about passage rites, sensual liberation, alchemical transformation, and radical mind-shifting to overcome stagnation and blockages and re-wire your nervous system, Nydia guides you to re-connect with your body's intelligence and womb wisdom, re-align with your unique path of soul, desire, and purpose to discover new perspectives, vision, and clarity and redesign the heart-centered life of your dreams!

Connect with Nydia: https://www.healingartsbynydia.com

Chapter 11

The Elements of Poetic Healing

K.J. Kaschula

My Story

I like to imagine myself in a beautiful garden surrounded by perfumed wildflowers, buzzing bees, dancing twittering birds, and a gentle breeze who inquisitively watches from the trees. Time exists not in this garden—day and night do. They are brother and sister playing a game of tag, forever trying to catch the other and only exchanging tags at twilight. I imagine my soul, my human breath, breathing—in, out, out, and in. This is home; this is my personal space where I can connect to the All, to what is and what shall be. At night, when brother sun tags sister moon, I imagine my fire coming alive. It is warm and inviting and speaks many truths of my will and of my deepest desire. As its gentle flames lick the delicious glittering stars of the forever night sky, crickets orchestrate the next act of my breath, of my home, of my connection, and of my passion.

"Life seems nothing more than a quick succession of busy nothings," said Jane Austen once, speaking the truth of mankind and womankind through an age that almost seems forgotten to our human memory, if not for the historians who record past happenings.

"Busy nothings"—*busyness,* a term I've come to equate with my current lifestyle of late—a good busyness through, when I reflect upon where I've been and where I'm going. However, although one becomes busy or is busy, it seems vital to return to our centre—our core; for we as an individual require our very existence to return to a balance, to re-locate our humanity and our very purpose for being here, for being now.

And so, I'm drawn to the elements, to the points of connection of Mother Earth, to help re-align my personal *busyness* and bring me back from the simple "busy nothings" of life.

I call upon AIR:
the very breath I breathe as sit in my meditation garden.

And I call upon EARTH:
my home, my planet, with one foot in South Africa and the other foot in France.

I call upon WATER:
to connect me to the now and to the ether—to my past, present, and future.

And I call upon FIRE:
to connect me to my burning passion: to write, to create, to inspire, and to be the cause of hope and change.

And I gift to you, dear reader or listener, 'The Elements of Poetic Healing' to help you in your quest to rediscover who you are, to reconnect, and to rejuvenate your soul. May the following words guide you as you return to your centre from life's "busy nothings."

The Poems

AIR (breath)

Breathe.
In. Out. Out. In.
Feel the movement, feel the AIR.
Inside the body, outside the body.

AIR dances like Wind and whispers to the heart.
"Play me a song," she calls out.
As her breath, your breath beats in and out.

Drum. Drum, drum,
the heart calls to her breath.
Drum. Drum, drum,
the heart calls to your AIR.

Breathe.
Breathe in. Breathe out. Out, in. In, out.
Feel the movement, feel your AIR.
Inside your body, outside your body.

AIR still and silent for a moment,
listens to the whispers of your heart.
"Hear my song, hear my story," he calls out.
As his beat, your beat breathes in and out.

Drum. Drum, drum,
the heart begins in the silence of her breath.
Drum. Drum, drum,
the heart begins with the listening of AIR.

"'Tis the story of you, 'tis the story of us.
We are one, you and I.
Lovers of a forgotten world.
When your AIR leaves this space.

and you dance among the flowers, trees and busy bees,
so will my beat, your beat, beat a forgotten tune.
Forever it calls to you.
Forever waiting for your return."

Drum. drum, drum,
the heart sings her song.
Drum. drum, drum,
the heart sings their song.

"Hear our song, hear our story," he calls out,
as his beat takes her breath, and they dance.
In and out, out and in.

"When you return, my love, my AIR,
we dance in beat, and we dance in breath;
you remember who you are in this world
as well as that world."

"And we dance amongst your soul,
and we dance amongst your light,
and we dance amongst your thoughts,
In-Between the stars and In-Between universes."

Drum. drum, drum.
Drum. drum, drum.

"But fear not, my love, my breath, my AIR.
For my beat, your beat
will beat each time you whisper to my heart.
each time you call out
each time I sing our song,
and I will breathe in
And I will breathe out
Your AIR, our AIR."

Drum. drum, drum.
Drum. drum, drum.

"'Tis a beautiful song, 'tis a beautiful story," she calls out.
As her breath, his breath beats out and in.
"And I thank you, my love, my beat, for singing this tune.
But alas, I must return to the flowers, trees and busy bees,
And dance amongst them as I remember
your beat, your drum, your hum."

Breathe.
In. Out. Out. In
Feel the movement, feel the AIR
Our AIR is inside our body
Our AIR is outside our body.

Drum, drum.

Drum.

𝓔𝓐𝓡𝓣𝓗 (home)

Upon this EARTH I walk. *From tile to carpet to wooden floorboards.*
There is song in the air. *A honk, a siren, and a cellular-ring.*
As I sip EARTH's water, *filled with coffee grounds,*
birds traverse the skies; *chemtrails pointing their direction of flight.*
A vast sea *of concrete grey stretches out*
with waves *of church bells who ring at the hour.*
Rich earthly aromas fill the air *perfumed by a cooking pot upon the stove.*
We will gather tonight around the firelight and *listen to stories around the black box.*

This is home.

Within this home I walk. The green grass between my toes.
There is music in the air. A tweet, a chirp, and a robin's twitter.
As I sip my morning brew, filled with nature's tea leaves,
birds perform aerobatic manoeuvres; seasons pointing their direction of flight.
In the suburb of my garden, fields of green EARTH reach out,
as the airflow of Wind's dances caresses then kisses my cheek.
Spices float upon the air, awakened by Grandfather fire.
We will gather tonight under constellations and hear the stories of our day.

This is EARTH.

WATER (connection)

I am the spirit of WATER
I am the memory of your past,
the memory of your presence,
and its future.
I connect to the All,
and the All connects to me.
I know the stories of the plants,
the stories of the animals, the insects,
the beasts, the birds and the fishes.
Most of all, I know the story of you.
I am the spirit of WATER,
I know the laughter and the pain
of mankind and its Mother Earth.
I know its triumphs and its downfalls.
I move through time,
and time moves through me.
I heal that which is ailed,
And what is ailed is healed through me.
I purify and cleanse,
again, and again.
I am the spirit of WATER,
the unacknowledged traveller
the unheard storyteller.
I am a force upon this world
who gives life and starves it.
I am the spirit of WATER,
I soar with the clouds
and dive deep into the rivers, lakes,
and oceans blue.
I am the spirit of WATER
I whisper unknown truths
of this world and of you upon it,
of its heart, of yours and of mine.
I am the spirit of WATER.

FIRE (passion)

Burn bright
Ignite that light
Start with a match
Hear that scratch
Feel that passion
Fuel that FIRE
Burn bright
Ignite that light

Burning bright
Keep that light
With your candle lit
Let your soul emit
A passion, a FIRE
Your own heart's desire
Burning bright
Keep that light

Burn brighter
Grow higher
Gather around the campfire
And let loved ones inquire
About your passion
About your fire
Burn brighter
Grow higher

Feed the brightness
Bask in the lightness
Transend
And welcome friends
To your passion
To your fire
Feed the brightness
Bask in the lightness

Spark bright
Ignite a friend's light
Let them yearn
To burn
In passion
And in Fire
So, Spark bright
In many coloured lights ignite.

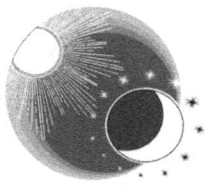

Dear Reader, now it's your turn to write! Use the blank space below. Try not to censor yourself.

Draw a picture of you in your own meditation garden where you are able to connect with AIR (breath), EARTH (home), WATER (connection), and FIRE (passion).

K.J. Kaschula
Brave Kids Books Publishing Director
Children's Book Author, Illustrator, and
Book Designer

K.J., or Kelly, grew up in Gauteng, South Africa (her first home), where she found herself gravitating toward the arts of storytelling. She created *The-Super-Dooper-Secret-Collection,* a series of children's illustrated books following the secret adventures of Little Lizzie, who encounters magical creatures never before seen by kid-kind! She's also the mastermind behind *Brave Kids: Short Stories to Inspire Our Future World-Changers,* a collection of short stories written by authors from around the world, uniquely crafted to inspire hope and change for a better world. When Kelly is not playing with stories, she is knee-deep in publishing, acting as Brave Kids Books Publishing Director and working behind the scenes for Brave Healer Productions. If you are looking for Kelly and can't find her in sunny South Africa, then she's most likely sipping coffee in Paris, France (her second home) with her husband.

Connect with K.J. Kaschula: https://www.kjkaschula.com/

Chapter 12

What Else Are You Feeling?

Centering in Your Medicine Wheel

Emily Atlantis Wolf

"The world is not conclusion."
~Emily Dickinson

My Story

"People who are stuck are failing humanity," he said, sitting with his arm over the low-back teal, upholstered chair. The lamplight of the bronze justice statue shone in his clear blue eyes.

I smiled as I pulled my arm off my eyes, laying on the orange IKEA sofa sleeper along the back of his chair. I lifted my head to look into the face of this man, my son, twenty-two years old, who had endured the abrupt ending to his senior year in 2020, a bout of long Covid that took his smell, taste, and ability to focus his mind, and a mysterious, debilitating fatigue that lasted two years.

Yep, he's recovered. I was there through it all. I'm the rock in my little family of three. Four if you include me.

But now was my dark hour.

The results of the 2024 election left me feeling crumpled—ruined. My first thoughts were: *This isn't my reality. I opened the wrong door. I slipped into this nightmare when I fell asleep. How do I get back?*

I felt like a gorgeous, blooming persimmon-colored marigold ripped out of its roots by a drunk, angry man who rubbed off all the petals in his doughy white hands and threw them on a slab of sidewalk.

All I could do was stare at the lace-white ceiling in my living room after my son left to meet up with his cousin. I cooked and baked for twelve days to cope with my despair. I fed my son steak, tacos, chili, and chocolate chip banana bread. I gave away a massive yellow Pyrex bowl of dark chocolate mousse to my friend for her college kids. I taught myself how to make oat milk. I made lime-ginger cranberry sauce for Thanksgiving and ordered brisket and turkey.

I exhaled into silent emptiness. *What am I feeling?*

I feel like an upside-down sea turtle
at the lowest level of the ocean,
surrounded by pressurized blackness
knowing there isn't enough oxygen to make it back to the surface.

Could I feel worse? Lower?

Wait, let me check. Lower, lower. No, this is the lowest.

Okay.

I sighed and made the sound like you do when you're pretending to be a sputtering motorboat. Then no sound for a healthy silence.

What else do you feel?

I feel glad to be on this couch and not drinking poison, smoking, or doing drugs anymore. I'm happy to have a century house. I'm grateful for my kids, who seem to be more resilient than me. I'm happy I have inherited my mom's toes because they are adorable. I'm grateful for my health.

That night was the beginning of my recovery. I opened the dark door of despair to let my feelings surface and smash like a breaching whale. My internal ocean of emotions returned to normal crests and falls. I survived the storm. Now I could choose my next galvanized action.

The Poems

Calling In the Direction of The East

(Raising arms and facing east)
We greet the direction of the east
With love and gratitude.

Hail to the rising sun, the first light!
We bow to the long, gold rays,
That activate our internal movements
And summon our eyes to rise.

Welcome spirits of the element of water.
Welcome the ways of dreaming,
Of remembering our gestation,
When we formed our body around a single cell of being.

We honor the natural rhythms of growth,
Of time to form and flow into cellular patterns
To become heartbeat, hand, and spine.

We honor movement and gyration
When we mimic the energy flowing through waves,
Allowing the same energy to flow through our limbs,
Surrendered to the ecstatic, electric feeling of aliveness.

We soften our imagination to remember
When our bodies had fins, scales, and tails.

We acknowledge the incessant curiosity
That pushed us above the surface of the water
To seek new ways of being, breathing, and living
And how we continue to pursue self-discovery.

We come back home to the direction of the east,
To honor our own beginning.
We honor the tribal family who cared for us at birth,
When we struggled to breathe air instead of water.

Thank you to the mother who carried us through,
Thank you for nourishing our womb waters,
And surrounding us with a cushion against the world.
Thank you for saying yes to our birth,
And your blood, sweat, and tears bring us forth.

Thank you to the hands that touched our skin and rocked us to sleep,
Thank you to the smiles that comforted our awakening.
Thank you to the arms that carried us outside,
And the ones who protected us before we could speak.

We lift our hands in prayer with sacred smoke,
And honor our primordial womb.
We drum and dance and sway to celebrate
The waters surrounding the Earth.

Welcome sea turtle with your lessons of patience and longevity,
Welcome whale and your living record of Earth's history.
Welcome dolphin and otter with your teachings of play,
Welcome protective primal forces of the shark and stingray.

Welcome jellyfish, mother of coral, who remembers the beginning.
Welcome octopus and your teachings of highest intelligence.
Welcome eel, Earth's first snake.
Welcome fish nations who feed us all.

Come to us, spirits of the East.
Help us begin our journey,
Give us guidance in our dreams,
Support our new ideas.

Bring in the season of spring,
Of hope for planted seeds.
Bring us water for our growing,
And first flowers after snow.

Be the rain that helps plants sprout
And rise up to the sky.
Be the mist on the mountain
That quiets the land.

Be the storm that washes us clean,
Reminding us who is queen.
Be the snow that falls in a sweep,
Reminding us to stay in our deep sleep.

As we face the East in reverence and awe,
We ask for spirits to come to us now.

The gates of the east are open.

Calling In the Direction of The South

(Raising arms and facing south)
We greet the direction of the south
With love and gratitude.

We greet the middle-day sun, the rays of heat,
That light our work and progress,
The strength and warmth to journey far,
And activate our cellular immunity.

Welcome spirits of the element of Earth,
Welcome the ways of doing, of inspired action,
Putting dreams in motion,
Tending the garden, clearing the path.

We lift our hands in prayer with sacred drums,
And honor the place we build our homes.
We drum and dance and sway to celebrate
The forests, jungles, and rivers of the Earth.

We greet the season of summer,
When all living beings tend to their work,
Finding their mates, creating families,
Exploring new territory and blossoming into fullness.

We honor the nation of trees
Who stand between Earth and sky,
We honor the stone nations
Who watch and observe.

Welcome great buffalo nation,
Our provider and friend.
Welcome deer, moose, antelope, and elk.
Welcome raccoon, fox, otter, and beaver.
Welcome bear and your cave of dreaming.

Welcome long stretches of land,
Trails of migration, interconnecting paths,
Prairies, meadows, deserts, and plains.
We honor space for all living beings.

We honor the direction of doing and productivity,
The bee collecting nectar and pollinating flowers,
The beaver finding trees to chew and stack,
The shaman birthing a hoop drum with songs.

We honor children who are running and laughing in the wind,
The father who is teaching how to spark a fire,
The mother who is showing how to sew clothes,
And the crone who is pointing at plants to mend bones.

We honor the river cutting into the rock,
Creating snake shapes of undulation,
Giving us valleys with fertile banks,
Minerals from mountain's memories of storms.

We honor the lava layer that rises
To spray out new lands,
The liquid insides of rock,
Shaped by father's hands.

We honor the crystals that are forming
In pockets of pressurized heat and gas,
Sacred geometry hardening
To record knowledge of the past.

We honor this time of long light and short nights,
When the work feels easy, everything feels possible.
When all living beings relax and enjoy being alive,
The stretch between birth and death.

We honor the mystery of attraction,
The dance of magnetism, the nature of play.
The glance of beginnings, the calculating considerations,
The longing to know more, to desire and please.

We honor the spin of mutual connection,
When two circle and spiral, push and pull
On each other, creating friction and tension,
A glorious game in every dimension.

We honor proximity of lover's bodies,
When scent is an ally and vibrations are felt.
We breathe today because they came together
At last, and became one force of creation.

As we face the south in reverence and awe,
We ask for spirits to come to us now.

The gates of the south are open.

Calling In The Direction of The West

(Raising arms and facing west)
We greet the direction of the west
With love and gratitude.

We bless the sun who blazes as she falls,
Descending into darkness
Signaling us to finish our work
And prepare for endings.

Welcome spirits of the element of fire,
The burning and releasing,
Transformation and desire,
Until all the world is heat and light.

We greet the mountains, caves, and alpine lakes,
Our places to retreat and reflect.
Our places of solitude, of quiet rest.
Our place to observe all we have finished, or yet to be done.

We honor the direction of the crone,
The one who endured, the one who tells tales.
We honor the ones more fragile and frail,
The ones more spirit than muscle, less bone and more air.

We honor the slowing, natural pace,
And writing our stories in books and letters,
And remembering our work and magnetic dances.
We listen to the wind, calling us home.

We honor the dying embers, full of spark and blue light,
The hottest form of fire, the carpet of light.
We scry into the radiating lines - alive!
And see our guides, healers, and helpers,
Our animal ancestors, our friends at last sight.

We welcome the wolf, the way-shower and pathfinder,
Who ventures alone and returns to the pack,
With wisdom of safety to lead the way back,
The one who goes first, who finds what's new.

We welcome the goats and rams,
The mountain lion, the puma, the jaguar, and lamb.
The moth and the bat, the fox who stationed between night and day,
Between forest and prairie, together we pray.

We honor the season of fall,
The fire-colors of leaves that ignite
And live their lifelong dream of flight,
Leaving behind the next sleeping bud.

We welcome the direction of circles,
Of gathering around fires,
To share stories of our day,
And celebrate our work.

We shake our rattles full of seeds and pebbles,
Chanting and singing to pass to each other
The ways of our ancestors,
What we need to remember.

We honor our mortality, our short visit to Earth.
We recognize the fragility of the web where we danced.
We bless the people who helped clear our path.
We give thanks to our children who we leave here,

The one we created or were made aware.
We honor our parents who created our birth.
We honor their parents and the lines extending back.
We honor our work on the web, our rest, and goals.
We see into the future when we are only souls.

We honor natural endings of seasons and cycles,
The sunset, the last crest, the last butterfly, the last breath.
We honor our last flames, last sparks,
And settle into the embers of our last dark.

As we face the West in reverence and awe,
We ask for spirits to come to us now.

The gates of the west are open.

Calling In the Direction of the North, the Above, the Below, and the Within

(Raising arms and facing north)
We greet the direction of the north
With love and gratitude.

Blessings to the moon, the sun of the night,
That calls to our tides and feminine rhythms.
Wrap us in your white light,
Bathe us in your reflective wisdom.

We greet you with whistling words and tones
As we breathe in love
And breathe out love
For this visit that, looking back, felt quick to our bones.

Welcome spirits of the element of the air,
Welcome guides who ferry us through the great dark,
When our body is returned to Mother Earth,
And our spirit returns home to dream of new starts.

We honor the time of rest and pause,
The age of reflection when we review our actions,
The documentation of lessons in the Akashic books,
The stones of karma rolled from one tally to another.

We honor the formless, the other dimensions,
The intuitive sparks that change our directions.
We acknowledge the knowing and the unknown,
And feeling into wisdom from maps we've been shown.

We welcome the silence,
The hush after death,
The moment after the waves falls,
The exhale's end before breath.

We welcome our ancestors,
The family known and remembered,
The storytellers and storykeepers,
Our ancient brothers and sisters.

We welcome the great teachers
Who walked the Earth before us,
Our guides and helpers
That led us forward each day.

We welcome the eagle, hawk, and condor.
We welcome the heavy clouds and the thunder.
We welcome the cold winds that push geese to the south,
Along with hummingbird, goldfinch, and grouse.

We welcome the nation of winged ones
Who carry our messages to the sky,
The ones with long feathers and hollow bones,
Who are more sky than body.

We greet the direction of the above, of Father Sky,
That hovers above us with a protective eye.
We welcome your vast placidness,
To our noisy chatter, to our busyness and distraction.

We embody the above in our Earthly body,
The connection to celestial realms,
To see with widest sight,
To use our love to shine on all beings.
We thank our guides, the legion of angels,
Who kindles our reason to breathe, our divine purpose.

We greet the direction of the below, of Pacha Mama,
Our abundant mother, creator of our borrowed body,
Who loves all her children, the two-leggded,
The four-legged, the winged ones, and the swimmers.

We embody the below in our body,
The connection to tribe, to creation and expression,
To our will, our ability to choose a next action,
We thank our guides, the nation of dragons,
Who teaches us to unite our power and be sovereign.

We greet the direction of the within,
The divine spark that we carry in our mobile sanctuary,
The spiraling path of discovering our own knowing,
The soul, the spirit, the immortal light.

O'Mitakuye Oyasin,
We are all related.

The gates of the seven directions are open.

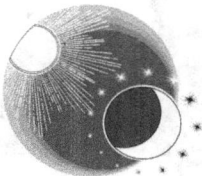

Dear Reader, now it's your turn to write! Use the blank space below. Try not to censor yourself.

With the seven directions open, ask yourself: "Given infinite time, money, and resources, what would I start doing today?"

Emily Atlantis Wolf teaches people intuitive techniques so they can make decisions with natural confidence.

She climbed corporate ladders in civil engineering and financial services until 2009 when her mom died, causing her to pivot into the healing arts, becoming a Shaman, Master Breathwork Facilitator, and Licensed Medical Massage Therapist.

Since 2010, she has helped over 3,000 clients confront and care for their physical and metaphysical pain. From chronic muscle tightness to trauma and unexpressed emotional energy, Atlantis combines practical and intuitive modalities. Part of her secret is connecting to spiritual realms using breathwork, drumming, fire ceremonies, and the guidance of galactic dragons.

She offers group coaching, writing courses, breathwork events, and retreats. Sign up for her email list to receive a free video showing you how to use drumming and a backyard fire to release one piece of stuck energy.

Connect with Emily: https://www.atlantiswolf.com/

Chapter 13

I Think I Killed My Father

Finding Self-Forgiveness and Redemption

Jacqueline Diaz

This chapter is dedicated to Kasey LaLa, whose love, smile, humbleness, and kindness touches everyone she meets.

My Story

Daddy, you look so peaceful.

There are so many things I wish I could tell you.

I rubbed my father's cold, stiff hands, staring at him in disbelief. He lay there, motionless, surrounded by white satin and polished mahogany. His lips curled into a faint smile, almost as if he were amused by something only he could see.

You look so dapper. The last time I saw you in a suit was years ago on those church Sundays. You wore them with pride.

The tears fell silently as I stood there, frozen, as family and friends trickled in. They all took turns approaching his casket like it was some exhibit.

They must know. I did this.

People went up to the pulpit to speak about the man my dad was. The loving, strong-willed, giving man. I couldn't go up there. Shame kept me glued to my seat.

What could I even say?

At the cemetery, everything felt like a nightmare. As they lowered the casket into the ground, my sobs pierced the air, raw and uncontrollable. It wasn't like when Mom died. I kept my cry private. This was different.

The truth is it wasn't just sadness. It was guilt, heavy and unbearable.

My dad had been sick for years. His kidney transplant gave him many more years, but his body began to fail. He was bedbound. He needed round-the-clock care. Dad asked me to visit. Just us. I was excited. It wasn't like him to want father-daughter talks. I won't share our conversation. That's ours. But I left fuming. I stormed out.

How dare he? I won't speak to him. I'll teach him a lesson.

That was the last time I spoke to my father.

Two weeks later, my eldest son asked me to come inside when I dropped him off at dad's. "Come inside. Just say hi to grandpa."

I refused.

If he wants to see me, he can call.

One late night, I saw a missed call from him.

I'll call him in the morning.

I never got the chance. Instead, I woke up to a frantic call that he had passed.

I killed my dad with my silence. With my pride. I could've visited him more. I could've loved him better.

The guilt has consumed me. I think about that last conversation constantly.

My dad was a stubborn, deeply religious man, and we clashed a lot. I realize that the things that drove me crazy about him are the things I see in myself.

The journey to forgive myself has been long. But I've learned that people love in their own way. Not always the way we want them to. My dad loved me. His love was tough and unyielding. A love that built my moral compass. A love that would've gone to the ends of the earth for me.

To those I've hurt because I didn't recognize your love, please keep loving me in your way.

And to those reading this searching for redemption, learn to forgive yourself first.

The Poems

Dear Brother

O brother, dear brother, in spring's gentle bloom,
We dreamed of tomorrows that never made room.
Through good and bad, chasing shadows of the past,
With hearts heavy, wondering how long it would last.

O brother, dear brother, we wrestled as kids,
But grown-up battles left guilt where joy hid.
My best friend, and confidant, my shelter in the rain,
Your laughter, your light, easing my pain.

The parties, dear brother, filled with cheer,
We had each other, and no need to fear.
In the quiet of night, after the fun,
Our bond unspoken, stronger than anyone.

O brother, dear brother, when storms came to stay,
We held each other, kept the darkness away.
In sorrow, we laughed, in struggle, we smiled,
Hope bloomed eternal, across countless miles.

In happy times, dear brother, we cherished the bad,
To keep us grounded, the memories we had,
Then came a blow that shattered my world,
Misunderstandings, egos, whispers that swirled.

We drifted apart, lost in our pride,
Two souls adrift, no harbor in sight.
I drowned in whiskey, you in your pain,
We found each other, but never the same.

O brother, dear brother, I miss those days,
When we lived in harmony, in simpler ways.
Life has moved on, but my heart still aches,
For the spark we shared, now easily breaks.

O brother, dear brother, with the same blood,
Before I leave this earth, if only we could,
Be like before, in another lifetime's beat,
I'd choose you again, my brother, so sweet.

Blue Lily

My body froze as you clutched your chest,
Gasping for air, in panic, distressed.
Sirens screamed through the quiet night,
I stood there shaking, holding on tight.

Relief came over me when I saw you again,
In a hospital gown, no longer in pain.
Days and years followed, filled with joy and grace,
You pursued piano, your childhood embrace.

You were there for graduations, beaming with pride,
Watched your grandkids grow, always by our side.
Sunday brunches, our sweet routine,
Laughter and stories, our bond felt serene.

You remained a homebody, content in your way,
Gardening, caring for father each day.
We told you to travel, to see something new,
But you found peace in the simple things you'd do.

Shopping for trinkets, a simple delight,
Promises made for vacations in flight.
But now, my vision blurs as reality hits,
My lily, once pure, was tainted, adrift.

That night, the sirens actually ceased their call,
Entering your room, a haunting pall.
My lily, so pure, was cold and still,
The birthdays and brunches, they never will...

You never saw those graduations,
Or heard the laughter of celebrations.
Those are all imaginations in my head.
Now I'm haunted by words left unsaid.

I thought we had time, I thought you'd stay,
But now reality's come to take it away.
You were my lily, once vibrant and true,
Now blue like your lips... fading from view.

And though you're gone, I hold you so near,
In the quiet, in the heartache, I wish you were here.
My blue lily, torn from the bloom,
The world feels so much darker without you.

The Cockatoo Dance

Have you ever seen the cockatoo dance?
Heads swaying back and forth, feathers in trance?
It reminds me of us, our love, our fire,
A rhythm so deep, born from love and desire.

But like those birds, we spun and we clashed,
Over words that burned, over dreams that crashed.
I wanted to love you, to hold you close,
Yet fear made me question the thing I wanted most.

We were made for each other, there's no denying,
But we let pride, like walls, keep us from flying.
Every argument, every fight we'd begin,
Only pushed us farther, kept the love locked in.

Still, I can't forget how you made me feel,
Your touch, your gaze, so achingly real.
And though I lost my way, blinded by doubt,
It's always been you I couldn't live without.

Yet even in the midst of our pain and strife,
Our love stood tall, the anchor of my life.
I fight every day to right the wrongs,
To prove our love is where I belong.

I see you, I feel you, even in the pain,
And I know we can find ourselves again.
No matter the scars, the battles we've faced,
Our love is timeless, it can't be erased.

Like the cockatoos, ready to dance,
Ready to love, to give us a chance.
Best friends through dark and light,
Even when grand gestures were out of sight.

In you, I found my safe place, so dear,
Though my heart aches with the mistakes I fear.
I never want to lose you, my love so true,
Despite the flaws, our love pulls us through.

The cockatoo dance, our timeless move,
Like holding hands, like hearts that groove.
I want to dance with you, through every season.
No matter the faults, no matter the reason.

As we grow old, with silvered strands,
Still swaying together, hand in hand.
Let's seek redemption, and forgiveness to find,
In the rhythm of love, hearts intertwined.

Our story is not perfect, it's broken and flawed,
But it's ours, and that's enough to call it a draw.
This is our love story, our eternal chance,
Forever entangled in the cockatoo dance.

The Pearly Gates Trial

Father. Lord. God. Judge.
As the guard of these gates,
I stand before you, to sentence her fate.
This woman, a dreamer, a heart full of care,
Yet guilt and regret have led her to despair.

A mother of three, her life spent in shame,
Consumed by the past, she lost her own name.
No legacy left, no great deeds to recall,
Just echoes of sorrow in the silence of hall.

Those she has left mourn out of mere duty,
Once a bright spark, now a shadow of beauty.
Her laughter once danced like the sun's golden ray,
Now darkness surrounds her, and joy fades away.

She stopped living fully, her spirit confined,
By chains of regret, she fell far behind.
A caring, sweet soul, once vibrant and free,
But her sins became anchors, so heavy, you see.

She struggled to love, even herself she denied,
If she cannot forgive, why should you, Lord, abide?

Father. Lord. God. Judge.
I plead on her side,
For deep in her heart, a true love did bide.

Yes, she faltered, yes, she erred,
But her remorse shows that her heart still cared.
Through all of her trials, her love remained true,
A flame still flickering, yearning for you.

Her loved ones are dear, her love runs so deep,
Though lost in her sorrow, her heart still does weep.
Grant her another chance, let her soul mend,
To live out the joy that she failed to defend.

Father. Lord. God. Judge.
Show mercy today,
Let her heal and forgive, let her find her own way.
Allow her to blossom, to rise from her pain,
To rediscover her life, her joy, and her gain.

Then thunder rolled forth, a voice filled the air,
As the heavens did shake, all creation laid bare.

"My child," spoke the Lord, "I will not condemn,
Nor let you pass through, but I'll see you again."

"You'll return to the earth, to your body you'll go,
To mend all your wrongs, to love, and to grow.
Forgive yourself now, let your heart once more sing,
Live with the passion, the joy that you bring."

With a final decree, the voice wrapped around,
And she opened her eyes, to life's tender sound.
With hope in her heart and a new path to tread,
She'd rise from the ashes, alive once again.

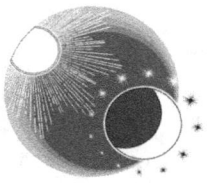

Dear Reader, now it's your turn to write! Use the blank space below. Try not to censor yourself.

Write a letter to yourself. Explore the profound themes of self-healing and forgiveness. Acknowledge your mistakes and the lessons they brought. What would you say to a friend who was struggling with the same feelings? Offer yourself that same compassion and understanding. Allow your heart to forgive.

Jacqueline Diaz is a thought leader and advocate for creating more inclusive workplaces that embrace neurodiversity. As co-owner of Strategic Talent Acquisition: A Recruiting Firm, and founder of The Steven Spectrum Career Project, a nonprofit dedicated to integrating neurodiverse individuals into the workforce, she is committed to empowering people from all backgrounds to thrive in their careers.

A champion of mental health, Jacqueline understands the vital connection between well-being and professional success. She boldly challenges the status quo, advocating for workplace cultures where mental health is a top priority.

Beyond her advocacy, Jacqueline co-authored the bestselling *The Ultimate Guide to Leaving Your Legacy,* where her chapter is titled "Neurodivergent." She also wrote *Jacob's Melody: Harmony in Autism,* a children's book about how an autistic boy finds his way through music. Her mission is more than just inspirational; she strives to create tangible, lasting change that promotes success for all.

Connect with Jacqueline: linkedin.com/in/jacqueline-diaz-85023953

Chapter 14

Reconciled. . . No More Fear

Melanie Barnes, Da Evangelist

My Story

From the impressionable age of ten, I was immersed in the world of Christianity, chicken dinners in the annex, and black patent leather shoes with scuff marks because they stuck together when one foot would rub close to the other. I was hooked up to the feeding tube of organized religion and fed a consistent diet of regurgitated information and toxic ideology with an enormous side of fear.

We attended church five out of seven days, off on Mondays and Tuesdays. It felt like a job with double shifts on weekends. Some days, we started early in the morning and left after the streetlights came on. I decided: *God must work from home on those days.*

Can't you picture Jesus as the first remote worker? All our plans were centered around my mom's church activities. So, the running joke was Jesus got a 3-for-1 deal with us because when my mom got "saved," the entire house got "saved."

Church was often enjoyable and became a staple in my childhood. My favorite memories were singing in the choir and sleepovers that turned friends into family. My love for God and fear of being sent to Hell led me to a young life of service and sacrifice. If church had consisted only of music, good food, and fellowship, it would've been perfect. Unfortunately, that wasn't the case. Good food and good times were side dishes. Fear was the main course, and I ate of its bitterness 'till I was full of doubt and lacked any sense of self-worth. Fear drew me to the altar and also pushed me away. Every Sunday was the same—hellfire and brimstone.

You'll burn in Hell if you don't know Jesus! I made up my mind—I needed to make sure Jesus and I knew each other. I spent many Sundays at the altar washing away the sins of my young soul. It was damn near impossible to have a normal childhood with the constant threat of death looming. Fear consumed me and became my crutch. How could I grow into my own if I couldn't see beyond my present experiences?

Choosing what felt right wasn't allowed. Even choosing a career was questioned: "Did you consult God and get an answer?" Gifts come from God, right? So, it seemed natural that it would be God's will for me to pursue my talents. There's a twofold scripture that says God will give you the desires of your heart. Meaning, our desires not only come from God but also are given by God. I didn't understand that as a child. I also didn't understand fearing God. It never made sense. I am an extension of God. So why would I be afraid of me? Why would God create me, then have a problem with me and sentence me to eternal damnation? These were questions I needed the answers to, and I am happy to say that I no longer have the question, "What will God say?"

The Poems

Decision. . .

I had to make a decision. . .
So I stopped trying to prove my worthiness and just accepted it.

I stopped trying to defend my position and I just held it.
I stopped trying to maintain my focus and I just kept it.
I stopped bringing up the past because I can't change it.
I had to make a decision. . .
I stopped complaining about the situation and handled it
I stopped letting fear rule me,
 stood up for myself and took back control
I stopped procrastinating and started building
I stopped settling and I started practicing the power to choose.
I stopped perpetuating the lie and decided to live in my owned truth~~~
I had to make a decision. . .
I had to face the thing that threatened to kill. . .
That which tried to hijack my identity. . .
So I Am no longer waiting for someone to tell me who I am. . .
I am no longer seeking your approval.
I am no longer waiting to be validated by you.
And I thank God I no longer care if it's me you're not choosin
But what I am doing. . .
Is defining myself,
embracing my identity,
living confidently and comfortably in my
owned truth.
but first. . .

I had to make a decision
I had to face the thing that threatened to kill me.
That which tried to hijack my identity
fought against my authenticity and made me my worst enemy

while I questioned
"my" life's validity
I had to make a decision to let go of past ideology
that confused me while uncovering answers and diving deeply
Intentionally, disrupting the disbelief
within me. . .
While posing the question to myself. . ."Sis"
"Are you really ready to be free?"
I had to make a decision
See I could yell from the mountaintops like Martin the King, "I Have
A Dream," but was I willing to do the work by calling on my ancestors
to empower me? Was I willing to undress myself and soul search, deeply
letting go of the infectious dis-ease of that, which held me in captivity?
Or would I bow out cowardly and wear a sign that said, "In case of
emergency, please do not resuscitate me"
I had to make a decision. . .
to only envision the greater version of me
then take meaningful action through spiritual practices
that revealed the truth about me
By exposing the higher me
I had to make a decision. . .
and what I found to be most consistently is that
Spirit was and is always with me
Constantly reminding me and
Forever reassuring me
that there's simplicity, my child. . .
even in life's complexities
I just had to decide to trust Thee
Trust that Spirits got me to stepping out on faith
 to do that which was calling me
walking into the fullness and the depths of me
choosing to show up as the true me
Because my 3rd eye can now see
signs and wonders come forth in synchronicity
like 555 and 333
Things are always, always, always working out for me
because I decided to break free

I had to make a decision
Now you can find me Centering,
Aligning and grounding
Positively impacting those around me
by walking freely
intently living authentically
while leaving indelible impressions on those that can see
 their reflection of the Divinity in me
I had to make a decision and once I made the decision
I realized the whole time
The decision was waiting on me.
da evangelist. . .

See. . .Reconciled Thoughts. . .

My thoughts used to be consumed with
the thoughts,
that I thought you were thinking about me. . .
had me feeling like there was no gravity
Because it felt like
I was losing the very essence Of me.

See I wasn't in touch
with reality.
My self-esteem and
my own thoughts of me played second fiddle
to what I thought
you 'might' be
thinking about me.
You maybe wondering
How could that be?
How could a stranger's thoughts and opinions
of me mean more to me than my own
when they don't even
know me.

Well the way it works
really isn't much of a mystery.
You see I digested
what I was taught. . .
and once it was consumed, it infected me.
I was brainwashed
into believing
that I was always unworthy and never enough
and in that space
the pain was constricting
and oftentimes
self inflicting. . .
Yet I still wasn't able to
set myself free
Because now fear
had taken over and incarcerated me.
Held me captive in anxiety.
And left me feeling uncomfortably me
I was stifled and afraid. . .
Afraid to leave the comfort
of the very thing that restrained me.
I was caught up in the midst of
a rigid dichotomy

Now fear kept me company thru all those years
with no reciprocity
Because I foolishly continuously looked
for help from within the same community.

Finally things became too heavy and tiring.
I needed to break free.
I needed to get past all the limitations and expectations
that had been placed on me.

And I'm giving thanks because I'm starting to see
that the damage wasn't done irreversibly. . .
Because now the pain of staying the same
had become greater

than the pain to change. . .
And how I weighed and viewed the opinions
of others
was no longer
leaving a stain. . . I was free. . .
So I began to ask questions. . .
and let Spirit guide me.
Because I was starting
to get a glimpse of the truth
that was already inside me.
I began to have a vision
of the greater me.
Opening up my third eye allowed me to see
That I was already free. . .
But I still had to Disrupt
how I saw me.
So as I began to
crawl out of the box of mediocrity
that contained me. . .
I decided to take a look
at the younger generation because you know
they came free.
They helped me begin to see the value,
the significance and
the importance in me.
Some may think it's strange to proclaim that I learned from those
Who are younger than me. . .
But As the scriptures say, "A child shall lead the way,"
As the wisdom in their hands unfolds,
They're leading us to truth untold
while breaking down barriers and molds.
Now. . .In my seeking I also sought teachings of those who came with a
message
that unshackled me. . .
got the shackles off my feet
and empowered me. . .
Helping me to see the true me. . .

You know. . .
The beauty in me,
the brilliance in me,
the love in me.
They taught me to know me and to trust me.
To listen to the still small voice that is within me.
They taught me that it was ok to be comfortably, me.
They were just the vessels
that I needed to see so that I would stop. . .
trying. . .to kill me.
da evangelist

Spiritual Birthright

Unfortunately religion doesn't give us all the facts
it's great at creating a foundation
but that foundation has structural cracks
and there's something critically significant
that we need as spiritual beings
that the foundation lacks and
it's incredibly important that we do our due diligence
to research and dissect the hidden truths from within these so-called facts
I'm not here to deflate anyone's bubble
or cause your faith to crumble
but because I believe your soul deserves the truth
I just wanna give you something to think about,
even if that something creates within you reasonable doubt
because contrary to popular belief
religion isn't based on genetics or heredity
unfortunately it's mostly regurgitated information
that's been passed down from generation to generation
making it a predominantly learned behavior and
the worst part of it all is that it
never really teaches us
to take accountability for ourselves

but rather instructs us to only rely on
an external savior
thankfully Spirituality picks up
where religion leaves off
and combining the two
along with
the creative power of our
Own imagination breeds harmonious self-discovery
and a greater sense of self-trust
and yes in Jah I trust...
but my own spiritual awakening is still a must so. . .
for myself, the paradigm. . .
I must adjust
so I'm leaving behind condemnation and distrust
and I am taking responsibility for my life
and learning to live intentionally
which has me. . .
vibrating at a much higher frequency
consciously, deliberately connecting and aligning with the divinity
seizing moments and opportunities
I'm creating new habits
and engaging in spiritual practices. . .
like journaling, meditating daily and
speaking positive affirmations over my life consistently
and what I've found
is that these things have given me the opportunity
to live my life honestly and openly
without shame or the pain of self inflicted suffering
Now over the years
as I've engaged in these practices consistently
Spirit has been revealing itself to me frequently
by infusing my intentions with
love and tranquility
circulating thru my entire body
illustrating to me that we are All particles of the Almighty
And honestly this makes sense to me
much more than religious rhetoric

Spirituality provides
a sense of stability
see cause now I'm gaining clarity
and the dots are finally starting to connect. . .
I feel alive and born again, but for real this time
and it's not at all what you'd expect
I didn't have to pray the gay away to access life's higher frequencies
I just chose to lock—into the truth about me
loving myself unconditionally
embracing the reality that there is no separation between Spirit and me
. . . (beat)
I'm living authentically
By reprogramming old data and showing up in 5D
where I live with the expectancy that things will always work out for me
I'm participating in life with vibrancy and vitality
and now I have the audacity to believe in me
to believe that I'm worthy
that I'm more than enough when I show up in the power of me
just as I am
operating in my isness making truth my business
Premeditatedly choosing me
while Source is constantly reminding me that because I am an extension
of thee
I'm God in the flesh the composer of my own Symphony
now some might not like me speaking so freely
I understand
trust me
I used to be afraid to speak words like these. . .
because religion says it's blasphemy. . .
but I'm challenging and uprooting generational beliefs
that no longer serve me
you know the ones that cursed the very existence of me?
Well finally I'm asking myself what do I believe
what do I want to see growing in my garden of creativity and possibility
I'm planting seeds of purpose and
letting my heart speak freely willfully allowing
my feelings to lead me

Unwaveringly believing in
all kinds of possibilities because whatever my powerful mind
can conceive and believes intensely
will soon become my reality. . . I'm manifesting
I'm carrying a newfound sense of peace and empowerment with me
waking up from the illusion of 3D
deactivating old beliefs
by fine-tuning my desires because love leads me
So in this dance of purpose and desire with mindful footsteps
carefully choosing each step moment by moment
while resting in the security of the All-Knowing
we must meticulously and passionately navigate the tapestry of this
beautiful
 journey we so endearingly call life
my brothers
and sisters
this is our
spiritual birthright. . .
da evangelist

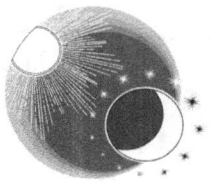

Dear Reader, now it's your turn to write! Use the blank space below. Try not to censor yourself.

Reflect on a time when you may have felt disconnected from your true self. Write about how embracing your authenticity helped you walk in your truth.

Melanie ~ "Da Evangelist," is a seasoned stage, film, and TV actress with over two decades of experience who recently showcased her versatility by writing and producing the comedic short "Miss Gloria's Life Advice." This piece garnered great enthusiasm and interest at LA's View Park Collective Film Festival. With a rich background, Melanie has captivated audiences in over 20 off-Broadway and regional theater productions, earning notable roles in Roommates, The Laundry Room, and Lorraine Hansberry's A Raisin in the Sun.

A five-year tenure with the New York-based Afrikan Women's Repertory and recurring roles in the Emmy Award-winning "One Life to Live" and NBC's "The Office" showcase her versatility on both stage and screen. Melanie's expertise lies in creating humorously nuanced characters with depth and soul.

Beyond acting, she is a comedian, a passionate writer, and poet, infusing her performances with the same humor and humanity that defines her characters.

Connect with Melanie: https://linktr.ee/brnsmln45

Chapter 15

Transformation and Metamorphosis
Michol Mae

My Story

I joked with a friend, "I'm not even starting a new chapter; I'm in a whole new book or series." That's how drastically my life changed.

If I'm honest, it feels like I've lived a few lifetimes within this one. I've changed subtly and drastically throughout the years. I transformed and morphed at each stage, trying to find ways to balance the shadows and light of life.

Everyone has a story, agreements, and frames of reference that shape who they are. I was the victim of abuse as a child; this fundamentally changed me, shaping me in ways I didn't fully understand until much later.

As a teen, I lost my mother and rebelled against the passive, people-pleasing child inside; the landscape of my life forever changed. You'd have seen me wearing all black, eyeliner used to draw on my face or to darken my eyes. I struggled with self-harm and suicidal tendencies. My mother's gift, nurturing my creative talents, saved me a few times.

I transformed from a teen into adulthood. In my 20s, I was a free-spirited artist (when time allowed). I held down several jobs and put myself through college. I changed my major from Music and English to Business and Tech because "What are you going to do with that degree?"

I experienced my first loss to suicide just before my 30s. This transformed me again. Becoming a homeowner, I embarked on a self-healing journey while staying as busy as I could. My favorite method for dealing with trauma and grief at the time was avoidance.

Suddenly, two years later, I became a parent, triggering the second largest transformation of my life. I took in a seven and eight-year-old, keeping them out of foster care and raising them as if they were my own. My experience driving me to ensure that they never felt less than loved completely by me. Becoming an overnight parent was a dramatic metamorphosis that, strangely, I didn't feel. I simply became.

If metamorphosis is defined as a change in physical form, structure, substance, or an alteration in appearance, character or circumstance then we all most certainly experience this.

The most dramatic metamorphosis for me would be after the death of my 15-year-old boy to suicide. I was fundamentally changed at my core. I'm not who I was, nor am I who I'm becoming. This resurfaced when my girl left home. Left with no children, I faced an identity crisis.

When you say the word Metamorphosis, most think of the caterpillar to the butterfly or the tadpole to the frog. Occasionally, they think of the coal that turns into diamonds or the seed into a plant or tree. I often thought of how frightened the caterpillar might be as it was surrounded in the darkness, uncertain of the upcoming changes. I've thought of the seed buried under the weight of the soil encased in darkness, straining toward the surface, never knowing if it will reach the sun.

The Poems

Cocoon

It's ugly, the sticky gooey inside of this cocoon,
I don't yet know what it is I'll turn into.
It's painful, the oppressiveness of this space,
I'm not sure I will survive this change.

Was this my choice or something destined to be?
Could I have chosen to stay the same ol' me?
Should I, could I, would I, have been happy,
If I chose to stay the same because it seemed easy?

Is it easy not growing, not moving forward?
Blaming others for their cruel words,
Giving away my power to everyone else,
Tearing away strips and pieces of myself?

Striving to be perfect, because then maybe, I'll be loved,
Afraid if I make a mistake, I'll be worthless and judged,
That doesn't seem worth staying in that same space,
Yet, I questioned it, because this new space is filled with pain.

Pain, as I confront all of who I used to be,
The good, the bad, and everything in between.
Pain, as I tear away everything that doesn't serve me.
Fear, because I'm now surrounded by uncertainty.

I don't know who I will be when I emerge,
Will who I was and who I'm meant to be, merge?
Or will the old me be gone forever? Why do I mind,
If I must shed the old me to allow my soul to shine?

Grief, that is why I mind. It settles comfortably inside,
Reminding me of everything and everyone that has died,
From the younger versions of myself, to those I loved,
To the moments I was denied a much-needed hug.

Further, I grieve that which would have been,
Then I ponder that which could have been,
As I mourn that which should have been,
I embrace the grief as I settle back into the cocoon again.

There is no shortcut to this metamorphosis,
No guarantee that I will even survive this.
Only the knowledge that I could not stay as I was,
Driven into this cocoon, knowing it was a must.

That I must endure this darkness and blight,
Knowing I'd once again see the light,
Even as the uncertainty plagued my mind,
There was a flicker ever present telling me this was right.

Yet, I still do not know what I will become,
I understand this transformation is an act of self-love,
A breaking down of old harmful beliefs
That will lead me to a greater inner peace.

It's messy, I've cried, and I've screamed,
As I reviewed every agreement to which I agreed.
And all of the times I would simply concede,
Harming myself just to keep the peace.

At last, I feel something break loose,
I see a tiny ray of moonlight in my cocoon.
With shaky hands I push my way out,
Standing in the light, the agreements disavowed.

It's time to make new agreements with myself,
Agreements that are worthy of being upheld.
It's time to walk once again in the light.
Time to unfold my wings and take flight.

Empty Nest

A parent's job is never finished,
And the love for your child remains undiminished.
Or so they tell you from the start,
And you comfortably give your kids all of your heart.

You take them to magical places to play,
And watch them growing up day by day,
Not realizing that you somehow lost yourself,
Little by little as they need more and more help.

Even if you noticed a time or two,
You'd quickly wave it away, focused on them anew,
After all, you were more fulfilled the more they grew,
And it was so subtle the way your inner-self withdrew.

As they got older there were more tasks to complete,
Getting busier and busier until the old you was obsolete.
All your dreams and goals now firmly in the backseat,
Even the promises of future time for dreams ceased.

You love your kids so much, it's a sacrifice worth making,
After all, these are impressionable minds we are shaping,
There is nothing more important than the children we are raising,
They'll be the ones running the world one day, theirs for the taking.

What a transformation we go through, becoming a parent,
Subtly or suddenly our futures become transparent.
We know on a deeper level our life has changed,
And our mission, if we accept it, is to keep the kids safe.

So we move with every intention of safeguarding,
Without a single thought that one day we'll be discarded.
Focused on all the wisdom we must ensure is imparted,
Even when that wisdom is barely or casually regarded.

It's no wonder that we are eventually lost one day,
When our kids are ready to move away.
Over the years we stopped considering this possibility,
Consumed with our day-to-day responsibilities.

Struck by the silence of the now-empty house,
Suddenly missing even the frustrated shouts,
Feeling empty as you wander aimlessly around,
Wondering if the pieces of the old you could be found.

Yet, you know you cannot be who you once were.
You have lived a lifetime since, and so much was learned.
In the time between who you were and who you are,
The loss of yourself to the role of parent spiraled down too far.

Now you are left with an empty home and an empty heart,
Still, the parent in you hoping they'll have a successful start,
Torn, because they may need you or want to come home again,
Stuck in this perpetual limbo, you find yourself backpedaling.

Even as they drift further and further away,
You put in the hard work of healing, working towards being okay,
And you start to think back on all the things you delayed,
Some you choose to discard but some still hold sway.

There is a tug at the corner of your heart and your mind,
A piece of you locked in the darkness coming out into the light,
It tastes freedom again and rejoices, finally free,
Now that the nest is empty, it's time to revisit being me.

In Between

It's dark in the uncomfortable space in between,
In between who I'm becoming and who I used to be.
It's uncertain, it's unclear, this path I've taken,
Determined to continue forward, to heal my own foundation.

Reminded of the caterpillar that grows wings and flies,
Or the tadpole that became a frog snatching flies from the sky,
Even the diamond is born from intense pressure, it's true,
I tell myself, I can survive this metamorphosis too.

I've been lost my whole life it seems to me at times,
Sure, I always had passions that made me come alive,
But those were all shunned by society, labeled a waste of time,
Worthless, they said, the very things that made my soul shine.

It's no wonder I struggled, stumbling into adult life,
Wearing this mask, conforming to their expected disguise,
Struggling to correct in myself something that wasn't broken,
Accepting their words, conforming to their notions.

So in between we settle for a time,
Doing what's expected of us, time flying by,
Some of us may stay here our entire lives,
While others, become tired of wearing society's disguise.

Stuck in between my core and society's expectations,
Between my own dreams and what they deem appropriate aspirations,
An undercurrent, a desire to break that which restrained generations,
At my core I felt something terribly wrong with these imposed limitations.

It's messy rebelling against the very things everyone knows,
It's uncomfortable for most to venture into the unknown,
Our biology telling us to fear it along with the idea of being alone,
Yet, we must all learn to find comfort in both if we are to grow.

I found myself in between again as I stretch my soul further,
Healing myself from previous agreements that were the precursor,
To many situations where I gave too much of myself to nurture,
Others, who would take more than they'd give and harm me further.

I can't cast a stone in their direction or the direction of my parents,
Everyone in this world is living their life from their own frame of reference,
Each with their own traumas and experiences that shape them.
What else could a control freak do but take control again?

I commit myself to my own healing to help stop the cycle,
To embrace a life that's about more than just survival,
Teaching the teen from my past the answer is not suicidal,
And becoming more adept at stopping my own downward spiral.

I sit in another in between at the edge of dusk or dawn,
I feel as though I might get a glimpse of a world just beyond,
I wonder if the fairy rings they blame for people disappearing,
Are really magical portals that take you places more fulfilling.

There's a balance to be had from the darkness and the light,
We see it in nature, the universe, and our own life,
Neither need be something we simply survive,
There're examples that show us in both we can thrive.

Chapters and Series

How many chapters does my book have,
Is it a series that I will one day rejoice I had?
How many versions of myself will I see,
Before I pass the threshold to the otherworldly.

From subtle changes to the obvious,
From knowing my direction to feeling lost,
I've ridden this rollercoaster we call life,
Uncertain if it'll suddenly take flight.

I imagine from the outside looking in,
Sometimes my rollercoaster appeared wildly careening
Myself a tangled mess of arms and legs,
Hair whipping about my screaming face.

Not all transformations were so dramatic,
Others saw me secluded, almost hermetic,
Withdrawing into myself, loved ones asking, "Can I help,"
There was nothing they could do but they meant well.

I turn the page, another chapter written.
Is this the last book in a series or a premonition?
Perhaps the prequel or the start to a new life,
Do I dare to believe this one will see all the wrongs right?

I'll start a new book in a new series; this is the first chapter,
No longer codependent looking for happily ever after,
Stronger now, than ever before, I see the truth more clearly,
The rose-colored glassed discarded, they no longer serve me.

These changes are obvious, I have been transformed;
Remade and changed at the level of my core,
The momentum carrying ripples of change throughout,
As self-compassion becomes a tool to erase self-doubt.

Gratitude becomes the sword I use against the darkness,
Creativity a valuable tool I use when there're emotions to process,
Self-love techniques—something I struggled with—eventually deployed,
Connection became an alternative to the grief I used to avoid.

When gratitude seemed impossible glimmers would do,
I nearly lost my desire to create in the most difficult times too,
But my creative drive, it seems, was too powerful to subdue,
When all else failed, I'd write away the impending sense of doom.

When I couldn't process or understand why this was happening,
I wrote, painted, or drew to help the process of re-examining,
I wasn't too stubborn, shy, or prideful to seek out help,
Sometimes things get too big for you to handle by yourself.

That wasn't a small feat for someone so fiercely independent,
Someone afraid to let anyone close or be remotely dependent,
Because previous chapters taught me it simply wasn't safe,
My trust issues were so vast, to do this was very brave.

Yet, the help I sought helped me reprocess the chapters past,
And while I shed that which no longer served me, something relaxed.
Part of myself had been holding on to so much for so long,
I knew I had to close this series, complete this chapter, to move on.

I completed another chapter of my life; I turned the page.
Being so transformed it was more than a mere chapter could contain.
All this pain, all this healing, a whole new series had begun,
Dedicated in it's entirety, not to who I was, but to who I'll become.

Dear Reader, now it's your turn to write! Use the blank space below. Try not to censor yourself.

Close your eyes. From a place of self-compassion, think about a transformation or metamorphosis you've gone through; imagine if that version of you could travel to you now, or if you could travel to them, what would you say to each other?

Michol Mae is the founder of Lady Mae Impressions, an international bestselling author, award-winning poet, educator, renegade artist, and musician. An intuitive, she weaves wisdom, experiences, meditation, shamanism, sound, and energy healing into her novels, poetry, music, and other artistic endeavors.

Her mission is to bring awareness to emotional intelligence, suicide, and mental health through her creative arts. She shares her journey through her arts in the hope that it will inspire, heal, and positively impact those that resonate with her works.

Michol loves all furry friends, and you'll find her cats, Mac Lir and Cheeky Neeky, and other family pets on her social media. In her "spare" time, you can find her fixing up the house, writing, riding her motorcycle, dancing, baking, spending time in nature, and practicing her many crafts. She shares the tools she uses to heal and find peace on her Journey Through.

Connect with Michol: https://www.ladymaeimpressions.com/

Chapter 16

Beyond This Place

Lyn Veneziano Fry, MBA, MSGT Ret'd

My Story

In our four room grade school, in Kylertown, we were seated alphabetically, so I was almost always in the back of the room. I became very shy; often living in a dream world.

I also experienced fear of speaking up, being bold with my ideas, or raising my hand with confidence, even though I often knew the answers.

Most often, I sat next to the classroom bookshelves. I loved the smell and feel of the books. We never had many books at home. We had magazines like *The Farm Home Journal* and a local paper, *The Grit*, which was my reading material. Seeing so many books in the library and classrooms was exhilarating.

My favorites were geography and history books and or stories about people from other states or countries—*It would be so awesome to travel to foreign lands and places outside or within the U.S.*

As soon as the teacher pulled down the world map, I was off on a daydream in those classrooms with their tall ceilings and huge windows, beckoning me to venture anywhere but the confines of my small desk.

I loved school; loved learning. I was extremely curious about the world outside my large family, our farm, and the small rural towns of central Pennsylvania.

After graduation, I didn't have money for college nor did I feel smart enough to attend, so with only a few options for jobs in our area, I accepted a job working in a sewing factory doing piecework for men's suits.

After a year or so—with exposure to a world other than school, church, or home—I became bolder and felt visible, and realized travel *was* possible for me. I considered joining the Peace Corps, which involved travel, and helping Native Americans on reservations out west.

My father served in the Army during World War II. When I was younger, I tried on his hat and jacket over and over, admiring it as I stood front of the closet door mirror. *Imagine, me, wearing a uniform, serving my country as he bravely did, being seen with a chest of medals and an arm of stripes.*

It became an intriguing desire tugging at me stronger than any fear of leaving my family.

"Please sign my enlistment papers," I pleaded with my parents. "In six months I turn 21and won't need a signature; I *need* to do this."

I joined the Navy which started my journey of seeing many places that were part of my adolescent daydreams.

Years after leaving the Navy, I was again filled with wanderlust. I joined the U.S. Air Force, where I was stationed in several more states and countries all over the world, even going to the war zone in Afghanistan before I retired with that coveted chest of medals and those many stripes down my arm.

My wanderlust continues as I use all modes of transportation, traveling with, and to see family and friends enjoying our beautiful country and the diversity of this spectacular world.

The Poems

Snowy Boughs

Snow covered boughs
heavily laden
with their showy frosted burden
bend in reference
to Mother Nature's
unquestionably
powerful
yet mystical
presence.

My Escape

I escape
in the various movies I watch
I escape while walking in sand or reading a classic book
I escape while window shopping
or sipping a cup of hot tea in a nook

I escape in excuses
in trying tales of woe
I escape in my writing
and when dancing on my toes

I escape in the mountains
on steep rugged trails
I escape in rivers
and in boats with sails

I escape in the clouds
so puffy and high
I escape in a rainbow
where the gold is nigh

I escape into freedom
a freedom that envelops my mind
lifting me to places of beauty and aah
where I can relax and slowly unwind

All the imaginative glory
these places in my mind
end as if a tether, pulls me back
to the harshness of reality
and a world that is unkind

I look around for another escape
I am seduced by my paper and pen
as words magically appear on the page
I am *free* once again

Torment From Within

do You see *me*, i feel so small
do You want *me* to reveal my truth at all
do You see *me*, are You aware
do You want to know *me*, do You really care

do You see me through hidden identity
or do you only see who i pretend to be
do you see i am brave, courageous and true
do You also sense i am afraid of You

do You *know* me; it is also a truth i fear
do i take a chance and make it all clear

i hide behind the smile You see
if i let You in who would i be
or is living in Your perceived blindness
my deliberate identity

Ecstasy

Our mutual desire
binds us
intimately
as the essence that guides us
to expressing our needs hidden
in the depth of our being.

Flushed by your gaze
you lift me
to endless ecstasies.

Delicate lace and soft silk press
against your dark satin skin
electrifying the moment.

The depth of our desires have
barely been touched
as we experiment
as hesitant new lovers.

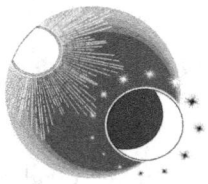

Dear Reader, now it's your turn to write! Use the blank space below. Try not to censor yourself.

When were you so sure of something you *needed* to do, be or see? Did it drastically change the direction of your life?

Lyn Veneziano Fry grew up on a 160 acre farm in rural Central Pennsylvania. After she served in and retired from the military, she made her home in Lake Stevens, Washington. She enjoys hiking around Puget Sound and the trails of the Cascade Mountains.

After a diagnosis of osteoarthritis, Lyn made it her mission to strengthen her body by building muscle to live pain-free and remain physically active. Besides writing, she loves everything Christmas, gardening, dancing, hiking, coordinating events, nature walks, and world travel.

Lyn wanted to help others continue being active so she became a certified trainer with MindfulOnlineGym.com as well as being a certified personal Law of Attraction Coach, Art of Feminine Presence coach/teacher, and CEO of Lightness of Spirit Personal Coaching.

Lyn is converting her five acres into a retreat/event center for her coaching business.

Connect with Lyn: lightnessofspirit@gmail.com.

Chapter 17

The Alchemy of Hands and Heart: Unraveling the Knots of our Past

Stacey M. Gayer, PT

My Story

A tree trunk sprouts down from my pelvis, and roots travel through the bottom of my feet—my root chakra connecting me to the molten energy of our Mother.

Oh, Great Spirit, surround me in a ring of healing emerald light; surround me with angelic white light topped with the protective violet flame of St. Germain. Spirit team, please come be with me and guide me.

I am ready.

We make an unspoken pact to enter this "dance" together, connected and guided by Our Mother's Energy. Rooted in the Earth, I become a conduit, my hands bridging the energy between her and the unseen forces guiding us. She stands facing away from me as I place my hand gently on the crown of her head. Through my palm, my attention is drawn slowly, like a magnet, to the left side of her neck. There are no words, just feelings. I feel the tension beneath my fingertips as though her body wants to speak–waiting for permission to release.

She lies face up on the table. Heat from my healing hands begins to seep into her body. Our energies communicate with no words. Her body's layers and textures guide my hands like sinking into wet sand. Her tissue leads my hands to the next tight spot–unwinding. I'm not in charge. I disconnect from my thinking physical therapy brain wanting to fix and heal. Her body runs the show. She stirs. Her breath catches. A deep groan escapes as if the Earth itself is exhaling through her. Her body trembles beneath my hands. A pulse of heat rises as trapped memories push to the surface. The air between us hums, vibrating. My breath deepens as her pain courses through my hands.

Can I hold this for her?

Long, slow exhale to let go of what isn't mine.

Her eyes slowly open as she returns to the room after a brief slumber. I whisper, "Take your time and let's stretch together." She rises from the table feeling lighter but asks herself, "How do I maintain this physical and emotional release?" It's a gradual inner knowing. But, as we move together to lengthen our limbs and torsos in the stuck spots like trees rustling in the wind, a deep knowing emerges. This tree dance teaches us: The body remembers, the body releases. I give the impulse, but she is her own healer.

The Poems

Earthdancer

The rustle of
Dancing branches
Delicious crimson and magenta
Tickle the window to
My Soul
Chirps beckon the morning
Nature's symphony
Surrounds
My arms become
Those branches
Dancing slowly
Lengthening
Unwinding
Releasing
The "stuck" spots
What would these spots say
If they could talk?
As my pelvis gyrates
And my body moves
This spinning dancing top

Lowers to the Earth
The grass tickles me
And my breathing deepens
Slows....
The smells and feels of
Mother Gaia
Accelerate
The letting go
Deep gasps
A scream erupts
Tears burn my cheeks
Past pain
Leaves me
And then
Uncontrollable
Laughter
Deep past trauma
Escaping
An inner smile
My spirit sprouts wings

Cocooning for Care

Universe calling....
Expansion and
Contraction
Usual patterns
Double Leo, extrovert
Egoistic, attention-seeking
Dance party gal
By nature do, do, do
Go, go, go
Breathe, stop
What does my soul need?
Calm, peace
Reboot, recharge
Alone in the flow
True independence
Relying on self
Place of creativity and passion
I am finally, truly listening
to my true heart's calling
Smell the flowers
Pause, what's next?
No more filling the void
with activities, energies that
do not serve me, feed me
Cocooning to care for me
so, I can care for others and
Mother Gaia

Healing Heart

It beats strong
But
Rusted barbed wire
penetrates my heart
The anger and pain
built this force field
Never again
A lock and key
below the belt
No pleasure
No more pain
Locking out the world
Can I ever trust again?
Never no one
A warm smile
cracks the darkness
My heart letting a glimpse of light in
pulls free a bit of wire
Some blood is shed

Scary to shed the armor
His strong yet gentle hands
sink into my shoulders
My feet are caressed
A deep moan
His hands massage my heart
Internal CPR
Another piece of barbed wire
extracted from deep in my heart and
soul
The barbed wire
slowly falls
Heart scars permanent
My heart slowly healing
but never forgets
His touch
A wrench to the wire
One at a time

Body Barometer

Deep ache in my sacrum
My pelvic bowl swells
My left foot
I know my spots
It is not
the body talking
It's my emotions
Speaking through my soma
The unconscious thoughts
bark at me
in my "places"
Does that happen to you?
My PT mind
wants to stretch it out
A temporary fix
If I shift my mindset
Meditate, breath
Unwind, let go
Let God
Let my Spirit team
Guide me
The true healing
The magic happens
I am transformed
The pain
The tightness
The discomfort
Dissipates
And I am
Dancing joyously
Free again
Thank you
Great Spirit!

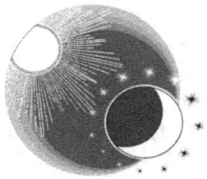

Dear Reader, now it's your turn to write! Use the blank space below. Try not to censor yourself.

Ask your body where you are holding your emotions and memories. If you then asked what emotion and/or memory it's holding there, what would it say?

Stacey's story begins in the Washington, DC area with her first business as a personal trainer. Her expanding love for health and wellness led her to Philadelphia, where she earned a Physical Therapy Masters from Thomas Jefferson University. She practiced in Pennsylvania for over 20 years and spearheaded the development of a Pelvic Health program at a local hospital.

Returning to the DMV (DC/Maryland/Virginia) in 2022, Stacey acted on her dream to open a Holistic Pelvic Health practice, **Core Healing Physical Therapy,** combining hands-on modalities of myofascial release, visceral manipulation, and crani-osacral therapy, & specializing in holistic pelvic health for all genders. Each client collaborates with Stacey to develop their individualized treatment program to address the root causes of pain and illness.

When not working or facilitating workshops, Stacey exercises in nature, travels, meditates, and dances to live music, continuously exploring communities through-out the world and following her deep passion to serve.

Connect with Stacey: https://staceygayerpt.com/

Chapter 18

Motherhood Don't Come With No Manual

Princess Best, "The Healacist"

My Story

My mother is laughing at me from the grave. This intrusive thought comes roaring back every time I feel like I'm failing as a mom. I sit on the bed, wrapped in the plush purple covers I inherited from her after she passed, scratching my head and twitching my feet. I force deep breaths, counting backward, "Ten—nine—eight—seven—six—five—four—three—two—one," to stop myself from going off on the beautiful little brown girl I birthed, the one I call my bestie. I love her with my whole soul, but love and frustration seem to exist side by side.

Can you hold space for love and, at the same time, see your child as a manipulator? My daughter, now in her tweens, reminds me of my own rebellion, and my mother's warnings echo in my mind. "You'll see when you become a mother, you're gonna get everything back you've given me." It was the classic Black Mama script I heard for years. "Oooo, I can't wait until you have a daughter," she'd say with a knowing chuckle. "Momma Myrt" was always so sure she was right, and I was determined to prove her wrong.

My whole life revolved around showing her that Black mothers and daughters could get along, that we could be friends, respect each other, and support one another. I wanted my mother to be my best friend, but we never made it that far. That dream, however, came alive when my daughter was born on November 4, 2012. "I'm gonna be the HipHopMomma," I declared, ready to balance motherhood, friendship, and trust, determined to prove to the world—and to my mother—that it could be done. For seven years, I poured myself into that mission.

But then, the unthinkable happened.

It was a Thursday when I got the call. "Have you talked to Mama? Have you heard from Myrt?" "Yeah," I replied. "I saw her on Monday. She had a doctor's appointment today, so she's probably there." Myrt was diagnosed with Stage 4 lung cancer the previous year, but she was in remission. Still, I decided to check. On the way to Baltimore, my hands gripped the steering wheel as I called my ex to calm my nerves. When I arrived, the apartment staff opened her door. "Best, are you here? Are you here?" I heard them call.

Then, a silence. "Ms. Best, she's in there, but she's unresponsive."

I collapsed to the floor, disbelief gripping me like a vise. My heart shattered as I realized I could no longer prove anything to her. As I cry the ugly cry, I flash forward to the present, where my daughter and I are at odds, bickering in ways I never imagined. I've said unthinkable things and reacted in ways I swore I never would.

And then it hits me: My mother IS laughing at me from the grave. But not because I failed to prove her wrong—because I finally understand. This wasn't about proving anything. The healing I was meant to do wasn't for her approval. It was always for me.

Momma used to say, "Motherhood don't come with no manual," but perhaps it does come with a prescription. Hence, "The Healacist." Thanks, Momma.

The Poems

She Changes Everything

She changes *everything*
She changed what fed her
What she ate
She changed what entered her
What left, what stayed
She changed her moves so that she could *disrupt* her
Patterns and cycles
She changed her autopilot cycles,
Distractions and DICKstractions,
She became the *manifestation* of her attraction,
She became the *joy* in her laughing
She started fasting
Talking to God (which should be on the regular), however,
She be *bullshitting*
Now admitting that her *spirit needs tending too*
Them cycles have a *season* boo,
The laundry is clean, rinsed, and dried too,
I don't need a *new* me,
I need a *renewed* me
Not a *reset* but a *mindset* shift ruling,
My thoughts, my words, my actions…
Put into APPLI-CATION
No longer lying to myself with this degree in *acting,*
She changes because it was time,
The rhyme, the reason, the season has passed
The lesson is learned
It's my birthday because it's a *new year*
Why? Cause SHE IS I.
SHE CHANGES EVERYTHING!

5 Words I Never Thought I'd Say to My Daughter

5 words I never thought I'd say to my daughter,
"I'm going to kill myself."
She wasn't raised how I was
'cause disobeying, my momma, certainly woulda got a belt.
"(You're) gonna have problems with her when she gets older!"
My momma's words whisper from the grave like a witch casting a curse
Did she just smirk? Oh, she's getting bolder!"
Teeth Smacking. . .Oh, she's a manipulator! We're gonna need to reset and reverse!
"Go do your chores, J!"
"I'm not gonna tell you again!"
"Mommy. Oh, my back hurts. I've got to go to the bathroom."
"Chiile! My patience is wearing thin."
"If this was your father or teachers, you'd fall right in line."
"Why you so ungrateful? Why I gotta ask you to do things ten times?"
Caramel frappuccinos, fancy restaurants and $1000+ birthdays.
"I don't have a stable job right now. Do you know how much I have to work to pay our
bills every day?"
Chest pounding, heart racing, yelling at the top of my lungs.
"Mommy, you're scaring me!"
"What little girl?" I snapped; I was done!
"You're scared of me? The one who takes care of all your needs? You know what? Don't
even talk to me!"
She pleads, "Mommy, please!"
"Well if you won't talk to me, can I call Dad? So he can pick me up, please?"
"I'm gonna kill myself! Go be with your dad!"
"Call him because I'm getting ready to leave!"
"Mommy. No I can't live without you, *no!"* I pushed her off, *"Girl bye* get off me please!"
Never thought I'd be *that* mom, can't believe what I said.
My momma laughing at me from the grave. How can I hear the voice of the dead?
Failing as a mom, self-fulfilling prophecy.
I contemplate, if I go through with it, who would find my body?
Remembering the unforgettable stench and smell when I found Momma,
I don't wish that on nobody.
Worried that she would be worried, I decided no. I'll just go home.
Came in, Jazz music playing like she's in a zone.
My sister and best friend tag team to "Auntie Activate"
Told her to do her chores and let me breathe and meditate.

I lay down to reset and reflect; she enters silently, gives me a sweet kiss.
Woke up, came downstairs, don't you know? She hadn't washed one *single damn dish?*
Ain't that a bitch?
Hmph! I laugh. I hear my Momma laughing at me from the *grave.*
I realize now she's laughing *with* me…
"Baby, motherhood is a job that **don't** pay."
Well, amen and Ase.
Thanks Momma.

The WombPrint

If they only knew about/
If they only talked about/
If they weren't shamed about/
Their sacred womb
If they only knew about/
If they only talked about/
If they weren't shamed about
Their sacred womb

If I could talk to my unborn children
The first thing that I would ask is, for my past, am I forgiven?
And would they listen? Or be scorned that I aborted?
Scared to death to be a single mom, like the norm, unsupported
I couldn't of thought it, so I boarded that plane/
Bought it for $300/getaway/escape the pain
Memorex tape replaying "Girl you got shit to do"/
"Your whole life will be rearranged, be about them kids and not about you"
Don't forget the shame that you feel when you miss taking your pill
Or you SKIPPED taking your pill, acting like you ain't know that pregnancy's real
Still, if you'd'a known about ovulation/
High fertility/Pregnancy only comes on certain days when
The moon plays music, you thought you was just horny
Her speakers full fuse screaming, *'reproduce homie'*
And it's lonely/in the karmic thoughts of your decisions
If you knew then what you know now, would you take a different position?
I get to twitching sometimes when I hear a vacuum
Abortions/rape/molestation, so much trauma in this trapped womb
Enough to consume your womb with dis-eases
They gon' send you to the hospital soon, like you was Yeezus

If I could talk to all the taken children
Erase all the separation that was created by CPS systems
and do deep incisions, into the the heartspace (chakras) of our sistrens
and fill them with Te Fiti 'til they grow what they are missing
Listen, her-decision may not been the one you chose/Why she have dem babies but can't
take care of them tho?
Then send them off to school wit' dirty clothes, smelling like mold/Her teachers
presume her moms a lazy ratchet ho
No compassion tho, sisters addicted to drugs and alcohol
Don't want to get involved, quick to make that CFSA call
Like foster care safe, it's where some of our girls get raped
The cost might be much less if we invest in mom's mindstate
But since that outcome's slow, we just do what we know
Put a band-aid on the problem, we know eventually grows
And where you think it goes? Our mental health unfolds/
Our trauma dismissed as *"anger,"* we are MISdiagnosed

If I could talk to the neglected children
and tell all their mothers how important it is to emotionally listen
Don't take full position, as though survival is your mission
'Cause in your "busy-ness," so many things you could missing
Don't be dismissive, like what they're going through is small
What's annoying to you might mean the world to them and all
Sometimes you let girls fall, sometimes you pick them up
Be present or else they might think that you don't give a fuck
and that's why some girls cut, "sit yo ass down and shut up"
Depressed and stressed mothers ain't got time to give hugs
If they struggle with self-love, then it's hard to pass it on
Disconnected from our wombs, this hold here is really strong
I'm not here to say you're wrong, that you're not a good mom
But we must heal our wounds, create mother-daughter bonds
('Cause) our anatomy's the roadmap, we got keys to this legend
But (we) can't navigate it clearly without nurturing protection
That's when motherhood gets hijacked with fear-based projections
Daughters in airplane mode, waiting-waiting on connection
Heal the girl within, means healing our wombs
Heal the girl within, means watch what we consume
Heal the girl within, means let go of the shame
Heal the girl within, means know the root of our names
Heal the girl within, means let your girl play games
Heal the girl within, means releasing the pain
Heal the girl within, means RELEASING the pain
HEAL the GIRL within, means RELEASING THE PAIN!

If they only knew about/
If they only talked about/
If they weren't shamed about/
Their sacred womb
If they only knew about/
If they only talked about/
If they weren't shamed about
Their sacred womb-man, WOMB-man, WOMB-MAN

Girl Get Up

Ok B.A.G.lady's time to get in formation
Ok B.A.G.lady's time to get transformation
Ok B.A.G.lady's time to get transmutation
Ok B.A.G.lady's pass on this liberation
Carry them bags, don't be sad girl, gon' get up!
No more sad ladies, baglady's, girl get up!
Ditch them rags, pick up glad, girl gon' get up!
Flip that B.A.G. to a B.A.G. (Broken Ass Girl to a Boss Ass Goddess)

When Mother Earth is knocked down, there's a disruption to soul
Seen eight trees on the ground, but who heard it? No one knows
See when a matriarch breaks, on her face it rarely shows
Navigating from broken branches, appearing as whole
But it don't hold up and it don't hold weight, at this fake rate, your bag gon' break
Go grab some jade, recalibrate, you're off-balance in heart rate
Challenge the enslaved, passed down outdated ways
That gave *praise* to a mama for how much shit she could take
Meditation break/walk by the lake/never do it 'cause you work too late
The kids need help in school and food/Excuse, "There's just no time in the day"
But how you gon feed/
communities/
must have no leaves/
you evergreen?
You in the weeds/
you need to freeze/
breath is on wheeze/
end on your knees
Push and deplete?/
Heal and Receive?/
Sis wanna bleed?/
Sis wanna breathe?

Sis you need a H.E.A.L. plan, your self-care on lean
Sis is sinking/
what she thinking/
light is blinking/
ignores the ring
Says it nothing/
gets in the ring/
says it's no-thing/
continues to sing

Ok B.A.G.lady's time to get in formation
Ok B.A.G.lady's time to get transformation
Ok B.A.G.lady's time to get transmutation
Ok B.A.G.lady's pass on this liberation
Carry them bags, don't be sad girl, gon' get up!
No More sad ladies, bagladys, girl get up!
Ditch them rags, pick up glad, girl gon' get up!
Flip that B.A.G. to a B.A.G. (Broken Ass Girl to a Boss Ass Goddess)

Sis if it's up, then get up, if it's up, then get buck
If it's up, then get up, before your ass get stuck
Mama is a leader/we need to relieve her/we need not deplete her/or she gon' get sick
Everything/is nothing and all things/trust half of what you hear and what you see
After the splinters, healing will spring
Change come from BossAssGoddesses eventually, we're evergreen, n'aw mean?

I seen mamas go through hell, I've seen mamas go to jail
Them B's be back by dinner time, baking biscuits like all is well
That's a witch's spell, you don't get to witness, hell
Mamas put out of tons of fires, never caught a whiff or smell
Mama don't be living well, stress be leaving her triggered
Bills, kids, family, heath, work, sometimes/hurt from niggas
Self-esteem low, made some bad money decisions and now the green low
House burned down in a fire, her car repo'ed
Her knees need surgery, her kids special needs though
IEP's, anxiety, get high to be at peace yo
Nervous system shut down, they thought she'd stay asleep though
Abusive relationship knocked her down, she not weak though
Divorced, of course, just like her parents, glaring sequel
Loss of her job, on God, on God how we gon' eat though?
Emotional eating, non-substance addiction is *lethal*
Therapy needed *repeated* in *depleted* people

Revive my breath, deny my death
Got one last damn nerve left, her must curb, de-stress
So overwhelming, it's absurd, life a full-court press

It's a mess, a reflex of my vexed choices
Pray for voices to tell me where to step and what's next
Then exploit it with excuses, intelligence, *hoteps*
Now avoiding the healing, prolonging me being blessed
That's the void Erykah spoke about, pack light, yes?
Keep on choosing what hurts me, why won't I focus on self?
Don't you know in your healing is the revealing of wealth?
So if your physical's pivotal, then your mental is critical
I spit this lyrical spiritual, triple threat to umbilicals
Fuck being cynical, I'm Ma'at, metaphysical
Find the truth, analytical, check the root of my crystals
My mini-me, a magic miracle
Pointing me at the pinnacle
I receive, its medicinal
She's the key, inexplicable

Ok B.A.G.lady's time to get in formation
Ok B.A.G.lady's time to get transformation
Ok B.A.G.lady's time to get transmutation
Ok B.A.G.lady's pass on this liberation
Carry them bags, don't be sad girl, gon' get up!
No More sad ladies, bagladys, girl get up!
Ditch them rags, pick up glad, girl gon' get up!
Flip that B.A.G. to a B.A.G. (Broken Ass Girl to a Boss Ass Goddess)

Sis if it's up, then get up, if it's up, then get buck
If it's up, then get up, before your ass get stuck
Mama is a leader/we need to relieve her/we need not deplete her/or she gon' get sick
Everything/is nothing and all things/trust half of what you hear and what you see
After the splinters, healing will spring
Change come from BossAssGoddesses eventually, we're evergreen, n'aw mean?

What about the leaves on trees with broken branches
Where do these BossAssGoddesses go after, they've done their dances in the wind
Will they cry or simply die?
No they gon' heal today, yes we gon' heal today!

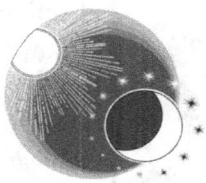

Dear Reader, now it's your turn to write! Use the blank space below. Try not to censor yourself.

Sometimes, there are people who must die (literally or metaphysically) so that we can live (figuratively). Identify and reflect on one or two people in your life that had to "die so that you could live" and why?

Melissa Princess Best, also known as "The HEALACIST" and HipHopMomma, is a transformational performing artist, educator, and spiritual healer. With over 20 years of experience, she specializes in empowering women and girls through creative arts, focusing on self-awareness, mental health, and personal development. Princess is the author of My BARZ Heal Scars: The WombPrint to Healing The Girl Within and the Executive Director of The Healacist Institute, working with schools across the Washington, D.C. area. Known for her dynamic public speaking and arts-centered approaches to healing and education, she has been featured on HBO's The Wire, TV One's Stage Black, and Ford national campaigns. Melissa Princess continues to lead creative social-emotional learning workshops and facilitates healing through the transformative power of hip-hop, theater, and poetry.

Connect with Princess Best: https://www.youtube.com/princessbestspeaks

Chapter 19

Pause and let Nature Inspire your Inner Cosmic Chalice

Korinna Zoya Hunter

My Story

It all started as I lay on my bunk bed and gazed out the window facing the front garden. I saw this huge butterfly before me. It appeared one meter in width, and I stared at it in wonder. It was so beautiful; it brought beauty and hope to my innocent six-year-old self, who was told she was wrong, that she was lying, and that my way of being wasn't right.

At last, I knew this was a visitation from a spirit. I knew it was real; my eyes weren't making it up. My naïve self so excitedly went to tell the human souls around me, "Hey, I saw a huge colorful butterfly visit me by the window."

Of course, there was no "Oh, how wonderful." Instead, there was silence and a change of topic, as if what I had to say wasn't of enough significance.

Then, I had another similar experience. I once stepped on a bee. Bee lovers, I hear you! Just bear with me. My younger self didn't know any better, so I stomped on the bee and killed it. Its body became whole again, and then before my eyes, I saw a golden white light forming around the bee and could see its body levitate.

How could this be? I thought I killed it.

I realize now that what I saw was its aura. From this point, my thoughts and perspectives on life were challenged.

What I spoke went to deaf ears. No one cared for my opinion. My sensitivity wasn't recognized, so I never received support for nurturing it or how to develop my intuition. How I wish I knew then what I know now. How I wish I knew how to regulate my nervous system, preventing any shutdown from happening. But my small self didn't know how, so I learnt to thrive the only way I knew.

I became a people-pleasing person. I did exactly what I was told—both at home and at school. I learnt the hard way that when I spoke my mind, I was physically or emotionally bullied. I became a people-pleaser to survive. I had to unlearn this in order to relearn. That became my mission—to self-heal and teach others how to.

Not surprisingly, by the time I was seventeen, I realized I wanted to become a spiritual healer. Now, in this present timeline, I've reclaimed my personal power, sovereignty, and self-worth and am passionate about helping other highly sensitive souls.

I'm now a certified Spiritual Healer. I'm trauma-informed, use somatic tools, heal with sound using my voice (the sacred sound of the universe), channel my higher self, and allow nature and beings of light to speak through me, including the bees and their Queen Bee Melissa! Some have described me as a natural shaman and pure source channel.

The Poems

Self Weaving Book of Life

Today I shall weave a story for all
A story that will weave more than just mere words and phrases
A story that will weave magic and healing for all
Today I shall co-create with nature
Weave the colors of my soul and allow nature to be heard
Weaving this book of no beginning nor ending
A book of no yesterdays and no tomorrows
A book that is weightless, yet carries so much depth!
A book that potentiates
That matures itself
The never ending story of our soul
That change and move with the wind and breath of life
The breath of our desire
For I am eternal, for we are all eternal
As we are sentient beings
Not just you and I
But all of nature
Nature speaks, nature has a voice!
Move over mind,
Blank, clean open canvas am I
I have no quill or ink
But the artist is here
Ready to quench my thirst and hunger to create,
And pulled to the light I am
Ready to birth something new,
Something unseen but felt,
Experienced and lived within my core
As I am a vessel
A vessel of light, of love
Sunlight and moonlight
Infinity shades of light am I
Infinity shades of potential
Layer upon layer
Falling leaves floating, pilling one after the other
I softly yet gracefully land onto her lap
To the Earth Mother beneath me
Cupping and covering my bare naked soul

I tasted her ambrosia, her divine fragrance
Remembering my call
Having my cup yet filled again and again with this eternal light, with this divine nectar
My hunger and thirst has been quenched
I am ready to pour, ready to give a droplet of my divine nectar
Thus, the weaving took place,
With this invisible yet colorful thread
Nature's vowels spoken, weaving its voice
To all who will listen
Complete total surrender and innocence
Allowing what needs to unfold, to unfold
No ego, nor mind
Just being and coexisting
Enjoying this mere presence
This Now moment
Where time stands still
Where all possibilities are endless
And ready to potentiate
My message is this
So, co-create Now
Ask and it is delivered
Let go of any unrest
Steer your divine engine to the direction that brings more peace, joy, freedom to your life
Light engineers are we
Like these fallen leaves, fallen feathers
I too shall fly free one day
We too shall fly free
Taste the scent of freedom
Taste the scent of here and now
Forget about what flavour will be of tomorrow
What is the flavour of now?
The colors of my soul have been threaded
The book is coming alive
I, we, have a choice
Let go of control and just be
Set yourself free
Completely surrender
Like the surrendered fallen leaf
And smell the heavenly scent of your divine essence
Feeling the warmth of your heart
Remembering your true home

The Shadow Lady

Darkness falling around me, as I stroll through these woods,
A warm hand suddenly fleeting past my shoulder
"Hush, don't speak and close your eyes my dear"
Silence went over me and I shut my eyes as told
Surrendering to what will come
"Move your hands closer to me, don't be afraid"
"I am a friend from afar,"
"I have been watching you"
I feel her leathery hands brushing against mine
And feel the cold metallic touch of what could be brass or silver
A goblet of some sort is being offered to me
"But wait?". . .
"Hush, and just take a sip of this fine nectar"
"Oh, it tastes like". . .
"I know what it tastes like my dear"
"But I want you to tell me what you see?"
As I sip this mysterious sweet nectar
My taste buds dance with excitement
Senses heightened
I feel this flower opening up
Absorbed in so much radiant light
So much energy flowing through my body
My internal rivers running wild with excitement
This Goddess-like being is merging out of this flower
Eyes gazing torward me,
Moments of silence,
Tears start streaming down my cheeks as I digested the spoken words
I soaked everything in, saw all I needed to see
Surrendering into this peace
Finally, I know who I am
The lady in the shadow now speaks
"Ah, so now you see!"
"I am pleased. You may open your eyes my dear"
I open my eyes to thank this mysterious lady
But, not a single soul in sight!
Just a gush of wind blowing past me and a shimmering golden light
Did I just drink from a golden chalice?
I noticed a spill on my linen dress and smelt that sweetness
Oh, it was real!
For now I know this shadow lady
Was indeed my messenger
To awaken and remind me of my divinity

Love & Possibilities of Potential

So let's begin with this 4 letter word love
Love, that humble sound, yet such a powerful word
Love holds one of the highest vibrations and energies known to man
And is capable of healing the whole world, even the universe!
We are born out of love and our aim is to return to love
For that is where we reach our eternal heaven
Where we find complete freedom.
Have you ever wondered what brought us here?
How we are existing now in this very moment?
It's not because two people decided to tangle,
But I am talking about a different tangle here.
A dance of creation itself

There are so many theories of how the world began
Was it the Big Bang, Adam and Eve and the serpent, or Lord Brahma?
I do believe there was a desire from a higher intelligence, call it God or what you will
it is not so important.
I believe that the creation itself was born out of love, out of a desire, so love had to
co-create with this hidden intelligence to bring the world into existence.
So, a type of tango, a dance of creation took place, possibly a combination of
the Big Bang theory and Adam and Eve or other.
So whatever theory it may be, love was at play and co-created with the desire
of the universal desire for life and so this world, this universe and the vast universes
around us were born to some extent out of love.

Let's go back to love
Love holds a certain valour, a divine essence, a fragrance that is worth more than
the weight of gold or even diamond!
But love really serves as a protective shield, serving like an armour, like
the valour of gold, God's armour.
A fine receptive antennae, coupled with laser precision,
Cutting across all barriers, timelines and dimensions.
Let's focus on the heart itself
We may see the heart just as an organ
But there are different fields, dimensions within the heart
Imagine if we tap into all the fields of our heart,
Prayed, set our intention to the universe with our hearts fully open and connected
Praying with our hearts with complete consciousness and awareness!
Those who are termed pure at heart or pure channels
Are able to tap into these fields, to Source itself
And when they pray, they really pray, their prayers
Travel straight to source, to pure God, Creator source consciousness
Serving as divine antennae's, channels

Imagine now the potential if a collective of heart-activated, pure channels were praying
or setting their intention for global healing or healing a loved one,
imagine how powerful would that be?
We probably have heard of a few cases where someone prayed for a miracle or the
impossible, yet it was delivered!
Imagine that, being amplified by the power of a thousand or more, pure source channels
Serving for the highest good, and magnifying the field even more!
Imagine the potential of that

Love is our *secret power* indeed!
This is why prayers work, but it is also to do with faith, having faith, and surrendering.
So let's all work on opening our heart
Feeling that freedom that once was felt
It is time to amplify your love field
Amplify your heart antennae
Really listen to her
Speak to her
Find peace within your heart
And ask your heart to always show you the truth,
Allow you to feel the truth from within
And to help you heal all those inner wounds that are left unhealed

Do you remember when your inner child believed in magic?
Well it's time for you to believe in that magic again
And co-create with this magical heart portal.
Your heart holds the key
The key that you have been searching for in all the wrong places!
Seek love within your temple before you seek love from an outward source
No one, not one single being can fill that void for you, can fill that empty spot
Stop using the band aid approach

Live your best and fullest life Now!
Honoring yourself, honoring your heart!
Seek freedom and love from within yourself first
Then the right people will find you and be part of your life
We often forget how powerful we are
And need constant reminders
I myself included
But I have learned to accept and be happy with this vessel of mine
Love is like a remembrance of home, our eternal home
A remembrance of our divine essence and potential
Be that potential.

Bird of Prey

My left wing carries not only yesterday's wind but ancient knowledge from all the continents that I have flown.

My right wing carries the promise of new lands and worlds yet for me to explore.

I have a natural beauty that you human folks cannot copy.

My eyes are beautifully and perfectly ornamented, born with natural beauty and natural eye enhancer that humans try to copy with your manmade eye shades so you can look like a bird!

My yellow chest reflects the sun I carry inside, my golden palace, and the magnet that guides me.

The brown of my feathers reminds me to stay grounded and never lose sight of my innate nature and assures my commitment to the life that was given to me.

Every dent I have is a challenge overcome, a proud scar I bear and wish not to hide.

My soul and driving force is run by an invisible magnet that resides within me. How would I otherwise know which way is north or south?

I may not speak the human word, but nature understands my calls, and my calls travel far and wide to reach my brothers and sisters.

My ears warn me of impending danger and nature warns me with her moves, with her shaking vibrations.

I hear her screams, I know she is forever looking after me as I look after her.

My sharp claws are my anchor to this harsh land and let me feel the creation that formed it, the earth beneath me connecting me to my core, to the very essence of my creation.

My sharp claws are also my defense and means to catch my prey. After all, I am a bird of prey!

My beak is not my only means to feed, but with my beak I also create my perfect home; I fetch what I need to survive and use it as a weapon if needed.

And in my beak, I can create new life by cracking those shells to drop the seeds into the soil to create new homes for my offspring.

My eyes are also my weapons. I spot a prey from miles away, I work out the needed distance and seconds of my flight as timing is very crucial in order to succeed with the hunting.

My eyes unlike you humans don't dart from my mission, they are solid and focused and they never let me down. I rely on them to spot my prey and go for the hunt!

Beautifully created, aren't I?

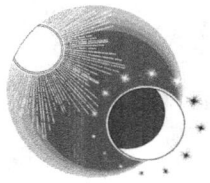

Dear reader, now it's your turn to write! Use the blank space below. Try not to censor yourself.

Focus on any animal or an avatar of your choice that would help you embody a certain quality or aspect to bring that much needed healing and balance in your life.

Be the new Avatar of your life.

Breathe it, feel it, embody it. Grab a journal book and write down the possible steps to get there; write down the vision of your embodied future self, and then say out loud, "It is done. Thank you," three times.

Korinna Zoya Hunter is a natural-born healer and co-author of the Amazon bestselling, *The Energy Healer's Oracle Vol. 1* book. She is a certified spiritual healer and mentor, Self-Directed Healing practitioner (Somatic healing) Multi-dimensional Healer and Light Language Channel.

People are drawn to her natural unpretentious down-to-earth nature. She executes a natural warmth and makes everyone feel safe and at home. She is very compassionate, non-judgmental, and has an uncanny way of getting to the true root cause of any issue. So whatever is going on in one's life, big or small, Korinna has a vast set of tools and knowledge at her disposal.

Korinna's special interest is supporting the highly sensitive souls, the spiritual seeker, for those seeking healing or support on their soul mission, awakening their gifts and so much more. If her poems move you and you intuitively feel drawn to her please reach out.

Connect with Korinna: https://www.cosmiclightkatalyst.com

Chapter 20

A Moving Life – Between Wonder and Tragedy

Dr. Pamela J. Pine

My Story

Maybe I should've come back as Leonardo da Vinci. I've been trying to figure it all out for a very long time. His genius would help, but I do get closer each year.

Memory: Despite being far more comfortable with animals, I sit (age ten) with other campers and counselors in the woods at a Camp Silver Lake fire circle in upstate New York a little after dusk. It's a time on the cusp of hippiedom and flower power, and we're discussing lyrics from popular songs. And I am, by the look on my counselors' faces, nailing the philosophical meaning of the words. *Wise beyond my years,* their faces are saying. *Right,* a part of me thinks. Another part notes: *A little too proud.* But I knew either way, I was born this way.

And then I was encouraged, thank goodness—not all are so fortunate.

Raised by an artistic (speech therapist, actress) mother and scientist (chemist) father, I was exposed to both worlds from a young age. *Scientific American* magazines shared space with art books on our living room marble coffee table. I took music lessons on multiple instruments and was brought to museums and Broadway shows. My father brought home non-explosive lab experiments to demonstrate scientific principles, like the one with the blue fluid in the test tube that turned green when I stood on my single bed to hold it up to the light streaming in from my small, high bedroom window. They signed up me and my sister for a global mail club, through which we received each month treasures in the mail of silkworm cocoons from Japan, brass trinkets from India, and small carved wooden statues from Africa.

This upbringing cultivated my innate desire to understand the world through multiple lenses—art, science, and philosophy. I was encouraged not just to observe but to try to improve less-than-ideal conditions, less by words than by examples: Mom working her speech therapy magic with deaf kids, starting the Golden Age Club for local senior women; dad close to tears recounting his refusal to conduct experiments on beagles. All this led me to work in places like Yemen, the Congo, Ecuador, and New Zealand on issues ranging from leprosy treatment to child abuse prevention.

Throughout life's journey, we constantly receive input to process, react to, grow, and heal. My diverse experiences provided a large canvas to learn from and contribute to as I continue figuring out the human condition. Though still a work in progress, I'm getting closer to understanding with each passing year. My path has allowed me to explore healing—both for myself and others—by engaging with different cultures, tackling global challenges, and reflecting deeply on the human experience. While I don't have Leonardo da Vinci's legendary genius, I have wide-ranging curiosity and strive to comprehend the world through multiple disciplines.

The poems that follow reflect my ongoing journey to make sense of life's complexities and find meaning amidst struggle. They are an invitation to explore the human condition together—our shared joys, pains, and quest for understanding. Though I'm still seeking answers, poetry offers a way to distill insights and connect with others navigating similar terrain.

Ultimately, my goal is to keep learning, growing, and hopefully leaving the world a bit better than I found it. By sharing my reflections through art and action, I hope to encourage others to embrace life's journey with open minds and compassionate hearts.

The Poems

The Subjects of Poems

The subjects of poems
Are like roses
What fascinates
Resembles the deepest red blossom
That arose from dirt and seed
To become the richest bloom

A Moving Life – Between Wonder and Tragedy (a poem in six parts)

Part. 1. Inseparable

You left out the art books
And Scientific Americans
The back porch window open
That connected my childhood room to it
To the room that you built -
Where the classical music played
On the big stereo
Where the exotic plants lay about -
That opened onto the wide, green backyard
With the two giant willows
In front of the brook
Down the field from the school
Where you taught.
My days' activities
Before school chorus

After school art
Evening dinners of politics and prose.
How could I have grown up
Otherwise
Thinking a difference was mine to make
The world was mine to be in
How was I to know
That life was not made of art books
And studies
Of Broadway shows
And museums
Of intellectual discourse
Of do-gooders
And plenty.
I watched you verbalize your way through
As the other was resigned
The only one, the "he" of "you," who understood
From poverty and war
That the world is beautiful
And pathetic
Together
Love and betrayal
At once
Wondrous and tragic
Inseparable

Part 2: I See the World and The World Sees Me

I don't need to close my eyes
To reach each enchanting New World
As I did
Each one, each time
Into the beginnings, middles, and ends
Their signature sights, smells, memories
Embedded

Mexico
I was 13

A bus-full of girls traveling the U.S.
Over the border to Mexico
At a Mercado
Brightly painted, flowered trays
Hand-stamped thick leather purses
Bargaining for the first time
Feeling awkward and unkind
I still got took!

India
I was 16
"The driver" picked me up on arrival
I smiled to little acknowledgment
He took my bags
Put them in the trunk
Traveling down the walled Arabian Sea
Arriving at my temporary Bombay home
Down into the gray, shadowed parking garage
Honking before every turn to ensure our safety
In the elevator, up to the 9th floor
The flat smelled like curry
I slept for one and a half days
My Indian hosts thought I was sick
But smiled when I thought I was dying
When my urine turned red
After eating so many red mangos
College with my Indian sister
Hysterics with my first real friend group
Studying Indian classical dance
Fingers, arms, legs, head and eyes all going hither and there
Adopting a scrawny black alley kitten
To our mom's mild horror
They are family

Yemen, oh my beloved Yemen
I was 23
The start of nearly 10 years abroad
A November arrival

Arms strangely seeming light blue
Next to the browned skin of the "old recruits"
Where
I came to speak Arabic
تحدث أو مت (tHdeth aou mat, speak or die)
I would say
I learned to treat leprosy
Fleas and bites
Everywhere my clothing touched
Sickness
My neighbors' two children
Dead of cholera
But, too,
The kindness of strangers
The work with those I loved
Who would hate me
Had they known

All the rest of the beginnings
And the middles and ends
Have their own stories
The work with poor women in Morocco
With rich women who despised them
Conducting training in basic business
Apiculture and doll-making
The dogs I tearfully left there
Teaching in Japan
Gasoline dumped on my new leather boots
The breakup and fast departure
Changing Egypt
Lesson 2010:
This can happen to a country in 30 years
Haiti and an earthquake
Disaster everywhere
World: Why are you not working together?
You have no right

Just back in the U.S. of A.
I was 31
Shock
At a school much too competitive
Much too soon
Working with an established colleague
I smile
Move very close to him to talk
Hold his upper arm
And address him
As he steps back
Shakes his arm loose
Wearing an uncomfortable look
Oh yeah, we don't do that here, I think
I come to speak about "the Americans"
It doesn't include me

Parts of me spread from A to Z: Albania, Bahrain, Bangladesh, Botswana, Canada, Cyprus, the Democratic Republic of Congo, Ecuador, Egypt, England, Ethiopia, France, Germany, Greece, Haiti, Hungary, India, Italy, Ireland, Japan, Jordan, Kenya, Mexico, Morocco, New Zealand, Oman, Poland, the Philippines, Qatar, Russia, South Africa, Scotland, Spain, Switzerland, Thailand, Tunisia, Turkey, United States, Vatican City, Wales, Yemen, Zambia.

I awoke one morning
And saw my thoughts
As if fabric in those shops in Thailand
Stacked, horizonal, on poles
Each long piece
Wound over and over
On itself,
Each in its place,
Ends of cloths hanging down,
Waves upon waves,
Multicolored, paisley, other-patterned
One upon the other
Together but of their own threads

They flow, draped over each other
Changing their stature and effect
With each breeze that comes
With each person that comes
With each person who goes
With every opening and closing
Opening and closing
Opening and closing
Of the door

I see the world and the world sees me
With the joy
My heart also sinks
In equal measure
There are too many pieces of me
Scattered in these places
I have never completely come home
How could I?

Part 3. The Personal Hits

I learned
And grew
I was offered softness
And avoidance
Told half-truths
And outright lies
Manipulation became no surprise
Through a tale worthy of Shakespeare's gifts!

And now
I'm tired of betrayal
For any reason
For any turn of a phrase
For any self-preservation
For any gain that's sought
Due to any excuse.

It's exhausting to deal with people
Who think it's all just fine
To hold one up to glory
And then just change their mind
When convenience strikes
And something else arrives
That shines a bit more new
Or glows a bit more bright
For the moment, eh
In any case.

So, take your ways away,
And let me live my days
With less disappointment
In those who spin a tale.

The personal hits
I can find wonder elsewhere.
Better not to have to wonder
If you're indeed just true -
Everyone has an excuse,
We're all survivors of something
I wouldn't do it to you.

Part 4. To All of Us

I asked a question:
Can I ask a question?
In the time that ensued
There would be no answer
I realized there never would

I have looked for answers
I have searched the oceans, stars, and Earth
Reviewed the animal kingdom for wisdom
Drew on mythological and magical beings
That have helped unravel mysteries
But will I ever get a leaning?

We were but pups when…
Sweet and playful
Puppy-fur softness…
And hard scars for a lifetime
Under where the fur grew over
Do we see the scars that are concealed?
Do we let them show?
They do: when the fur parts.

I asked myself questions:
Should I keep my house as is?
Should I invite you in?
Can I bear *your* scars?
Have they made you ill?
Will it make me sick?
Do I take the risk?
Do I let you in?

I built a new house
Around the old one
And in its renovation
I hit a holding wall
Around which I strongly built

Perhaps we can meet down the road, in my yard
Inside the white fence
I have oil to rub to ease your scars, and mine
But you will have to endure the strain, and I—
I will take the path less pained,
And that will make all the difference.

Part 5. Nothing Has Changed – While It All Has

Someday soon
As soon unravels
Things come to be like dreams
Not enough to hold
But to be remembered
Faintly
Disappearing
Like vapor
Over years
As details blur
Edges soften
I think
Maybe there is no point in trying
To hold it all
It is an exercise in futility
As smoke dissipates
No container can capture it
It will fade
Into thin air
And then
It will be
Gone
It all scatters and settles
Like particles in the wind
Gold dust in an open hand

Pollen on the wings of bees
We come to ourselves
Finally
Appealingly
Simply
With recognition
Whether we're lucky -
Or not -
And learn
What of this life
We aim to be…

It's dark again
As I awake
As the seasons change
The cats stretch
Unperturbed
As before
Though now shadows persist
Where there was light
Making their mark longer, earlier
The time is as it was
Just a short while ago
Nothing has changed
While it all has

Part 6. At the Core

I thought
It had gone
But see, some remains
Like all that grows
And dies
There are remains
From the birthing

That core piece
Once we're done
With the cover ups
The striving
The creating
The achieving
The settling of scores

Who we all are
At that first learning
Remains
Both growing
And rotting
And disappearing
At the core
Mine, you ask?
(Did you ask?)
Mine is the sadness
The fault line
Where it spews
That sense of responsibility
For it all
I was taught
It was compounded
It baked
Under years
Of pressure
What a surprise
To find a piece
Still lurks
And here
After all these years
It sits
I see now
What happened.
Now
This is my mission
For the now
To leave
Those remains
Dearly beloved
To leave them
Well behind
In my mind
In my heart

In my soul
It's down to the core
Nothing left to eat
I'll keep a few seeds
The ones that show promise
The ones that bring forth
But the rest
I'll throw
Time for a new orchard
While I think of stories
That make me ashamed
To be human
But I also know
I have learned
It's affinity
And communication
And an empathy
For the human condition
That binds us
And keeps a soul
In wonder
Birthing it all.

The Silent Point

The silent point is
Like the boiling point
Or the freezing point
That point that is
A thing of nature
A metaphysical reality
An evolutionary throwback
That happens
When speech is no longer –
When it is neither required nor available
When there is a change in structure
When emotion is
And peace unfolds
The essence of self relaxes
And attempts at words
Bring funny babblings and non-sequiturs
And "I love you" is
But silent

Dear Reader, now it's your turn to write! Use the blank space below. Try not to censor yourself.

What, in prose or poem form, expresses your understanding of the life you've lived so far? Has it been a kind journey, a tough one? Where and how has the healing occurred? Is there something you can say that sums up one or more major lessons for you so far?

Dr. Pamela J Pine (PhD, MPH) has been an international health, development, and communication professional throughout her adult life, concentrating on enhancing the lives of the poor and otherwise underserved groups. For the past two and a half decades, her primary focus has been on the prevention, treatment, and mitigation of child sexual abuse (CSA) and other adverse childhood experiences (ACEs). She is the Founder and Director of Stop the Silence®, now a Department of the Institute on Violence, Abuse and Trauma (IVAT, https://www.ivatcenters. org/stop-the-silence). She is also a public health professor and a life-long multi-media artist, which she uses in her work to raise awareness and open hearts and minds toward action. She is a bestselling and award-winning author and an award-winning photographer. She is a recipient of the Lifetime Achievement Award in Advocacy from IVAT. She speaks professionally about her knowledge, work, and life.

Connect with Pamela: https://drpamelajpine.com/

Chapter 21

Poetic Introspection:
Di-Verse-Ify Your Journaling

David D McLeod, DD, PhD, Certified Master Life Coach

My Story

I spent the first 40-plus years of my life struggling to live up to the conditioning, training, and expectations of people around me.

- *You must be nice.*

- *Your needs and desires are secondary.*

- *You're supposed to keep everyone happy.*

Messages like these echoed endlessly in my mind. And, heaven forbid, if I slipped up or dared do something for myself, an alternate—and more sinister—tape loop would chime in:

- *You are so selfish!*

- *Who do you think you are?*

- *Stick to the plan, loser! You must do what everyone else tells you.*

I squashed my wants and needs; I stuffed my disappointment and anger. By the time Mom passed in 1992, I was miserable. The messages had morphed into limiting and debilitating beliefs about myself; the inner voice sounded like a whiney little brat:

- *Nobody loves me.*

- *I'm totally invisible.*

- *Nothing I want matters.*

- *I don't matter.*

The plan—listening to the external world to determine what I was supposed to be doing (indeed, to know **who** I was)—was clearly a monumental failure. I was ready to check out permanently.

But there was a quiet inner pull calling to me. For that first four decades, I paid it no heed, but once in a while, it got strong enough to grab my attention. If only for moments at a time.

I started listening, and what I heard was: *Enough. It's time to go!*

Go where? I fretted. *I'm stuck here.*

In 1995, I managed to extricate myself from my circumstances. Think *Escape from Alcatraz,* only with much less drama! I was 42 at the time.

I found my way to Silicon Valley—new job, new environment, new beginning. Alas—to my dismay—the pain of my existence shadowed me on the journey.

Ha! Joke's on you!

The unspoken message: *Time to do some deep healing work.*

Luckily, my soul guided me. I found books and seminars. I met teachers, workshop leaders, coaches, and therapists. I attended retreats and seminars. It was a whirlwind of ideas and understandings that helped me unravel my twisted, dysfunctional beliefs and start peeling away the false layers I had accumulated over the years.

In 2003, I finally reconnected with the real me. What a joyous reunion that was!

"At last," I rejoiced. "I'm done!"

Are you kidding? You're just getting started...

Nowadays, I have an introspection practice that combines meditation and journaling. Sometimes, while I meditate, my mind resists settling, so I just grab my journal and write out my thoughts to stop dwelling on them. This helps me arrive at a relaxed, meditative state. And then, when I read my journal later, I often find beautiful seeds of material that transform into poetry sourced from my soul. Quite a bonus!

Try this out for yourself. If you develop an introspection practice like mine, you'll surely find your own poetic seeds that will contribute to your healing.

Bless you, and bless your journey!

The Poems

empty calories

sometimes i get so busy—
this, that, the other—

you know, the **d o i n g** of it

that the noise grows loud in my head
drowning me in a flood of

> unsung truths
> and
> unheeded warnings

i don't mind—
 not really—
because i am the one
 who does it all
 who can be counted on
 the *good little boy*
this feeds me with something
 masquerading as love
 but which turns out later
 to be empty calories...

sometimes i get so busy—
this, that, the other—

you know, the **l i v i n g** of it
that i begin to repeat myself
running around in circles and wondering why

> everything
> feels
> like *déjà vu*

it's okay—

                     really—

because i am the one
      who does it all
      the reliable one
   the *people-pleaser*

and my appetite is sated (briefly)
      by words of acknowledgment & approval
which turn out later
      to be more empty calories...

        and then,
     (when fatigue sets in)
  i am surprised by my hunger and thirst
      and i wonder

                  why is it that
              all i hear inside me
                        is a

ticking clock?

Dominoes

When dominoes fall
 Gravity is the inevitable victor
When dominoes fall
 My world wobbles and spills me out
As I fall,
 As I flip-flop and flail
  Like a caber tossed across the sky
 As I am yanked
  Into the spinning vortex of my own confusion

Oh, look out!

Because the particles of fear-lint stowed away in my pockets
 Shake loose and succumb to centrifugal force
 To fly out
       Like contaminated snowflakes
 From the dark corners of my mind
 Into the stark hot light of endless scrutiny
 Where they pollute everything within reach

The pressure squeezes the channels of my breath
My skin puckers in small tight beads of rancid salt-water
 Color drains out of my eyes
And I fall, and I tumble,
 And the last mote of control vanishes
 Like a vestige of false imagination

(I have become one of the dominoes
But I don't just fall over like the others)

No...

I topple and crash to the ground,
And then I am again suddenly airborne
As if I have bounced, spun around, and slipped over the edge
(A caricature of a trampoline performer)
Into an abyss that is beyond my capacity to understand
It is brief, disorienting, yet strangely pleasant
(Like swimming in a syrup of warm atmosphere)
Until I notice the charged spikey ground rushing up
And threatening to disintegrate me
In an electrifying plasma of Domino Dust

But then,
When I surrender to the ultimate termination
When I release myself to what lies beyond
When I pause and remember to sneak a breath

Magic happens,
Because *you* are there,
Calm, quiet, present
With your loving hands holding me
And your heart beating softly next to mine
Calm, quiet, present
With your steady gaze warming me
And your gentle understanding smile washing over me
Calm, quiet, present
(Everything that a falling domino is not)

You are *(always)* there
Flowing your *satchidananda* divinity
Through the hollow bones of my body
Around the vapid chaotic spiral of my mind
Past the damp caverns of my heart
Into the sparkling fjords of my soul

Here, now:
Love blossoms again
In the fertile depths of this charged dust

Where dominoes once stood

sacred circle

this is a good place to die.

i sit cross-legged in a sacred circle of oaks.
    they bear the scars of a long ago fire,
        and yet they stand.
    the fire burned their feet,
    flames licked their trunks,
    heat boiled away much of their lifeblood,
        and yet they stand,
            strong and vibrant in spite of their scars.

i have my own scars...
    it is good to be surrounded
        (protected)
    by these fire warriors.

beyond the circle,
    fallen treebrothers lie all around
        in intermittent heaps of ash and char.
    if there is honor to their final resting position, it eludes me:
        i see twisted, mutilated bodies of loved ones among their number,
            and i am saddened...
    illusion? elusion?
        no matter, honor is surely here,
        so i open my heart to the essence of it.

— dayMOMENTS —
jays and squirrels hide-and-seek in upper branches,
    and occasionally knock a tired acorn to the ground;
        chattering and arguing, they crave an audience.

the breeze breathes
    and the trees whisper
    with their gentle swaying
leaves succumb to the wind
    to fly briefly and to float quietly down again
        coming to rest on the decaying leafmosaic where i sit.

a squadron of ravens scrambles into the sky;
   the birds skim as one,
   high above the tree graveyard,
   to another stand of trees in the distance.

flies and wasps buzz constantly and harmlessly —
   their occasional touch electrifies me
   reminding me that i am
     (dying)
   alive.

the sun burns through a hazy rippled layer of cloud
   and filters down through the leaves
   to warm my
     (spirit armor)
   naked skin.

for reasons known only to them,
   the ravens take to the air once again,
   and fly a tight bank toward the tree they left
     a few moments ago...

mother earth caresses me

mother comes to me in a blur of pain
   for a brief moment
   to hear my anguish and grief
i sob to her and share the artifacts
of the control she exerted.

she burns as i say goodbye.

i sit cross-legged in a sacred circle of oaks
   and feel immense smooth power flowing
     (through me)
   around me.
there is safety and vulnerability in this circle of solitude:
   four days three nights,
     meditating, fasting, questing,
     (unchaining the essential me)
   removing masks, peeling layers of shame,
   opening and cleansing.

— *nightMOMENTS* —

the sun descends slowly below the horizon
    charging the sky with a brilliant orange blaze;
    scattered clouds begin to
        (bleed)
    condense in the cooling atmosphere.

jays and squirrels settle into silence
    (worshipping beauty)
    saving squabbles for another day

flies and wasps suddenly disappear to their secret lairs
    and the loud chorus is taken up by crickets and cicadas —
    has someone flipped a switch?
    the sound resonates and reverberates,
        back and forth, back and forth,
        across the expanse of trees and open sky,
            surrounding me, penetrating me...
        reminding me that i am
        (alive)
    dying.

a few birds spurn the fading light
    and dart between trees,
        seeking a party to crash.

color drains out of the sky;
stars appear in the deepening darkness;
the moon rises, a folded disc, mottled and white,
    and casts a vaporous blue glow all around.

i look into treeshadows
    and i see the bobbing, scanning head of an owl —
it leaps from its perch,
    and floats briefly above the ground,
        only to hairpin back a moment later,
    a little feast wriggling in its beak.

the night ages and intensifies,
    and i sense the
        (intimacy)
    imminence of something drawing closer...

i am fascinated:
    the moon yellows and ripens
    as it slides sideways across the sky.

forest sounds barely register on my consciousness;
    they seem vague and
        (urgent)
    unimportant...

gradually, almost unnoticeably,
    the moon begins a lazy descent —
    the vaporglow dissipates.

before i know it,
    the moon is swallowed whole by the horizon,
    and i am swallowed whole by the darkness...

in the faint light that remains
    the noises seem suddenly very loud,
    and the music of the cricket choir
    infuses me with energy.

out of the corner of my eye,
    i catch a glimpse of silver fur
    moving within my circle.

the creature slinks toward me,
    unaware of my presence.

my mind plays tricks in the dim light:
        skunk?
        deer?
        fox?

when recognition comes —
        coyote! —
i gasp in surprise, and he is off like a shot...

father sky embraces me

father comes to me from a great distance
for a brief moment
to hear my hurt and sadness
i cry with him and share the artifacts
of the abandonment he inflicted.

he weeps and repents as i say hello.

i sit cross-legged in a sacred circle of oaks
and welcome the beginnings of
      peace
      serenity
      wholeness
      godbreath
(within me)
inflating the empty balloon of my soul.

there is silent tranquility in this circle of solitude:
three nights four days,
meditating, fasting, questing...
         growing.

here is where i begin
    i surrender my pain and shame and anger
    i discard my old self and give birth to a new one
    i glimpse the truth and embrace it
    i touch the essence of my heart
    i step beyond boundaries into possibilities.

loving grace is here now...
welcoming, inviting, empowering...
enlightening...

              this is a good place to be born.

recycled

when i die i want to be recycled

i'd rather not be vaporized in a furnace
because i will have to absorb so much energy
    just to turn to powder,
and when my ashy essence is tossed to the wind
i will probably poison a bird
    or induce an asthma attack in a child

i'd rather not be wrapped
in an overpriced piece of silk-lined furniture
and buried like someone's idea of lost treasure
because i will just take up space
in a place that you have called holy
    where my relatives will feel obliged to pay respects
    and stand solemnly overlooking a gravestone
      (inscribed with lofty and vague half-truths)
    and where future archeologists
  from some distant galaxy
will question our customs

(and maybe wonder
why i didn't rate a
more luxurious retirement)

no

if there is a component in my body
    that still works
      take it and give it to someone who needs it;
if there is some part of my temple
    that can serve a different purpose
      take it and put it to good use

then

wrap my naked remains in a simple hemp shroud
and bury me upright in a deep hole
        in the forest.
plant a redwood tree over my head
    within a circle of fiddleheads and fungus
    and let me nurture it and return the favor of support

        let me spare
                the bird and child
        let me give the archeologists
                something to really ponder

and if you come to visit,
feel free to climb the tree,
    but gently,
and please remember
to let the dog leave a mark

i will be watching

Dear Reader, now it's your turn to write! Use the blank space below. Try not to censor yourself.

Contemplate your life journey. Notice all the waypoints you have encountered, the cuts and bruises you have endured, the gifts you have received, the blessings of wisdom you have accumulated. Take time to express the thoughts, feelings, and words about these experiences. Perhaps one day, you'll find the courage to share them. I hope so—I want to learn more about you.

About David D McLeod

Fighter pilot. Best-selling author. Software engineer. Mentor. Aerobics instructor. Poet. Janitor. Lifeguard. Musician. Radio host. Graphics designer. Father. Student. Teacher. Photographer. Ordained minister. Yogi.

These roles—past and present—add up to a *LOT* of life experience, which David McLeod brings to bear in his capacity as a transformational speaker, life-mastery coach, experiential facilitator, and writer/storyteller.

As a Certified Master Life Coach with a PhD in Metaphysical Sciences and a DD in Holistic Personal Coaching, David creates and shares powerful *Life Mastery Tools* that enable adult men and women to transcend triggers, challenges and obstacles so that they can express and experience the fullness of who they really are and thereby manifest truly magnificent and fulfilling lives.

Connect with David: https://linktr.ee/yourlifemasterycoach

Chapter 22

In the Arms of Empathy
Pauline McGuirk Penedo

My Story

Starting a life in a new country was more challenging than I ever imagined.

Everything familiar was gone, and my life became divided into two parts: before the move and after the move. The "after" part forced me to confront my authentic self, using empathy as a shield against what threatened to break me.

It was my first time working as a server. I needed a job to pay for school, and this was my only option. One Sunday, during a busy brunch shift, I approached a table, "What will you have, sir?" The man looked up at me with a sly smile and a sparkle in his eye as I took his drink order. After serving him, I continued working but kept one eye on him. I watched his slumped posture as he hovered over his glass.

He's drinking too much. Why does he look so disheveled?

Sitting at the bar, signaling the end of my shift, the bartender strolled over. Motioning towards the man, he rolled his eyes. "Another one" Sunday morning, and he's already putting them back," he said with disdain.

Finding his way to the bar, the man had ordered more drinks while I served other tables.

I felt a wave of anger. "He's having a drink while he waits," the bartender looked confused. Feeling my emotions rise, "That's my dad! He's waiting for me!" His expression changed instantly, and his face fell in regret.

I felt the weight of the "Irish drunk" stereotype—something we had endured since immigrating to Canada. And while the bartender's assumption wasn't entirely wrong, it still hurt. Shame burned inside me—not just for my father, but for the judgment I knew we both faced. But it wasn't just shame. I also felt a deep need to defend him. I remembered the man he once was, the respect he commanded, and how much he was loved—before the move.

I walked quickly to my dad's table, trying to control my emotions. "Let's go, Dad." His big green eyes filled with surprise. Slowly, he rose to his feet. I took his arm to steady him, and we left the restaurant arm-in-arm. I held my head high, determined not to let the tears that threatened to expose how vulnerable I felt fall.

When he passed away a few years later, still battling the demons that haunted him, I was left with one burning question: Why weren't we enough?

I had to go back- *before the move* and learn to wrap empathy around my memories of him, the way he used to wrap his arms around me as a child. I let my emotions run free on white pages as I wrote my way to healing. Empathy was the antidote to my shame; it refrained my memories so I could find myself again.

This healing gave me my purpose: to support you as you develop empathy for yourself and let go of anything keeping you from becoming the authentic leader you were born to be.

The Poems

Between Two Lands

There's a place that exists for me—
it lives in the sound of my footsteps,
on worn-out concrete sidewalks.
If you listen closely, you'll hear stories:
chattering ladies, giddy children, forlorn men.
It breathes in the crisp morning air,
under skies of blue, fleetingly clear,
before they yield to greyer days.
The sun peeks over slate-tiled roofs,
and rusty gates swing, creaking in the breeze.
Narrow roads where top-heavy buses trundle along,
the faint scent of coal hangs in the air.
Anticipation of something new,
rooted deep in something old—
Awkward conversations flow
over fresh coffee in white cups,
steeped in the comfort of the familiar.
It lies not in the past nor the future,
but in the presence of now—
where songs and stories live.
It's the ocean's roar, my feet in the sand,
and yet, it leads to red and white lights,
a maple leaf held in my hands.
I remember life took me far away—
From pebble-dash houses on streets of grey.
Brightly painted little doors,
Freshly scrubbed windows and worn-out floors.
Small cement walls enclosed our days,
marked by struggles and money's frayed ways.

I remember grasping through my tears,
to hold on to the place I'd known for years.
As we drove away, fear welled deep—
I knew nothing would stay the same.
All that remained was a house, not a home,
and the garden gate's creak, swaying alone.
I remember love, a life wrapped in pain,
but I longed to see past grey skies and rain.
I left those arms empty, begging me to stay—
stepping into the unknown, he faded away.
I remember descending white stairs,
worn dull by time, with brown handrails.
I looked back, saw faces streaked with tears,
arms reaching, pleading, "Don't leave, please."
We looked ahead, onward we marched—
their cries dissolved into the dark.

I remember my heart breaking in two—
one half stayed in Ireland, the other with the new.
Tears streamed down my mother's face,
as the weight of her choice took its place.
She worried—would we have enough to eat?
Where would we live? Where would we sleep?
She carried us all, no sign of defeat,
and grey skies gave way to hot summer's heat.
It's painful to recall the feelings inside,
that took me away from home and my pride.
To remember that journey brings loss, regret—
my mother's heart, breaking, so full of fret.
As we crossed - the vast open sea,
we made our home in the North strong and free.
Let go of regret and mistakes or remorse,
Controlling my thoughts with all of my force.
I'll swim through the night, let the waves carry me,
and memories will flow, emptying into the sea,
They'll disappear into morning's light,
Lost in the water, they are now out of sight.

Let Her Sleep

Please let her sleep; she's worked all day.
Step aside, don't stand in her way.
Worn to the bone, she needs her rest,
can't you see she's doing her best?
You stand in her path as she struggles to speak,
but your once-strong frame is now terribly weak.
We understand you don't want to be alone,
but step aside, Dad, leave her alone.
I've watched her struggle under heavy loads,
from caring for those who need clean clothes.
Her arms are strong from lifting her bains,
but her shoulders droop, weary and strained.
I see her walk to the top of the hill,
her aging body is run through the mill.
She knows when she reaches the pink-sided house,
you'll be there, on her green-checkered couch.
She doesn't complain; the choice was hers—
she loved you once, maybe still does.
But broken and drunk, you're not the same,
a flicker of the man who once was her flame.
I tell her, "I'll stay with you, Mam, for the night,"
and in her bedroom, we turn out the light.
But the yelling continues from the kitchen below,
and we sit on the bed, rocking to and fro.
It's a typical night; it's always the same—
she gets no rest 'til he stops calling her name.

A Moment in Time

I see him from afar.
Unwashed clothes clinging to a broken frame.
Worn out shoes and stringy hair.
Face in need of shaving
cold, lifeless eyes,
walking through the darkness
Head down, avoiding the light.
It's where he's made a home.

He doesn't see; he has no eyes.
He hears no sound.
One foot in front of the other
A compass without a needle
any direction will do.
His story holds no interest to others,
he lives in a void.
He's forgotten the arms that once held him.
His life goes uncelebrated.

Who counts his years?
Who tracks his path?
Who would miss him?
if he simply disappeared.

I know his story.
I've seen better days.
When he walked a little taller
and leaned less into the wind.

He is the reminder,
that the darkness does exist
There's a beauty to his story.
If we took the time to ask
To look upon his troubled face
that covers what's within
To see a light that still flickered deep inside,
In the beginning, before his journey began.

He walked on into the night and never looked back.
Except for a brief moment with regret
for what he left behind.
I see him in every unwashed face in every broken frame.
Knowing that if I were to stop and ask,
their story might be the same.

In My Dreams

Your hair, so vivid, so clear,
In your green eyes, I see the fear.
Your presence fills the space,
Soothing words, the past erased.
Deep in my heart, I want to hear,
those words that make the pain disappear.
To know you cared, to be set free,
To carry on into eternity.

It wasn't you; it wasn't me,
It just was and no longer can be.
I've seen the mountains, I've done the climb,
Looking back, I wasted so much time.
I want to move ahead, to know,
I long for peace, to let you go.
I'll rise and fall on solid ground,
just to know what I lost is found.

I awake, and you have gone,
It seemed so real, your presence so strong.
I rise to start the day,
Those healing words, they fade away.
And so it is; it was just a dream,
that you appeared and sat with me.
When you spoke, I listened close,
To hear the words, I longed for most.

Between dusk and dawn, when I'm alone,
your outstretched arms, they call me home.
I see you clearly as if you're real,
and I listen closely so I can heal.
You walk beside me and take my hand,
I see you smile, and I understand.
You were broken and had to deal,
with losing all that made you real.

But now you're not so real to me,
And only in my dreams I see,
the one I loved before the strife,
that took you far away from life.
I want to sleep so I can see,
but you don't come so regularly.
Only when I'm in need,
you'll come to me so I can breathe.
You'll hold my hand so I will feel,
that I was loved, and you were real.

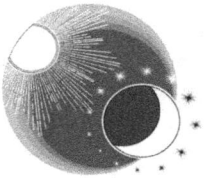

Dear Reader, now it's your turn to write! Use the blank space below. Try not to censor yourself.

- If you could receive a letter from your future self, what advice or insight would you hope to find in it?

- What guidance would your older, wiser self offer about what truly matters most in your life right now?

Pauline McGuirk Penedo

I knew I had to embrace my story. For years, I was stuck in a narrative telling me *I wasn't good enough.* As an immigrant and the daughter of an alcoholic, I battled that inner voice of judgment. Shame kept me trapped, but I came to realize that empathy is the antidote to shame.

When I explored who I truly am—where I came from and who my people are—I began to see myself and my family through a new lens. I realized that every experience was teaching and empowering me. I started celebrating the uniqueness of my path, knowing that no one else sees the world through my eyes or learns my lessons. Like a sunflower, I turned toward the light and blossomed as I embraced my experiences. I want you to know that it's possible to carve your own path, define your purpose, and achieve your dreams.

Connect with Pauline: https://littlehillcoaching.com/

Chapter 23

Finding Love Within My Soul

Jen Potter

My Story

I stood at the front of the room; all eyes stared at me. For the first time, I was nervous. I didn't know what would come out of my mouth. I waited my whole life for this moment. I hoped I'd be excited leading up to this, and I wasn't. *What is wrong with me?*

Eyes glistened as they waited for words to come out of my mouth. As I spoke, sweat dripped down my face. "Welcome, everyone. Thank you so much for coming."

Today was the day I began telling my story. While I have told so many stories in my lifetime, the ones I shy away from are the ones that affect me every day.

"What you see in front of you is the product of a little girl who has been broken into a million pieces and has spent her entire life creating a mosaic masterpiece."

I created a life I thought I wanted because the one I was born into wasn't so charming. Growing up, my mother was an abusive, alcoholic narcissist who only cared about herself and what the world could do for her. While I had an amazing dad, the damage my mother caused me before they divorced far exceeded any good he could do. I spent decades trying to find myself and the little girl who desperately needed to be loved. I never allowed anyone fully into my world, as I was scared, I'd be judged because of my mother and her actions. The same actions that haunted me and caused me so much mental and physical pain. Then, one day, I did something that changed my life. I started to write about my story and allowed myself to release the words into the world. I never anticipated that I'd share any of these stories. But as I started to heal, I knew sharing my story was how I'd continue to heal and let others know that they're not alone.

"For decades, I wished that my mother would die, that if she died, I would no longer live in fear and pain..."

I truly believed this until I started to heal, and then I found out she was dying. True healing comes from finding yourself, digging deep into your soul, and allowing the beauty that is inside out. With each word you read, may you find a piece of yourself and allow your soul to shine.

The Poems

Broken Beyond Repair

Visible scars of harsh memories
Painful—delicate to the touch
The skin ignites
Feeling it deep within your veins
Emotional turmoil stinging your soul
Teaching you how to feel
Piercing through your heart
Causing you to surrender to the pain by
That broke your beyond repair
Creating a beautiful chaos
That is made of you

Whispers of a Loved One

The gentle breeze of the wind
Cool air brushed across my face
I could feel her
Out reached her delicate hand
We connected
It was as if she was never gone

This time felt different
I spun her around
My lips kissed her shoulder
Longing for this moment
For it's been too long
Since I touched her skin
And could smell her hair
She gazed into my eyes
Are you ready?

I whispered in her ear
I missed this…
As a tear glided down my cheek
I took a deep breath
Slowly closing my eyes
I could hear her soft voice again
I love you, whispered in the wind

For in this moment
I knew it was not my time
She looked at me
A smile appeared across her face

I know!
I just wanted to remind you
You have more work to do
But I'll be here waiting
Just like this

Present

Cool morning dew
Wet grass against my toes
My body grounds into the universe
Reconnecting with my soul
For my heart and mind are scattered
Uncertainty lies in my insecurities
Trying to make sense of the chaos
Racing thoughts
Negative emotions
But in the stillness there is peace
The wind blows against my face
Birds chirp and crickets hum
I close my eyes
Fighting the urge to give up
I search for silence in my mind
My body calms with each breath
I feel the sun shining on my soul
The dirt beneath my feet settles
I'm calm and present

My Ocean

My heart calls to you
The way my soul calls to the ocean
Longing
To smell the salt of the sea
Feeling
The rhythm of the waves against my body
As I float effortlessly
Wanting
To feel as if I am one with the water
The way I feel when I am in your arms
You have become the ocean to me
When I go too long without being near you
I feel this strong pull at my soul
Sinking like toes in the sand
The waves drawing you near
As our love intertwines
Likes salt with the water
Our ocean is a constant
It is forever changing but remains the same
It's love grows strong and powerful like waves
And it's calm embrace allows me to feel
I am exactly where I belong

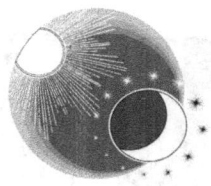

Dear Reader, now it's your turn to write! Use the blank space below. Try not to censor yourself.

In still moments of solitude, when your thoughts drift toward the feelings you've been pushing away, I invite you to pause and look inward. What have you been avoiding? Close your eyes, take a deep breath in through your nose, and exhale slowly. After a few calming breaths, open your eyes and let your thoughts spill onto the page. Don't hold back, let your emotions shape the words as they flow from your mind to the paper.

Jen Potter is an accomplished Author, Poet, Motivational Speaker, Ultrapreneur, and Business/Life Strategist. She is the Founder of Empower Your Epic Self Conference for Women and several other businesses. Her mission is to help people realize their ultimate potential while changing their thought processes both in business and their personal lives. She does this by inspiring others to dig deep within themselves to find their "WHY" and understand that when they start to listen to what they want, their lives will indeed change and they'll recognize that they have the potential to transcend the confines of their environment. She will always remind you to wake up every morning and live your best life; you live every day, and you only die once!

Connect with Jen: https://linktr.ee/jenliveyourbestlife

Chapter 24

The Fourth Face

Thais Conte

The Japanese proverb says we have three faces, but I believe we have four.

My Story

The ringing of the phone was rare, like a melody that broke through the silence. I'd rush to answer, knowing it might be months before I heard the familiar voices again. Letters were even slower—a stamp pressed onto an envelope, traveling across oceans.

Each time I packed my life into suitcases, it felt like tearing pages from a book no one would finish. My address changed so often that I stopped trying to keep everyone informed. The ink on return addresses faded, but the memories of true friendships stayed.

In every new country, I faced the mirror not just to learn a new language and culture but to meet the woman staring back at me. *"Come on, girl, fear and shyness won't help you now. You've got this!"* I breathed deeply, walked into rooms full of strangers, and introduced myself again. My voice trembled at first, but soon it steadied. With each move, I reinvented myself, shedding one skin and growing another, stronger but still open to what might come next.

Regrets? Yes, I have a few. But I'd choose this path all over again. Without the stumbles, I wouldn't be who I am today—a woman, yet stronger than I ever imagined. My strength lies in my choices and the ability to keep going even when the road ahead seems unclear.

After many moves, I faced a new struggle—trying to give my daughter a sibling. Between pills and injections, the endless routine, each one carried a weight that words couldn't capture. *"I just know this is going to work. I'm a healthy woman—only my age is working against me, nothing else. And I refuse to give up without a fight."* I was caught in a cycle of hope and heartbreak, and along the way, I found strength in the company of brave women who shared this journey, and for a moment, I wasn't alone.

Just when I thought I learned all my lessons, life brought me another challenge. After the pandemic, I faced cancer. *All this hair falling out is driving me crazy. This is true agony. Maybe I should just shave it all off now."* At that time, I had no idea that something even harder would hit me. Soon after, I froze at work, my mind completely blank. I couldn't remember even the simplest task. *How could I keep moving forward if my mind was failing me?* For the first time during treatment, I broke down in tears. Yet, these thorns—these painful moments—shaped me.

I know I'm not perfect, but I remind myself daily that I'm the best mother my children could have because no one loves them like I do. Now, I have one more reason to fight anything on my way, and I am sure better days will come.

True friendships didn't need my new address to survive. They found me through the echoes of shared laughter and memories, even from across the world.

And now, I stand here—grateful for every thorn and every petal—still growing, still reaching, thankful for the journey that led me to this moment.

The Poems

The first face we show to the world.

The Little Girl Inside of Me

On tiptoe, unseen and unheard,
She moves through the lives of everyone she knows.
Even when her tears fall like a tropical storm,
No thunder rumbles in her voice,
No lightning strikes in her movements.
Instead, a fever rages where lightning should,
And a sore throat whispers in place of thunder.
They think she is kind, but fragile—
A little girl clutching her mother's skirt,
Hiding within her father's shadow.
A people-pleaser who so often forgets herself.
She has stumbled seven times and risen eight,
Normalizing her pain,
Brushing off her battles as if they were nothing.
If everyone else hurts too, why should she make a fuss?
She doesn't pause to feel the sting—
Miscarriages, cancer, pains of the body, mind, and soul—
They're all just part of life's quiet, brutal rhythm.
Nothing has ever been easy, yet she endures,
Brilliantly navigating storms,
Even when everything was new,
Even when she was just a girl.
She's done it so many times it seems effortless,
Though each time the struggle deepens,
And the weariness grows.

The second face we show to our close friends and family.

All My Experience Combined Defines What You See In Me

She dances through life like a ballerina,
Pirouetting in both sunlight and shadow.
In graceful arcs, she flutters,
Elegant, sweet—a swan gliding over silver waves,
Until the black swan calls her to darker depths.
She makes friends as effortlessly as a hummingbird sips nectar,
Buzzing and humming in gentle, fleeting moments.
Once shy as a fawn, her timid steps are now the past,
Left behind like the worn footprints of old paths.
To some, she remains hidden,
Invisible as the soft rustle of owl feathers in the night.
They see only the quiet surface, the sweetness, the softness—
Assuming her easy prey,
Delicate like a deer under the watch of the waiting wolf.
But they don't know the full rhythm of her spirit,
The dolphin's gleam beneath the surface,
A sharp, quick flash of insight that cuts like a blade.
And in moments fierce as a lioness's roar,
She breaks the silence—her power echoing,
In a single, resounding beat,
Her roar shakes the forest,
As she stands, a wild symphony of all she has lived,
Unseen, unheard, yet always there,
The essence of all her experiences, rising.

The third face is one we never show anyone. It's the most faithful reflection of who we are.

The Search for Myself

Who am I?
A lonely soul, sometimes hurt, a fragile being,
Delicate as glass, yet forged in silent fires.
I am human, flawed and searching,
But when my sense of justice rises,
I separate emotion from reason,
And let truth speak through me, clear as dawn.
Such a sensitive heart, raw with feeling,
Yet reason stands taller, stronger,
A steady flame that tempers every storm.
Who am I?
I speak the truth, and strive to be fair,
But doubt lingers like shadows at dusk—
Is it worth it? I ask.
And the answer, a quiet whisper,
Reminds me to be true, to hold firm,
Not to let people or circumstance dim the best within me.
It's hard to see an enemy in your envious eyes,
For instead, I see someone burdened by shadows,
A spirit in need of light, and so I pity you,
Even as you hurl your jealousy like stones.
Where am I?
I live among the hidden,
Between my heart, my soul, and my mind—
My heart opens to all who carry love in their veins,
With light in their souls, and justice in their thoughts.
Alone, yet not alone, for something greater moves me,
A quiet force that pulls me onward,
A silent companion through the dark,
In search of the self I have yet to fully know.

The fourth face is how God sees us.

How the Father Sees His Son

He is my Father, who knows me better than I know myself.
I trusted in Him and had faith, even when I could barely grasp
The vastness of His love, or see the ways He worked within me.
Yet, I have always known Him as omnipresent, omnipotent, and omniscient.
That alone was enough to feel His protection,
To find the strength to endure, even when pain and solitude weighed heavy upon me.

So I thank Him, and I praise Him, my Shepherd,
For I am His sheep, and He cares for me with an everlasting love.
He knows my every sorrow, my deepest fears,
And the quiet strength that lifts me after each fall.
He guides me along paths of righteousness, for His name's sake,
And He understands that empathy blooms from shared trials.

He knows my sins, yet also my grace, for He sees my heart as no one else can.
So, with my soul laid bare, I call out to Thee in full vulnerability—my Friend, my
Master, my Father
With a grateful heart, I have learned
That I need not limit my prayers to grand requests alone,
For gratitude springs forth even in the smallest of things,
The daily bread, the gentle mercies, gifts undeserved.

He is a merciful God, who meets me where I am,
Not because of me, but in spite of me.

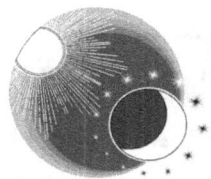

Dear Reader, now it's your turn to write! Use the blank space below. Try not to censor yourself.

Take a deep breath and tell yourself your three faces. Are you showing up as your most authentic self? Do you have a fourth face?

Thais Conte was born in a small town in São Paulo, Brazil. At the age of eight, she experienced her first significant move to northern Brazil, and from there, a journey of global relocations began. Over the years, she has lived in more than five countries and ten cities, gaining invaluable cultural insights along the way. Thais holds a bachelor's degree in business administration and, in addition to being a dedicated mom, she is an accomplished writer. Her diverse life experiences fuel both her professional and personal growth.

Connect with Thais: https://linktr.ee/thaisconte

Chapter 25

Healing While Grieving
Simply Sherri

My Story

Seeking Help

Me to Therapist: "I've been through a lot in the last couple of years."

Therapist: "Explain."

Me: "In the Spring of 2022, my mom passed; in the fall of 2022, my brother unexpectedly passed; in the Spring of 2023, my boss passed. In October 2023, I had emergency surgery, and while I was recovering, my bonus dad passed. Then, in June 2024, my godmother passed."

Therapist: "Wow, that is a lot."

My shoulders dropped.

Me: "So, I'm not being dramatic?"

Therapist: "No."

Exhale

Many of my friends are surprised to hear all that I'm dealing with; I never let pressure show on my face or in my actions. Stress and grieving have been a constant companion for the past six years. The pandemic/quarantine was just a backdrop to everything happening—from suffering through a series of medical challenges, my mother's health failing, and my stepfather's gradual descent through dementia, I could go on. I've forgotten what happiness feels like or not being on edge while waiting for the other shoe to drop. Living with this much stress takes a toll on one's physical and mental health. My waistline, medical tests, and the doctors' wagging fingers prove it. But when living in constant reaction mode, it's easy to forget the most basic self-care or find joy in the hobbies I once took more pleasure in.

The first step to healing is reaching out for help. This wasn't my first conversation with a therapist, and at her suggestion, I spoke to my physician. My doctor prescribed something to ease my undiagnosed anxiety, which has gone untreated for years. Depression has always been acknowledged, claiming anxiety is new. The medication helps relieve sleepless nights, making the following days more manageable. Plus, a well-rested mind makes better food choices; a well-rested body creates energy for movement, which all my doctors say I need.

I needed help from various professionals to reach my healing goals. Often, the first person I contacted was not the right person. They didn't understand my concerns and couldn't help me navigate my challenges. It's discouraging when the professional you hired seems to be giving prepared advice, nothing personalized. If the first person you speak to doesn't give you the answer you want, find someone else. It was my time and money; I wanted answers deeper than what I could hear from an untrained influencer.

The journey has included finding a workout routine I enjoy and can stick with; I love Aquafit. I'm improving my relationship with food; as of this writing, I'm feeling better than I have in a few years.

I deserve peace and happiness; both are within me to be found. I see days when I have a clear mind and am not waiting for another shoe to fall. I see days when I enjoy all my hobbies again. Six months ago, I wouldn't have been able to say this much.

The Poems

What is Grief?

what is grief but love persevering ~ WandaVision

Grief develops like a tsunami
Formed on aftershocks
There's no warning
The tide does not pull away from the beach
The wave overtakes you
Praying the receding waters leave my memories

Grief produces avoidance
Including your extended family
Sitting in the corner in tears
You want to attend the celebration
But the last time we were together was the worst day of my life.

Grief scrambles your mind
The brain doesn't quite work the same
Attention is fleeting
Memory no longer exists
The inner voice is always asking questions
Is this healthy?
Is it avoidance?
Is it toxic positivity?
Is it just overthinking?
Can it please stop?

Grief is a DJ
Curating your playlist
The O'Jays were once on repeat
After my mother climbed the stairway to heaven
They could not be listened to

Grief is not a sprint or marathon
It's a hike through the Himalayas
Every breath gets harder
I hear there will be beautiful scenery along the way.

And whether or not I want to, it's a journey I'm forced to take.

Dams

Before a dam burst
It heaves
Moans
Reshapes
Relaxes

There may be small leaks
water seeping
slithering along the facade
long going
unnoticed

Dams are built for protection
standing silent sentry
continuing its task as
as the pressure builds

The reservoir swells
The dam heaves
It breathes
the water escapes
Nature experiences relief

Dams are doubly destructive
When built,
destroying what previously existed
when cracking
Damaging everything in its path

Dams are built out of fear
The longer they stand
The stronger they are
Whether on rivers or eyelids

People are not dams
Fear not the outburst
What's broken can be repaired
What's left will be relief

Yes to Me

It's me
I'm the problem
I'm the one who has forgotten what yes to me sounds like

It sounds like

No, I'm not ok
Yes, I can use your help with this task
Yes, to treating myself better
Yes, to additional rest - TODAY
Yes, to my self-interest regardless of yours
No, that never made me selfish
No, I'm not going to be the bigger person or code switch right now

Yea, I've always been beautiful
Yes, I'm open to a loving relationship
Yes, I'll wait for the bartender to finish making this drink
Yes, I'mma pay for it
No, I didn't wear this outfit for you
No, my looks didn't change because I no longer wish to engage in this conversation
No. Don't ask again

Yes, to making my own money
Hell yes, this is how I'm spending it
Yes, to immersing myself in things I love
Yes to joy
Hell yes to my pleasure
Yes to how I get there
No, that may not include anyone else

Yes, to how I honor the god I worship
Yes to making space for your life's religious practice
No to whatever BS you are trying to sell me as religion

Yes to spending time with my friends
Yes, I'm open to hear what you need to talk about
Or no, right now might not be the best time; can I call you later?
Yes, I'm always here for you
I just need to remember to be there for myself

Sometimes saying no to you is saying yes to me
And if I say "Oh hell no"

Then yes, you fucked with the wrong one.

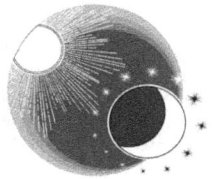

Dear Reader, now it's your turn to write! Use the blank space below. Try not to censor yourself.

Compose the conversation with a loved one you can no longer talk to.

With a stylish and alluring approach, **Simply Sherri's** writing style is not just accessible but also enjoyable, offering a revealing reflection of her world that resonates with everyone. Her poetry has the power to make audiences laugh, cry, and, most often, smile at the playful thoughts her words provoke. Sherri has been a shining star at various venues along the East Coast, captivating audiences with her unique "Love, Sexy, Classy Nasty" style—a poetic journey that is both humorous and heartfelt and a warm exploration of love and relationships.

Though well known for her love and erotic writing, Sherri is unafraid to examine the totality of a black woman's life, poetically illuminating subjects such as depression, misogyny, abuse, and surviving the political climate.

Sherri hosts Second Wednesdays at Busboys & Poets, 450 K St. in Washington, DC, and the Pajama Jammie Jam Slam at Busboys & Poets, Takoma Park, Maryland.

Connect with Simply Sherri:
https://www.simplypoeticentertainment.com/

Reclamation

By Laura Di Franco

It was an up-leveling of a different kind,
so intense I didn't recognize the signs.

The Universe always taught me the flow
spelled out what I needed to know:
the way it feels to transform
how it takes what is
and turns it into your dreams
and the life you were born to lead.

But I forgot.

Maybe. . .
. . . just maybe I prayed for it to happen this way
asked God to unlock the gate
so I could run free.
And she gave me exactly what I needed
to create everything.

It all came at once
a gift of chaos and pain
no explanation
only an answer to a prayer for my best life to arrive.
And suddenly what I truly thought I wanted. . .
. . . that well went dry.
I found myself at the bottom of a pit
so deep and dark
I didn't recognize me—again.

Damn, you did it again!

When will I learn?

You stole my identity
forced me to see a bigger, better me
the me who's actually meant
to do that dream I dreamt
once upon a time.

I thought I was her again and again.
Now I realize I had some expansion
to take on.
If I really wanted all that
I'd have to accept the fact
that there was more work to do
more fear to alchemize into fuel
a grander-sized heart and soul to grow
a more masterful circle to curate.

At this rate?
Baby, I'll be there in no time.
In fact, I've arrived today
in the reclamation of my voice
my worth
my dream
my chaos
my pain
my moment of waking
to the depth of WTF-ness
in my circumstance.

I laughed when I saw.
How could I have missed. . .
. . . everything carefully placed on the table
in front of my face
clear as day?
1.   Express your love and detach
2.   Set your boundaries and cast your line from there
3.   Let down your hair and surrender to the sweet spot
of letting go
4. Remember you aren't supposed to know the how;
It's always a surprise and delight

The Universe's fireworks show for your soul
is not a set holiday
or size
or color
or model or make.
It's always the awe and the joy
always the feeling of yes
of ease
of love expressed
always takes care of itself
and lets itself be known

Your doubt, fear, and clench
just brace around the clarity
you spend months blocking yourself from.
If you take off the brakes and break
so be it.
If you break
and everything comes crashing down
don't you get the Divine purpose in that soul-fall
and the power that has your back?

Aren't you ready to receive the support
you always thought you lacked?
Can't you see YOU are what's holding you back?

If the stuck spot feels bigger or harder this time
it's only because you thought holding on tighter
would be the only way to survive.
Instead, that old tactic
created cement inside
and weighed you down so hard
you struggled to rise.

So dreamer, warrior, world-changer, lover. . .
. . . let go.
Break the rules.
Let the old ways die.
Birth something new.

Don't over-analyze the mess.
Confess to the blankness.
Embrace and sit in the middle of it all.
Call the angels to your side.
Reclaim what's yours.
Fly.

What's in store will happily, easily flow
like a cosmic lazer light show
showing the way to the next dance step. . .
. . . as soon as you're ready.

And friends, I know you're ready to dance.

Let's dance!

Poetry heals.

What if that thing you're still a little afraid to share is exactly the thing someone is waiting to read to change (or even save) their life?

It's time to be brave.

This is way more than a book you have in your hands. It's a generous community of souls waiting for you to reach out, ask a question, or get support. Our poets aren't just authors; they're teachers, coaches, healers, and therapists. They are heads of organizations. They are leaders, mentors, and successful entrepreneurs. We want you to connect!

Go back through to the chapters that pulled you deeper and made you realize something about yourself. Contact our poets and let them know they made a difference in your life. Your reviews on Amazon are badass, by the way! I always tell my authors on our coaching calls, "If you're having a bad day (and don't we all?), go read the reviews!"

By the way, there's a big group of us here in the DC/Maryland/Virginia area and our *100 Poems & Possibilities* open mic event is usually in April to celebrate poetry month. Email us at BraveHealerTeam@gmail.com for details!

And please check out some more awesome things we're doing for poets. . .

Laura

Opportunities For Poets

The Warrior Love Poetry Page

You can **submit your poem** for a shout-out on our **Warrior Love Poetry Page** on Facebook. Please email that submission in the body of your email to BraveHealerTeam@gmail.com with:

1. Poem title

2. Poem

3. Signature/title

4. 50-word bio with one link

5. Photograph that accompanies the poem (please include photo credit line).

If approved, your poem will be posted on the page and you'll receive an email with that link. If you don't hear from us within 72 hours, please follow up!

Please make sure to like/follow the page before you submit your poem!

Go here to do that: https://www.facebook.com/warriorlove

Positively Purposeful Poetry YouTube Podcast

Do you have a poetry book you're promoting? Come **be interviewed** by Laura. Please email us at BraveHealerTeam@gmail.com with interest.

Make sure to subscribe to the YouTube channel before you inquire.

Go here: https://www.youtube.com/@positivelypurposefulpoetry8316

100 Poems & Possibilities for Healing Collaborative Poetry Book

Are you ready to join a global community of poets and authors and be published in our next bestselling, business-building collaboration? You'll find more info about all of our active book collaboration opportunities here: https://lauradifranco.com/expert-book-collaborations/

Or feel free to reach out by email: support@LauraDiFranco.com

Other Poetry Books from
Brave Healer Productions

My first four books of poetry were published under my married name and can still be found on Amazon. Don't judge, y'all. These books were me figuring things out.

Warrior Love, a Journal to Inspire Your Fiercely Alive Whole Self

Warrior Joy, a Journal to Inspire Your Fiercely Alive Whole Self

Warrior Soul, a Journal to Inspire Your Fiercely Alive Whole Self

Warrior Dreams, a Journal to Inspire Your Fiercely Alive Whole Self

When I took my maiden name (Di Franco) back, I wrote a book of love poems. And then, we created the first volume of 100 Poems, which supports our non-profit partner, The InkWell.

Warrior Desire: Love Poems to Inspire Your Fiercely Alive Whole Self

100 Poems & Possibilities for Healing Volume 1

Show Me a Boulder

By Laura Di Franco

Show me a boulder on a river
and I'll show you
the best therapist in the world

Her flat, sun-baked top
beckons me to sit with myself
longer than an hour

The bubbly rush
of mountain spring
the only words I need

I find a seat where I feel safe
This feels like home
And the voices start

I'm open to listening here
I'm curious—
allow my belly to soften with the exhale

Her flat lines and bold curves
spell confidence
I'm held

She's been there before
wracked by the storm
trampled by unconscious fools who leave trash

I trust her silence
Wisdom sparkles from tiny specks, cracks, and lines—
how I know what she's made of

Basking there, I notice
The trees give the breeze a voice
The birds make it a song

and my beating heart
syncing all along
belongs to the rhythm

Show me a boulder on a river
a seat where my soul
reigns queen

I connect with a higher self
who can do this life today
even when the battle comes

Remember, your words change the world when you're brave enough to share them. It's time to be brave.

With Warrior Love,

Laura

www.ingramcontent.com/pod-product-compliance
Lightning Source LLC
Chambersburg PA
CBHW071716140626
46557CB00012B/849

Praise for

Rise Together

"*Rise Together* by Laquita Dian is a powerful memoir of the author's transformative journey of endurance and triumph in the midst of profound pain following her son's life-altering event. The book is a beautiful exploration of love, courage, devotion, and resoluteness in the face of a family's utmost challenge. The author's writing is a symbolic helix, with mother and son forming the strongest and most beautiful of bonds. This book is an excellent source of inspiration and guidance for those who have been through crisis and for the rest of us who may someday encounter a life-altering event."

—DR. KATHLEEN SLIJEPCEVIC, clinical psychologist

"It has become abundantly clear that both the care recipient and the caregiver need to forge a partnership as two equal sources of inspiration to achieve optimum results. Aaron and Laquita are living proof of this vital principle. Reading Aaron's book, *The Rebellious Recovery*, gave me a tremendous appreciation for Laquita and her role as caregiver in the success of his recovery. But nothing surprised me more than the profound impact that Laquita's memoir, which you are about to read here, had on me. Each exquisitely written chapter was a cathartic experience, and I was moved to tears as I read it aloud to my wife, Alexandra, who had suffered a massive stroke and, she too, was moved to tears. The depth of Laquita's soul is boundless. Her indomitable spirit in the face of adversity within her family, her strength of character, her love, and her unfathomable purposefulness (her 'Why') is astonishing."

—RON SEIGEL, author of *Enlightened Caregiving for Men Who Care*

"*Rise Together*, just like *The Rebellious Recovery*, was one of those books I couldn't put down once I started. Laquita journeyed from heartbreak to hero. Her masterful storytelling invites readers into her most vulnerable moments and her most empowering ones. She's a role model of hope for mothers and certainly inspires us to be the 'all-in' facilitators of our own healthcare and that of our loved ones. *Rise Together* goes deep into the impact a health tragedy has on every member of a family, their mental health, and relationships. Her strength, spirit of optimism, and willingness to do just about anything to help her son realize new possibilities is awe inspiring. You can't finish this book and not believe with all your heart that anything is possible! As a mom of a child with a rare disease, *Rise Together* has inspired me to push for more answers, get involved in research, and explore alternative and nonmedical possibilities for managing, or even curing, her disease. She is a light, illuminating hope and possibility where most people see none. I'm incredibly grateful to know Laquita's story and to know her beautiful, loving soul."

—SHELLEY KELLY, talent representative

"Laquita's story is for every mom or dad, sibling, or friend who ever loved someone more than life itself . . . a story for everyone who faces demons and fights dragons, head-on, without restraint or reluctance, with no thought of the dangers ahead and no assurance of tomorrow. It's a story about a mother's fierce, holy battle for her children and, in the end, for herself. *Rise Together* is a road map not only for families facing spinal cord injury and addiction but for everyone; for certainly if one single mom can conquer these conflicts, then there must be hope for the rest of us as we struggle to find joy. Laquita's gut-wrenching journey is about finding peace and wholeness, as well as joy. Give this book to someone you love."

—DEBORAH FLYNN, western regional director Christopher
& Dana Reeve Foundation (retired), founder QUAD
Foundation Inc., mother of amazing C4–5 quadriplegic son

"*Rise Together* moved my very soul and gave me courage, inspiration, and allowed me to solidify even more that love, perseverance, and determination all work together for the greater good. I met Laquita in 2018, after my own son broke his neck. The terrible grief and emptiness of that trauma are indescribable; meeting another mother who understood that journey, as only someone who has traveled it can, gave me much-needed courage. Laquita lives with fierce love and courage and will inspire others to do the same. Everyone's life situations are unique, but Laquita writes with such humility, vulnerability, and insights for a better path forward that I believe this book can be a valuable resource for anyone facing life-changing challenges. Regardless of your circumstances, you need to read this book. It will infuse you with hope and a sense that you CAN overcome whatever life throws your way. *Rise Together* will impact many, and encourage them to rise from the ashes!"

—SHELLEY CARLSON, entertainer/singer, mother of C5 quadriplegic son

"I am truly moved by Laquita Dian's book, *Rise Together*, for so many reasons—most of which have to do with the amazing testimony about never giving up no matter what happens in your life. I was thoroughly moved during my entire read. There is so much about the experiences of Aaron's and Laquita's stories (together and apart) that serve as a model for everyday life. Each of us will have a hurdle to jump or a situation that changes how we go about our lives (events beyond our control). How we choose to respond to those challenges/situations/events is in our control—is our choice. I came away from reading this book wanting to meet Aaron; however, I feel like I have already met him because of the way Laquita portrayed him in her story. She shows him as driven and certainly touts his many amazing wins, but he is also portrayed as vulnerable. He has worked for everything he has achieved. During her story she shares some of her own vulnerabilities and challenges and how she was able to 'rise' above those to help Aaron reach his goals of independence. Aaron and Laquita truly set the example for the attainable and the tone of 'I am possible' from the seemingly 'impossible.' One of my favorite parts of this book was Laquita's reflection on 'redefining life': for me, it speaks to every type of redefinition life throws our way. To be able to allow ourselves the space to paint our own canvases how each of us sees fit. Our reactions are our choice. I so recommend this book to be able to share in Aaron and Laquita's story and their challenges and appreciate how love and perseverance facilitate change."

—MICHELLE MARSH, RN

Rise Together

Rise Together

The Art of Climbing Out of the Ditch

a memoir by

LAQUITA DIAN

PNEUMIND
LOS ANGELES, CA

Published by PNEUMIND
contact@pneumind.com
Los Angeles, CA
pneumind.com
@_pneumind

PNEUMIND books are available at special quantity discounts for
bulk purchase for sales promotions, premiums, fundraising, and
educational needs. Special books or book excerpts also can be created
to fit specific needs. For details and permission requests, write to the
email address above.

ISBN 979-8-9864880-5-9 (eBook)
ISBN 979-8-9864880-6-6 (paperback)
ISBN 979-8-9864880-7-3 (hardback)

Printed in the United States of America

laquitadian.com

—

Copyediting by James Gallagher & Adeline Hull
Cover Design by Aaron Baker
Cover Photo by Melanie Manson
Proofreading by James Gallagher
Book Design & Publishing by Kory Kirby
SET IN ADOBE CASLON PRO

rise

....

/ˈrīz/

verb

1. to assume an upright position especially from lying, kneeling, or sitting
2. to return from death

together

....

/tə-ˈge-thər/

adverb

1. in a body; as a group
2. in or into contact, connection, collision, or union

For Aaron & Arielle
Because We Can

Six questions of value in life to ponder

Of what is your spirit made?

How can we overcome struggles and suffering?

How do we find meaning in life?

How can we cultivate compassion and empathy toward others?

What is worth giving everything up for?

What is worth living for?

The answer to each is the same.

Only Love.

Contents

Author's Note

As I composed this memoir, the intensity of my experiences had such a profound impact on me that the act of writing felt like a vivid reenactment, like scraping the scab from the wound. As hard as it was to admit many aspects to myself, it was even harder to admit them to you. But I cannot share the victories if I don't share the raw, gritty, and ugly truths as well. It is my hope that in sharing my truth, you can move closer to yours.

Also, I chose to change the names of a few individuals, out of respect for their privacy.

My Why, Our How

Life is unpredictable, and it has a way of catching us off guard. It can bring us tremendous joy and happiness, only to turn around and present us with challenges that feel insurmountable. It's often in the midst of these challenges that we realize how precious life is, how important every minute we have on this earth is, and how important to us the people we care about are.

There is a driving force behind everything I do—it's what inspires me, motivates me, and is my reason for showing up every day to face the challenges life has given me. Love is my force, my through line that connects the various distinct and divergent life phases I have experienced, and *Why* I chose to do the things I do.

The word *why* has two different meanings; depending on the context in which it's used, it relates either to motivation and purpose, or causation and explanation. My *Why* directly relates to what motivates me to live and love courageously. *Why* is the key influence behind action; it's what inspires us to move forward and is the foundation for our purpose. How we take action and persevere through challenges, while staying true to our values, ultimately determines our outcome. The connection between our *Why* and our *How* is powerful, and together, they can propel us to go far beyond our perceived limits.

When the very thing I feared most happened, the only way I could help myself was by helping my young son. He had sustained a catastrophic, disabling injury that would require my complete dedication . . . to keep him alive.

I had always believed I would not be able to handle anything tragic happening to either of my children . . . until it did. I then discovered a well of untapped strength that I would never have been able to access or activate on my own accord.

With a rebellious spirit, my son and I refused to accept the severe limitations imposed by the injury, and catalyzed our own pursuit of recovery, on our terms.

Our SPIRIT permeated every step we took. It was our road map, our way forward. . . . The first and most important thing I could do to feel more in control of our out-of-control situation was to take a *Stand*, a vital action that helped me assert our values and beliefs to create a positive change. We opened our minds to *Possibility*, which allowed us to see opportunities rather than obstacles. When we began to *Initiate*, we transformed our circumstances into positive actions, with the *Reason* being the principal stimulus behind our *Intentions* and the steps we took to achieve them. Ultimately, the power of our *Spirit* lies in its ability to *Transform*, using our adversity as an accelerant to re-create and amplify our lives.

The words *inspiration* and *spirit* both share the same Latin root *spirare*, which means "to breathe." To inspire someone is to breathe life into them, filling them with a sense of purpose or enthusiasm. Perhaps within these pages you will feel your own spirit and the transformative power of connecting to your *Why*. My hope is that you discover, through mindful and deliberate action, that we *can* Rise Together.

> **"He who has a strong enough Why**
> **can endure almost any How."**
> ~ FRIEDRICH NIETZSCHE

The Ditch and the Can

June 2000

The particular day that I reached for a vodka bottle during a grocery shopping trip is burned into my mind. As if in slow motion, I watched as my hand grasped the bottle. I put it back twice, the rational voice in my mind-talk was reminding me of how dangerous this would be for me. The other more seductive voice convinced me that I would have only a little bit at a time for much-needed energy . . . and the bottle then stayed in my cart.

Alcohol is poison for me. I struggled on and off throughout my life with overindulging, using it mostly for energy and creativity, especially during times of distress. No matter what kind of emotional upheaval was happening in my life, two drinks and I would feel enthusiastic, free from sadness or tears. With it, I believed I could conquer the world and do anything I wanted . . . it did live up to its reputation of being liquid courage. Even more dangerous, the effect of alcohol taps into the thrill-seeking aspect of my personality, which I love even more. Like the lyrics in a country song, *one is never enough.*

I had managed to keep myself in check for the twelve months following my son's injury. I was committed to being fully present. I had even refused any type of pain medication after I sprained my ankle, because I feared I wouldn't hear Aaron when he called me, or that I would misinterpret any medical explanation.

Aaron's darkness and constant fight against me and my daughter, Arielle's increasing disconnection from our misery, along with my brokenness, finally penetrated, enveloping my psyche. I was searching for something, anything, to help me continue. A few drinks of vodka and cranberry juice would provide the energy and dull my senses in a way that otherwise had escaped me.

Aaron and Arielle's father, Dan, had returned to stay with us for a couple of weeks. My afternoon drink that commenced two days prior continued without pause. Somewhere around 4:00 a.m. on the morning of the third day of drinking, I decided I wanted to drive to Oklahoma to get a few of my belongings. Our apartment was extremely sparse, furnished only with the absolute essentials. Without telling Aaron, Arielle, or their dad my plans, I got in Arielle's little Dodge pickup truck, at morning's light, and headed east to Oklahoma.

I stopped at a market and purchased a six-pack of beer and an ice chest to continue my binge while driving. I was in a multiday-long alcohol stupor, and a welcomed sense of freedom came over me. I was on the road, singing out loud with the radio, slipping in and out of focus. I came back into awareness as I was traveling on an undulating two-lane road surrounded by a barren lunar landscape. I shook my head, not knowing where I was. I was supposed to be heading east, yet a road sign said south.

As I came upon a Border Patrol checkpoint, eight officers swarmed my little truck. I rolled down the window, laughing, flippantly saying, "Sorry I'm late."

The head officer said, "Ma'am, you need to get out of the vehicle."

At that point I broke down.

I told them I needed help.

The officer said, "Yes, I believe you do need help, but you are going to jail first."

Apparently, I'd been reported for swerving. I found out later that Aaron and Arielle had filed a missing person report as well.

I was handcuffed and escorted to a patrol car. I leaned forward to ask the officer who was driving where we were. He answered with a "sit back and be quiet." The two-hour drive, handcuffed, in the back seat of a patrol car, was shrouded in an alcohol haze I couldn't see through.

I was deposited in a minimum-security correctional farm outside of Calexico, which is on the border of Mexico and California. There were two benches and a commode in the women's holding cell. I was beginning to feel the ill effects of the three-day hard alcohol binge when the cell door closed, leaving me alone, with veiled reality beginning to creep in.

My poisoned body, cold and malnourished, began to tremble as my teeth chattered. I found a bit of comfort lying on the hard wooden bench, using a roll of toilet paper from the corner commode as a pillow for my pounding head. An officer appeared at the cell bars to tell me I could come out to make a collect call to someone to make bail for my release. I lifted my heavy head and said, "I'm not calling anyone."

Many hours later, an officer opened the cell bars and told me I was being released. It was six o'clock in the morning. I was given my belongings and a bus ticket for a ride to Calexico. The bus would arrive sometime between 6:30 a.m. and noon.

With an empty wallet and a broken sandal, I stumbled out of the correctional center security gates to wait for the bus on the side of the desolate two-lane country road.

The temperature was already in the nineties, as this was June in the Southern-Central Valley of the California Desert. In my alcohol stupor, I had dressed in winter clothing, a thick velour sweater and velour leggings. I had on three-inch-high thong sandals. The right toe strap had broken somehow. Not wanting to walk barefoot on the hot, strewn-with-broken-glass blacktop road, I hopped and wobbled, trying to keep the broken sandal on my foot.

I was a complete disaster, with no idea of where I or my car was, no money . . . and no idea of how I was going to face what I had left behind me.

By this time, I was physically sick, horrifyingly sick, although that paled in comparison to how sick my soul was. That sickness went beyond any sickness I'd ever known. I couldn't believe my actions or the abhorrent condition I was in. Demoralized, dehydrated, with a splitting headache, and dry heaving due to nausea, I lay down in the ditch next to the road.

The morning sun was scorching hot, made worse by the thick velour clinging to my body. I placed a crumpled piece of discarded cardboard over my head, trying to protect my face from the blistering rays. Lying in a fetal position in the dirt ditch, I began to beg to die, pleading with God to take me right then and there. I begged for each breath to be my last.

As death was eluding me and the breaths continued, I asked, out loud, for a sign. A sign that would let me know I should get up. I then heard a faint whistle over my shoulder. I leaned up out of the ditch and turned toward the whistle, but with the sun directly in my eyes, I couldn't see anything but the blinding brightness of the sun's rays.

I heard the whistle again, this time a bit louder. I feebly got up and then saw what I believed to be a mirage or hallucination: a man standing on the other side of the chain-link fence that separated us, holding a bright blue Pepsi can that was so cold ice was running down the sides. As I came closer, he stretched his arm over the fence, the Pepsi can in hand, and stated, "I thought perhaps you might enjoy this."

He had seen me—from the prison yard—in the ditch just outside the fence.

This was my sign.

The feeling of that Pepsi hitting the back of my throat, the effervescence of icy-cold carbonated sugar running into my sick stomach, was like swallowing a bolt of pure electrified life force . . . all the more powerful because it was handed to me by a complete stranger while I was in a dirt ditch. It was the sign I needed to get up, to make a pact with myself right then and there to begin to put one foot in front of the other.

The bus pulled up.

I stood up and got on.

I was dropped off on the main street of Calexico. Due to my mental fog and weakness and broken sandal, I stumbled into the first store I came upon. I asked the clerk for the location of the nearest Border Patrol office. The clerk didn't look up from her counter, just pointed in the direction of the office down the street.

At the counter of the Border Patrol office, I leaned into the window that separated the staff from the visitors, and asked how I would go about finding my car, which had been left at a checkpoint the day before. I was asked, "What checkpoint?"

I didn't know the location. I didn't know the license plate number of the car. I didn't know the year of the car. The only thing I did know was the make and the color.

The agent rolled her eyes and shook her head in exasperated disbelief of my lack of knowledge and mangy appearance. She shooed me away with a finger pointing in the direction of yet another agency office. This one was several blocks away.

Once again, I was limping along the hot streets, destination unknown, but somehow being guided by an emerging inner strength that was beginning to make its way into my awareness.

The second Border Patrol checkpoint, after hearing my story, did indeed take the time and effort to locate my car. The car was still at the remote checkpoint where I'd been arrested. They hadn't impounded it. This was the second of a number of very lucky, unlikely occurrences, which were my signs from the unknown elements we can define as God, angels, or whatever—the divine magic of the universe, I like to say. These signs had a visceral effect on me—do not stop, do not back down, keep moving forward, no matter what, and no matter how hard.

My next task was to find a taxi to take me to the checkpoint, which was two hours into the desert from Calexico. With a bit of optimism, I opened the back door of a taxi, got in, and asked if he could take me to the checkpoint. Because of the location, I would have to pay for both his way there and back—it was nearly a full day's work for him in drive time. I passed him my credit card for prepayment, and he pushed it back, saying he accepted only cash. My wallet had been emptied of the eighty dollars cash I had before the arrest—I suppose by the guards or someone in the prison colony.

After opening the door to hold my head out and dry heave, I leaned back heavily into the back seat. . . . Now what? The driver saw my empty wallet, empty eyes, empty soul.

Although I was fragile, something in me prevented me from getting out of the car as he requested. He threatened to leave me stranded if I did not find a way to pay him in cash. Though I did have a checkbook, I was well aware that the balance in the account wasn't sufficient to cover the amount demanded by the driver. Despite my clouded and foggy state of mind, I searched for ways I could acquire the funds I needed. Calling someone to help me was out of the question.

I asked the driver if he would take me to a grocery store and he agreed. The actual probability of getting my check cashed was next to zero. I was from out of town, a stranger in a new store, asking them to cash my check. The store clerk looked at both sides of my scribbled two-hundred-dollar out-of-town check, regarded my disheveled yet seemingly confident appearance several times over his reading glasses, opened the cash drawer, and counted out two hundred-dollar bills. I wanted to jump over the counter to give him a giant hug, but my exterior demeanor remained unfazed, as though I wasn't surprised at all.

I began to feel my inner power stir. That grocery store clerk was my reminder of a power I had lost sense of. I wanted it back. That power was the key to my family's future—to my future. My back straightened a little more as I walked to the waiting taxicab.

As I rode back through the desolate expanse of the desert, the vast void mirrored the depths of my inner turmoil.

I was a colossal mix of a disgusting disaster and a stirring, distant inner strength. These opposite forces kept colliding, one trying to overpower the other. Despite the tumultuous power struggle, the image of the Pepsi can persisted, anchoring me to a profound sense of self, triumphing over my self-deprecating feelings.

Two hours later we arrived at the Border Patrol checkpoint where I had been arrested. On the far side of the office sat the little truck that had chauffeured Aaron and Arielle for several years. It had been my first time driving it, and now it was sitting forlorn, waiting to be rescued.

The officers inside seemed empathetic as I was handed the key. One officer wished me well, another wished me help, and the third wished me a safe drive home.

Upon opening the door to the little truck, I was struck by the size of the ice chest still sitting on the bench seat. It was huge, taking up all but the small space for me to sit behind the steering wheel. As I lifted the lid, the smell of moldy water and old beer hit me between the nostrils. There were three opened and three unopened beer cans floating in the hot, melted ice.

I was surprised the officers hadn't thrown the beers away. I was also happy they had not, as it was a sobering reminder of my insanity and horrific negligence.

Repeatedly I grappled with the juxtaposition of emotions. This juxtaposition was center stage for the coming years. My task was to constantly keep the negative forces at bay . . . to remain in deliberate intention while walking a blistering path of fire.

My resolve took root when I opened the front door upon arriving home. I stood in the doorway inside the apartment, while Aaron, all one hundred pounds of him, sat in his recliner chair on the opposite side of the room.

Without a hello, he glared at me with fierce, hateful, yet desperate eyes, and screamed, "Just collect your things and leave again. I don't need you! I don't need you like this!"

My son's statement was the most devastating thing ever said to me, cutting even deeper coming from him. With every ounce of my being, I replied, "Aaron, you may not need me, but I need you, and I need to stay."

From that day forward I didn't make declarations of sobriety. I didn't say anything about how I was going to deal with my personal issues. I committed myself to action, not words.

I had stated my intended behavioral changes before and fallen short. Knowing that my children had lost their faith and trust in me was worse than how I felt about myself.

Now it was time for a different strategy. So often I believe we rely on words, as they state our intentions immediately, in an attempt to redeem ourselves. Actions take a long period of committed consistency to have any real effect. I've come to understand why words of intention are so heavily relied on. I've come to understand our need and attachment to short-term solutions and immediate gratification. It's easier. Long-term commitment is harder but that is where positive changes can occur. The process is the progress.

Integrity: Choosing courage over comfort. Choosing what is right over what is fun, fast, or easy. Choosing to practice our values rather than professing them.

~ June 2, 2000

There will be a time, not so far from now, that I will look back on this phase of my life. Instead of condemning it or beating up on it, blaming, or feeling immense guilt, I will feel appreciation for it. I will understand that a renewed desire for life was born out of this time period that will bring me to physical and mental heights I could not have achieved without the contrast that gave birth to this desire.

Larry

I was always a bit surprised at how easily I brushed off any negative statement from the medical staff treating my son. Generally, what a medical professional or doctor says is taken with seriousness and rarely dismissed with the disregard I exhibited. I would counter them with my belief: "Anything is possible." Over time I was even told by the medical staff I was doing Aaron harm because I did so many things for him and wasn't allowing him to face his reality.

I believed that if I became his hands, arms, and legs, it would allow him to pour all his energy into therapies, not waste what little energy he had on performing menial tasks that I could do easily for him, and perhaps help minimize the myriad of frustrations he faced every moment. I believed that if I could protect and help him maintain his spirit, he would prevail.

My stance was: he is my son; therefore, I will proceed as I determine what is appropriate for him. Yes, quite often their words would seep into my awareness, making me question myself. Was I doing more harm than good? Was I unwilling to accept reality? Should I back up and allow Aaron to struggle even more than he already was? Were they correct? I always came up with the same decision: NO; I will help him until the day comes that he can do it himself.

I didn't realize it at the time, but a life experience I'd had when I was a nursing assistant at nineteen years old, buried in my consciousness was informing my noncompliant self.

September 1975

As a young teenager, alongside a wanderlust nature, I had a natural inclination to nurture others. I decided I wanted to be a nurse. True to my mode of operation, I wanted to get right to it: get a job as a nursing assistant in a hospital and get my feet wet before attending nursing school for a degree. I got the job.

I worked the morning/day shift, from 7:00 a.m. to 5:00 p.m. My duties were to take vital signs, provide morning baths, change bedding, comfort with words of encouragement, and assist the head nurse with whatever she or he needed. Illness can bring out the best and the worst in people. Some were so grateful for the care, while others were incredibly demanding, with no amount of care being enough. This was my battleground for being indoctrinated in human nature at its most vulnerable time.

Four months into my new position, during the morning shift change, we were all told of a new patient who'd been transferred to our facility in rural Oklahoma the evening before. An eighteen-year-old young man, who had suffered a brain injury due to falling eighty feet from an oil derrick, which rendered him comatose, with a bleak prognosis for survival. He was basically brought to our facility to die, although he had lived for three months post-injury without life support. All staff were told not to go into his room per his family's wishes. I don't know what compelled me to do so after being told not to. Curiosity? Compassion? I'm not sure. All I knew was I had to see the patient who had been described as a "vegetable."

I opened the door at the far end of the hall to darkness, curtains drawn, not so much as a ray of light allowed in the room. The stench of old urine, feces, and body odor hung in the air. In the darkness I heard faint, rumbled breathing. I immediately pulled the curtains open for light. I found a once very handsome young man with a bruised, swollen face, blood crusted, dry lips parted ever so slightly, emitting a low growl with every breath. I couldn't help myself—I had to turn on the lights, turn on the TV, anything to provide a little life to the one lying there. After I washed his face with a cold, wet cloth and pulled the blanket over his shoulders, I said, "Larry, I'll see you a little later. I have some other people I need to go see about." I was talking to him as though he were awake and aware.

Upon my walking out of the room and shutting the door behind me, the head nurse saw me. She immediately came up to me. "What are you doing in that room! Did you not hear the instructions in our report this morning?"

With trepidation I replied, "I did hear the report, but it is my break time, and I thought I would just go check on him. I promise I won't go in except on my breaks or off time. I just really want to visit him."

She shook her head with a reluctant, "Okay," along with a reminder that that was the only time I could take time out of my duties to see him.

From that moment on, I was in Larry's room at every opportunity, even going in to see him on my days off. When I went in, I would open the curtains, turn the TV on, and talk to him about everything and nothing.

I didn't know him. He was uncommunicative, comatose, with supposedly no brain activity, just a beating heart . . . yet I went on as though we were friends having a conversation.

"Larry, it's such a gorgeous day outside! We should be out there instead of in this hospital room! I would love to know about your work at the oil derricks. My grandfather and uncles all worked in the oil field. Did you know you and I are the same age?"

I'd continue my babbling and inquiries as I cleaned and washed his body, brushed his teeth, and rubbed his arms, legs, and feet with lotion, feeling as though I was infusing his nonresponsive body with my positively charged energy. Days went into weeks with no change in his condition. Somehow this did not discourage me, and I continued on.

Embarrassingly Dismissed

At about the two-month mark of the same unresponsive Larry, something changed as I was going through our daily routine. Larry had an erection during the bed bath. This was the first sign of any type of energetic awakening beyond the rise and fall of his chest. Wide-eyed, I ran out of the room to the nurses' station, where the two head nurses were giving two doctors the daily patient reports.

Excitedly, I asked for their attention. "Larry just did something he has never done until just now. He had an erection while I was bathing him!"

They all looked at me and laughed like I was a complete imbecile, a mere nursing assistant—and annoyed for my naïve dumb ass taking their time with this nonsensical information.

The medical staff quickly dismissed me and my excitement. "That kind of response is natural, involuntary," the head doctor, with exasperation, explained.

I shook my head no, countering back, "I believe it is demonstrating his ability to feel. Something is waking up!"

The doctor's dismissal stung, and I was ashamed. I walked away, feeling defeated and embarrassed. My young, uneducated, inexperienced self knew they were wrong. I knew, in my heart, Larry was beginning to reconnect.

Much to everyone's amazement, Larry did indeed begin to improve, ever so slowly. I'm sparing all the details, but Larry, with the support of a walker, surrounded by his family, walked out of the hospital six months later. We all cried. Larry gave me a big hug and told me he loved me as we bid our tearful farewells.

As I reflect on this experience in my teenage years, I realize now the impact it had on me. Deep in my soul was a refusal to accept the status quo if it did not fit my picture. To stand up for what I believe in—to commit, to be proactive, to take responsibility for the outcome and work for a desired result. It astounds me now to think that this experience set me up for my biggest fight: my son's life.

You will find the depth of your strength when you fight for what you are unwilling to lose.

Scan the QR code and head to
laquitadian.com/photo-gallery for this book's
complementary photo gallery!

Rise Together

Part 1 # Stand

Possibility

Initiate

Reason

Intention

Transform

"Develop enough courage so that you can stand up
for yourself and then stand up for somebody else."

~ MAYA ANGELOU

Chapter 1:

A Rebellious Beginning

On May 26, 1999, I received one of those late-night calls you hope to never receive. Carolyn, the mother of one of Aaron's racing friends, called, telling me, "Aaron crashed today. He's going in for an MRI now."

A chill went through my body, which was odd, as we'd certainly had our share of broken bones, x-rays, and MRIs. I tried to dismiss the chill by blaming it on the fact that I was fifteen hundred miles away from him.

The year before, almost to the date, I had moved my family east, to a ranch in Oklahoma, near my mother and father's farm. They had gone back home, so to speak, after spending many years in California.

Eight months after calling the ranch "home," Aaron received the call every young, hopeful motocross rider works so hard for, a sponsorship from a team in Simi Valley, California. I helped him pack and put him and his dreams on a plane to return to our home state. He had received his professional license along with the number 249 for rider identification on the front plate of his motorcycle. He was on his way to create and conquer his desired world.

I replied to Carolyn, "Please have Aaron or a doctor call me after the results of the MRI have been read."

Minutes turned into hours before the phone rang again. "Aaron is going into surgery now," Carolyn reported, a quiver in her voice.

I didn't ask why he was going into surgery or what had happened—not one question. I suppose I was already assuming the posture of not believing or accepting what I was about to learn.

I mindlessly packed a toothbrush and pair of pajamas. The first flight out was at 6:00 a.m., and it was only midnight. . . . I began cleaning and straightening my home, listening to music, doing everything I could to busy myself, trying to keep the choking anxiety at bay and my mind from projecting worst-case scenarios.

My mother would be taking me to the airport, so I decided to go to her home. My sister, Julie, and her husband, Andrew, had booked the flight, knowing I didn't have the wherewithal to do it. They had called every hospital in the Ventura County area until they found Aaron. I hadn't even asked what hospital he was in.

My ranch was remote, with ten miles of dirt roads between me and the rural two-lane highway. With this out-of-body experience occupying and fogging my mind, a surreal sight came into view as I was driving down my road: the foreground of the 2:00 a.m. sky was lit up like a fireball.

I drove upon a distant neighbor's home, which was completely engulfed in flames, fire licking every structure and vehicle on the property. Fortunately, the owners were away, so they didn't witness everything quickly rendering into dust, destroyed, as though it had never been there. A family's home, lifetime of memories, and livelihood left in a heap of smoldering, smoking ashes. This scene was hauntingly reflective of what was happening in our own lives, a premonition of sorts.

At the airport, all my actions seemed to unfold in slow motion. I didn't want the hug I gave my mother to end. Through tears, I whispered like a little girl into her ear, "I don't know if I can do this, Momma. I am so scared."

She pulled me in tighter, a stern strength in her voice imploring me, her Southern lilt attempting to penetrate my panicking heart. "Yes, you CAN do this, Laquita Dian! I KNOW you can, do you hear me!"

Looking over my shoulder and waving to her as I boarded the plane brought me an eerie, hesitant ache. I wanted to run back to her, but instead my feet carried me forward. I heard her voice behind me, growing fainter with each word: "I love you. Call me when you get there. Everything is going to be alright."

The future had, just hours before, seemed to contain infinite possibilities. Now it was shrouded in doom and terrifying unknowns.

During the flight I called the hospital recovery room twice. I could have asked many questions but chose to ask only if Aaron was resting well, which he was.

Carolyn picked me up at the airport. I opened the van door to be received by red, tear-swollen eyes that appeared to have been crying for hours.

"This isn't good, is it?" was all I heard myself ask.

She replied, "No, Laquita, it's not."

She must have thought I was uncaring or completely nuts as I began chattering mindlessly during the hour-long drive to the hospital.

"Boy, I sure don't miss LA and all the traffic. I can't believe I'm back again. I was just here last week!"

Carolyn glanced at me with a pleading look, as if to encourage me to ask about Aaron, but I continued to babble. "Gosh, it's hot outside already. I thought Oklahoma was hot, but you know, it's a different kind of hot, sort of balmy and humid, not dry like it is here."

Every time Carolyn opened her mouth to speak, I would rush into another senseless spiel about my ranch or the different lifestyle

I was leading, not once inquiring about Aaron's condition or what had happened to him.

Subconsciously, I had a steely suit of armor enveloping every aspect of my being, preparing to fend off the piercing declarations that were to come.

The Grim Reality

I was met at the entrance to the hospital by Aaron's father, Dan. He was visibly shaken, and his first words to me were, "Aaron will dance again."

I put my hand up to shield myself and asked him what room Aaron was in as I continued walking forward. To my utter disbelief, I heard him saying behind me that Aaron was in the ICU.

As my pace quickened, my knees became weaker and I heard Dan behind me call out, "Room fifteen." The handbag I was carrying dropped out of my hand onto the hallway floor as I stumbled through the electric double doors of the intensive care unit.

Once inside, I immediately saw the placard with the label "Room 15." The sickness in my stomach and the ringing in my ears overtook me as I continued toward the room that held my son. I wanted to stop, so afraid of what I was about to find, but I had a strange sensation of being pushed forward against my will.

I entered the room, blood emptied from my head, and an arctic chill rippled through my body, numbing my limbs. My heart began to race as I felt a guttural scream, "NOOOOO," being forced from my open mouth, yet no sound came out. I kept shaking my head to try to clear my vision, yet it remained unchanged.

It was, indeed, my beloved son, strapped to a rotating bed with cutouts to immobilize his extremities. He wore a large neck collar, and a Hemovac tube had been inserted into his neck for drainage. There was a ventilator in his mouth, and a heart monitor with eight monitor pads placed in various spots on his uncovered chest, all wired to the beeping bedside machine. A clip had been placed on his index finger to measure oxygenation levels, and there was an IV in his arm, leading to three separate bags dispensing time-released drips of medication. A feeding tube entered his unscathed, smooth stomach. With his eyes closed, his stillness was as alarming as all the machines attached to his body, keeping him alive, producing breath and a beating heart.

As I was reeling, desperately trying to breathe, a nurse walked in to inform me my fifteen-minute visitation time limit was up. There was a waiting room down the hall, and I could wait there and come back in two hours for another fifteen-minute visit.

This news was as effective as CPR . . . although shallowly, I did begin to breathe again. I then asked, "Could you please bring me a chair? I am not leaving my son."

The nurse replied, "I can't do that. These are the hospital rules, and I need you to follow them."

I shook my head no, countering her, stating very assuredly, "I am absolutely not leaving. If you can't bring a chair, then you'll have to step over me. A court subpoena will be the only thing to make me adhere to such rules."

She reluctantly gave in and came back with a chair, which also served as my bed for the following twenty-one days. As she set the chair down, she looked at me with disapproval, stating, "You need to stay out of the way when we come in to take care of your son's medical needs."

I found myself standing on the bedside stool, desperate to reach Aaron. I began to rub the parts of his body I could touch—legs, arms, feet, hands, all of which were limp, lifeless, and as cold as ice.

Arielle and Dan had come into the room. Like me, Arielle was wrenched in sobs and disbelief of what she was seeing. She and I held on to one another as we surrounded Aaron's bedside. We tried to console one another while we attempted to take in Aaron's unimaginable condition.

Arielle cried out, "He's dead! Oh my God, he's dead!"

I took her shoulders and shook her. With her face in my hands, I bore into her eyes, stating, "No, Arielle, he is not! He is horribly injured. We need to touch him, let him know we are here with him. He can hear us even though it doesn't look like he can. He needs us to be strong. We need to be strong for each other!"

For brief moments, lucidness would break through the heavy haze of anesthesia, and Aaron would fix his gaze on each of us with love pouring from his eyes. His lips would ever so gently mouth, "I love you." His body was frozen, in critical touch-and-go condition, yet he was swathed in love and pouring that love onto his family. The image of the angelic look of his face in those heart-penetrating moments is indelibly etched in the photo journal of my mind.

A short time later the neurosurgeon came into the room, still wearing the surgical scrubs he had worn for the six-hour procedure of repairing Aaron's broken neck. The fourth and sixth cervical vertebrae had fractured, and the fifth vertebra was shattered.

"Please meet me in the conference room down the hall. I'll go over the post-surgery report," he said to Arielle, Dan, and me. We had just gone in and sat down when the doctor said, rather formally, "The surgery went well. However, you need to prepare for great changes in your life. Your son has a one-in-a-million chance of ever having any type of function, including feeding himself, from the neck-level down."

The declaration seemed to have been spoken from a far-off distance, each word drawn out slowly as if being yelled from the depths of a cavernous hole.

I felt an internal explosion that shot me out of my seat. "This is not my son you are talking about. Don't ever tell him this! I want to come back tomorrow and talk about the procedure and not your prognosis."

I stormed out of the room, slamming the door.

Realization

Once in the hallway, I slid down the wall, crying, in blinding pain. Feeling like I was teetering on the edge of a blackened abyss, a powerful awareness came to me: "There is no possible way for Aaron to recover without complete support. You must pull yourself together, or everything you were just told will be absolutely true."

It was as though an invisible hand had slapped me hard on the face, shocking and shaking me into clarity. I stood up.

What feels impossible will be,
until you summon the will to defy it.

~ Reflection

One of the truths I have held close to my heart since the dire prognosis was delivered to me is that when faced with a catastrophic injury, it is wrong for medical professionals to state hopeless absolutes. Hope for improvement must be left intact, with the use of "Possibility Outcome" rather than "Probability Outcome" language. I encourage the declared absolutes to be focused on the list of secondary complications that will indeed occur if one does not actively pursue a wellness protocol. With hard work and commitment, anything is possible. For me, functional returns are not the most important issue. Keeping the spirit intact, keeping the willingness to face another day alive and well is of tantamount importance. Hope and possibility are medicine. Hope provides a positive outlook one can focus on during the nebulous, rocky journey toward recovery. It was hope that lit our way on an otherwise blackened road.

Hope never leaves you in the dark. It is a ray to lighten up the darkness. Hope never fails.

An urge to turn Aaron's hospital room into a healing space overcame me. I became consumed with one thought: "We can do this." Feeling like we had no time whatsoever to waste, I asked Julie and Arielle to go buy a CD player and meditation music, including sounds of the rain forest, thunderstorms, and Native American ceremony music.

I transformed the hospital room into a healing sanctuary, with music and a trickling water fountain drowning out the sounds of life-support machines and typical hospital chaos. The music provided a soothing backdrop for Aaron's mind to find comfort from the confines of his traumatically injured, frozen body. My mind, also, was lifted with each note, which in turn allowed me to find a calm within the internal hurricane that battered my emotions and inhibited my ability to think and respond rationally.

A cocoon was created that separated us from the typical hospital environment—a cocoon wrapped tightly around us to aid in and promote recovery, protecting us from slipping into a dark, hopeless state of mind, and fending off exclamations of impossibility. It became our safe haven.

I operated in a surreal fog, accompanied by sudden, wrenching pain, which exploded into tears, in the initial days following Aaron's accident.

Grief is a silent intruder that slips into the corridors of your mind without warning. It's a stealthy presence, capable of seizing your emotions with an unexpected and ruthless grip. One moment, you may be navigating the routine of daily life, and the next, grief wraps its tendrils around your heart, stealing your breath away. Like a shadow in the periphery, grief lingers, haunting ordinary moments and turning them into poignant reminders of loss.

I would bolt out of the room so Aaron wouldn't witness these outbursts, as I felt it even crueler for him to see this when he was in such a helpless state. After gathering myself I would tell him, and myself, "Aaron, we can do this. I need you to focus all your thoughts and energy into your body, to help heal your body. Please don't think of anything or anyone else. We will all be okay."

I had conversations in the hallway with every medical professional treating Aaron. "Don't give him any negative information or prognosis of his condition. I want you to tell him anything is possible with hard work and a positive attitude. Please tell him you don't know what the future holds for him," I directed, committed to the stand I was taking.

~ *Reflection*

As a six-year-old girl, the oldest of my siblings, my natural reaction, when my mother and father divorced, was to take care of my mother and younger brothers. My mother and father had told me I was born that way, always wanting to take care of everyone in my family from the time I could walk and talk. He says I was a bit of a boss, but not bossy. I do remember never feeling like I was a child. I felt my mother and brothers were my responsibility. I was my mother's protector and confidant, taking care of her and her heartache.

~ *Proaction*

It is in the realm of proaction that we transform the tides of despair into waves of possibility. We become architects of our own destiny, reclaiming control over our lives and rewriting the narrative of our future. In this realm of action, we can navigate the uncharted waters with unwavering determination, embracing the challenges as catalysts for growth and seizing every opportunity

*to redefine what it means to thrive. In the face of adversity, it is
not the enormity of the challenge that defines us, but the audacity to
confront it head-on, armed with a spirit to persevere.*

A New Birth

On the third day, as Aaron's anesthesia and medications had begun
to wear off, I placed a chair behind the head of his bed. Music with
the sounds of thunderstorms filled the darkened room, leaving the
noise of the beeping heart monitor muffled.

I was massaging the top of his head, the only part of his body
with full sensation, and leaning my head close to his, whispering
a guided meditation in his ear, "Dissolve into total relaxation and
turn your attention to your heartbeat. Feel and observe the air fill-
ing your lungs. Imagine your body filled with the energy of white
light, holding and healing you." Aaron was immediately receptive
and naturally engaged in the process of promoting healing through
mindfulness.

I asked him if he was afraid. This question unleashed his pain. His
sobbing came from the deepest part of him. I asked many questions,
and he would nod his head for yes or shake it for no. I asked if he
was afraid of dying. He slowly nodded . . . yes.

Aaron was slowly declining throughout the night and into the
morning of the sixth day after his accident. Because of the respirator,
he couldn't speak. Our communication was through eye contact and
the clicking of his tongue. The cadence of his tongue click indicated
the urgency of his need.

As his oxygenation levels dropped, he didn't have the energy to
even click his tongue. His eyes were filled with terror. I kept trying
to reassure him that all would be okay, that there was a lot of fluid
in his lungs, and we needed to focus on putting all our energy into
assisting his body to absorb the fluid.

"Focus, Aaron, focus. Your lungs need all your attention. Forget about everything else right now," I would repeat over and over again while peering into his terror-filled eyes. Although frantic inside, I somehow maintained a sense of calm focus.

The oxygenation level numbers on the monitor continued to gradually fall as I stood helplessly watching the life force slip from my son. I wanted to pick him up, stand him upright, and force the fluid from his lungs, yet I could not.

I called for the respiratory therapist several times to relieve Aaron of the suffocating grip of the mucus he was unable to expel. Just as the therapist administered yet another round of treatment, Dan entered. Feeling like I was about to pass out, I told Dan I needed to leave for a few minutes to catch my breath. I quickly left the room.

In my memory, there is a complete blank space between leaving his room and then returning. In my altered state, I didn't realize the faint voice I heard over the intercom calling Code Blue was for our room. I don't know where I went. I don't even know how long I wandered through the hallways.

I walked back in as though nothing had happened. I was calm, without even a memory of frantically leaving or an understanding of why I left in the first place. It was completely out of character for me to react in that way; however, it was clear I'd been protected from what I was about to learn.

As I reentered the room, his father was pacing, rubbing his hands together. "Did you hear the Code Blue call?" he asked me.

In puzzled disbelief I said, "Was that for this room?"

"Laquita, he DIED. He was gone! I watched him take his last breath!" Dan exclaimed with a trembling voice. Aaron's greatest fear had happened . . . he had flatlined and died. Yet, he'd been successfully resuscitated.

I still didn't fully comprehend what his father said. I walked up to Aaron's bedside, looked into his eyes, and immediately saw that I was looking into the eyes of a very different young man. In his eyes I saw serenity, a knowing, a wisdom far beyond his years that had not been there just mere minutes before.

Through our eye contact I knew and understood exactly what I needed to do, for him, myself, and our family. I told him, "Aaron, it doesn't matter how long it takes. We are going to do everything in our power to get you well. I will be right here with you, even if it takes the rest of my life. I am here, until you choose otherwise."

His slow, accepting, grateful tongue click spoke volumes. Through our eye contact, we solidified our commitment to the pursuit of his wellness.

Within the intricacies of a caregiver's arduous journey, a concealed yet far-reaching prospect unfolds—an opportunity to uncover a deeper aspect of yourself and establish unwavering command over life's potentially overwhelming circumstances. This marks an occasion for profound self-discovery.

Part 2

Stand

Possibility

Initiate

Reason

Intention

Transform

"Whatever you can do or dream you can, begin it;
boldness has genius, power, and magic in it."

—JOHANN WOLFGANG VON GOETHE

Chapter 2:

Broadened Horizons

July 1980

I was twenty-four years old with a sixteen-month-old baby and four months pregnant with my second child when I made the decision to move to the Central Coast in California. I raised Aaron and Arielle on the exquisitely beautiful Monterey Peninsula.

My closest family member was in Southern California, a six-and-a-half-hour drive away; I became used to handling our life, emergencies, and childhood illnesses on my own, as their father and I were too dysfunctional to successfully co-parent. Dan and I had gotten to a point where a heated argument would ensue over simply saying hello. "Why are you addressing me in that tone of voice?" Dan would probe, sending me up on my self-protecting heels.

I was an eighteen-year-old when we married, but becoming a mother accelerated my ambitions to build a solid future for our family, while it seemed as though Dan was okay with just barely getting by. He hadn't given up his partying ways or carousing with his pals, whether it be a weeknight or weekend. His excuses enraged me, filling me with a fight-or-flight sense of being.

Having experienced the fallout of a shattered marriage, I was all too familiar with the detrimental impact it has on a young heart.

As much as I wanted to spare my children from such anguish, when I glimpsed into the future, I saw a path of compromised mediocrity. This felt more harmful than the prospect of their father and I not being together. I held on to the belief that by broadening our horizons and embracing new possibilities, the heartache would be buffered.

Given the disparity between their father's aspirations and mine, I was confident I could navigate our life more effectively on my own.

Peewee Racer

Aaron was just three years old when his dad bought him a Yamaha YZ50 with training wheels for Christmas. Dan had moved to the Salinas Valley, just over the hill from us. At the tender age of five Aaron began racing flat track at the Monterey Fairgrounds. He won almost every race and brought home trophies taller than he was.

I did go to a handful of his races, but it made me sick inside to watch him. I was acutely aware of the vulnerability of his young, small body against the machine beneath him. With every twist of the throttle, the cold grip of worry tightened around me. The waving checkered flag, signaling the end of it, could not come soon enough.

I wasn't there to see one particularly hard crash that landed him in an ambulance, fearing he had hurt his neck. The EMTs placed him in a neck immobilizer and rushed him to the hospital for an x-ray. The pictures revealed a clip attached to the skin. The alligator clip on the suspenders holding up his little pants had come apart, refastening to the skin on his neck.

Between this incident and witnessing the wide-eyed fear in Arielle's innocent face as she breathlessly recounted the story of her brother's crash to me—"Oh Mommy, you can't believe it! Aaron wasn't moving! He went in the ambulance!"—I refused to let him continue racing or riding a motorcycle from that point on.

It pained me to take away something he loved so much but I

could neither ignore the weight of my emotions nor dismiss the haunting whispers of worse case scenarios.

I immersed Aaron in other activities—soccer, baseball, gymnastics, camping, biking, snowboarding, skateboarding, guitar lessons, acting classes and travel. He loved them all, yet he loved the motorcycle more.

Carmel—Soul Home

Even though I had very little financial means, the abundant natural life that Carmel afforded us more than compensated for it. Our small community was rich in natural experiences. We made grand adventures out of the mundane, always taking advantage of the exquisite beauty we came to know as home.

I would find tiny one-bedroom homes nestled in the heart of some of the most coveted areas of the peninsula. A turn-of-the-century, bright-red-and-gold Chinese pagoda, accessed down a long boardwalk through the sand dunes of Asilomar Beach, was our home for a couple of years. A week-long school vacation found us camping on the rooftop of our carport, the vastness of the sea our picture-window. The sound of ocean waves lulled us to sleep and filled our dreams.

Another secluded treasure was situated on the coastline of Carmel Highlands, a home named the "Gate House" positioned directly across from a steep private cove of rocky cliff fingers jutting into the sea below. Point Lobos, labeled the "crown jewel of the California coastal state park system," was our neighbor. Just outside our pint-sized home, a Grecian-looking, beautiful rock outcropping, with the ocean's waves wildly slapping against it, served as our favorite spot for homework in the late afternoons. Ancient coastal trees took on sculptural shapes, further infusing our sense of wonder and appreciation for the natural world.

Overnight camping at Pfeiffer Big Sur State Park, tucked in

sleeping bags, under the stars, Aaron on one side of me, Arielle on the other, was always a beloved adventure. We found our sleep while taking turns weaving grand tales sourced directly from our imaginations. The serenade of crickets and gentle hum of the nearby river provided the perfect soundtrack to our stories.

However, no matter where we lived, where we camped, or what activities I entered him in, the fire for the motorcycle was never extinguished. And his anger toward me for taking it away from him did not dampen over the coming years.

"Why won't you let me ride my motorcycle?"

"I don't like you for keeping me from riding!"

"My dad wants me to ride it, so why don't you?"

These were just a few of the stinging remarks Aaron would throw at me.

Adventurous Heart

A few years after Dan and I divorced, I met a man who was to become one of the single-most-influential people of my life, Preston Carter.

I was exceptionally intimidated yet awed by Preston when we first met. He was the most colorful, worldly, multilingual, funny, larger-than-life individual I had encountered. His first comment, "Nothin' like true love and homegrown tomatas," accompanied by his crystal blue persuasive eyes, left me dizzyingly captivated. A cross between Indiana Jones and James Bond, his pursuit of me was electric and convincing.

When I discovered Preston was an importer of antiquities, oriental rugs, and treasures from around the world, my deepest longings pushed me to step through my feelings of being overwhelmed and outmatched.

From my earliest memories, a desire for travel, culture, and the arts was within me. It was a longing that shaped my dreams and my imagination and pulled me toward a world yet unknown.

However, up to that pivotal point of meeting Preston, my life had unfolded along a path that was incongruent with these aspirations that lay within my heart.

~ *Reflection*

 *My mother and father were youngsters of nineteen and twenty when I was born. Daddy was a truck driver in those days. Mother wanted to go with him on one of his cross-country trips but didn't want to leave me, a four-month-old baby. They decided to take me with them, against their families' pleas of, "You'll kill that baby! She's too young to go!" Dad relishes in telling the story of how I fared on that trip. He says the only time I fussed or cried was when he turned the truck engine off. As long as the engine was running, I was a content, happy baby.*

The Rug Washer

The first time I visited Preston's antique gallery I boldly announced that I would one day run his business. He laughed and told me it was no place for a girl like me; he employed only male nationalists from the countries he frequented. He flippantly said I could have a job washing rugs.

Much to his surprise I took him up on his offer. I retired my waitress position and became a rug washer.

I agreed to the new position with one requirement—that he include the country of origin and the date the rug had been woven on the tag with the customer's name and phone number. This was my introductory education that led me into foreign worlds. I soaked up the nuances of each rug I stroked with a scrub brush. I imagined the faraway land from which it came, and the landscapes and ancient architecture that inspired the designs. My mind's eye saw the women covered in their hijabs, burkas, and salwar kameez with their nimble fingers creating the masterpieces on the loom.

Our relationship was on a fast track when Preston invited me to go to India with him. Love and the world cracked wide open, and I took a swan dive deep into the pool of possibility.

The stark contrast between a life of no travel experience and the vibrant cacophony of honking rickshaws, clanging temple bells, and explosions of color and smells found in India, was nothing short of awe-inspiring. It was as if I had been reborn, and a portal of limitless potential had been unlocked.

My days as a rug washer gave me a sense of familiarity as I traveled with Preston to those countries I'd previously only imagined. My walls of uncertainty and self-doubt crumbled. I was no longer a foreigner in my own mind.

Looking upon this character who was now in my life had the proverbial light bulb effect. I was the night moth seeking light. He was the light and I was head over heels in love with him and the opportunities he offered.

Split Life

In no time my life felt like a fairy tale, caught in the whirlwind of travels all over the globe. Being on a short leash of financial anxiety was no longer an issue. I felt like I was strapped onto a rocket ship, hurtling from one way of life to a polar-opposite one . . . but my children's lives were split in half, one half with me, the other with their father, and those two worlds were as different as daylight and darkness.

As much as I loved my time traveling, working, and being with Preston, I couldn't bridge the cavernous gaps between my children's father and me. It was obvious that Aaron and Arielle were emotionally confused with the conflicting loyalties and the constant feeling of being torn between our opposing worlds. This was even more problematic than the stark differences themselves.

During drop-off and pickup, Aaron would try to run away, in the opposite direction, from their dad's and my never-ending arguments. Arielle would turn inward and painfully wail, her little heart so hurt.

I believed that our endless dysfunction and disproportions would lead to long-term detrimental effects on all of us, especially on Aaron and Arielle. Although Preston and I had talked about it, we weren't yet prepared to marry and blend our families . . . but I had to put an end to the madness.

I had been introduced to the world; it gave me a glimpse into how travel can hurtle you out of old ways of being and create conditions for new ones to emerge. I'd discovered a new confidence, and wanted to show Aaron and Arielle that the world had so much more to offer than the one they knew.

Having learned the art of importing, I realized the Indonesian island of Bali presented an ideal business opportunity for me: buying and exporting.

I felt the same draw to Bali I'd felt when I moved to the Monterey Peninsula with its stunning beaches rugged coastline, and varied landscape of hills and mountains, all providing a picturesque backdrop to its colorful, deeply spiritual, and unique culture—a paradise on earth. Carmel and the Monterey Peninsula had been described with the same words and imagery; therefore, for me, Bali wasn't so foreign.

At that time I felt leaving was my only answer, and Bali was on the other side of the world. . . . It seemed the perfect solution.

Mission . . . International

I didn't tell Aaron and Arielle we were moving. Instead, I told them we were going on a grand adventure, which excited them greatly. I proceeded to sell all our furnishings and belongings, keeping only what one piece of luggage and our personal backpacks could hold. I made a big mistake the day of the sale: Aaron and Arielle were there.

At first they were excited about helping and talking to people, but at ages eight and six, they couldn't quite understand why strangers were taking our things out of our home, one by one. They both did okay until Aaron saw one of his toys leave in the hands of another child. He had a huge meltdown, so huge that folks were trying to give back the items they were buying! I assured the buyers that all was okay and that my children were a little more sensitive because we were embarking on a huge life change.

I took Aaron and Arielle onto my lap and explained that we couldn't take all our things where we were going, and none of it would be important to us because we would be so focused on seeing and learning about new things. They both wiped their tears, and, with sniffles, gave me a look of loving trust and said, "Okay, when are we leaving?"

We then packed their favorite things into their backpacks . . . a little quilted bear pack for Arielle, a mountaineering pack for Aaron, and one suitcase for our clothing, along with the hopes and dreams no pack could carry.

Our flight was scheduled to depart four days later from Los Angeles International Airport. At that time my parents lived just outside of Los Angeles and were going to take us to the airport. My mother was beside herself with fear of what I was doing. Although she had gone through the same feelings with me when I moved to the Monterey Peninsula, four months pregnant with a one-and-a-half-year-old, this one was very different . . . halfway around the world. She told me I had no business taking my children to a foreign country so far away, that I was out of my mind. I heard, "Laquita Dian, just what do you think you are going to do? How are you going to support and take care of yourself and those babies?"

I said the same thing I said when moving to the Monterey Peninsula: "I'll figure it out."

Bro in Tow

I think my mother thought that as the time drew nearer I would come to my senses and realize just how ill-conceived my idea was. When she accepted I was going through with it without reservation, she asked me to take my brother along. "Laquita, please, please take Keith with you. He is in need of a change, and you need him for protection for you and those babies," she explained, attempting to convince me that a third-world country was not safe for a young, single woman with two towheaded children.

Even considering taking Keith was difficult. As much as I loved him, he'd been in the throes of addiction, and I couldn't see how he would be of benefit to us. I saw him as a huge liability and one more responsibility.

Upon arriving at my parents' home, I was met on the front doorstep by Keith. He gave me the tightest hug ever, saying, "I really, really want to go with you, Skeet. I need to go with you. I need a chance to make something of myself, and I never will as long as I stay here."

He promised me he wouldn't touch anything alcohol or drug related, not even a cold beer. I wanted to believe him, but I also knew how fleeting that promise could be.

We talked about it all through the evening. I wasn't easy on him. I gave him many different scenarios with horrifying outcomes arising from intoxication or drug possession as a guest in a foreign country and when going across country borders. He listened intently, but continued to assure me of his commitment to abstinence and how this trip would change his life in a way that nothing else could.

I began to see him as I saw myself. Desiring a total life change. "Keith, I know the feeling of wanting to change your life, that's exactly what I'm doing. I truly do want this for you as much as I want it for myself," I said to him.

I finally agreed to his going with us. I believed him, and I believed in his having a chance to turn his life around. . . . We would do it together.

At the airport we gave our mother and father goodbyes, teary yet filled with nervous excitement. We were embarking on the adventure of our lifetimes.

With Aaron holding my right hand, Arielle holding my left, we proceeded to the gate.

Arielle had sucked her thumb as a baby and hadn't yet given up the comfort her thumb gave her. I had been telling her that she would have to stop as soon as we arrived at our first destination, Singapore. "Ari baby, I know how much you love your thumb, but germs can love you even more, and they can make you very, very sick. When we travel like this, you cannot put your thumb in your mouth, because of the germs on it," I told her.

She enjoyed her thumb throughout the flight. Upon landing, I reminded her that she now had to stop. A number of times over the coming days she would start to put her thumb in her mouth and then pull it back.

The Adventure Begins

As we stepped off the plane and breathed in the humid air of Singapore, I felt a thrill of excitement mixed with a tinge of nervousness. We were starting a new chapter of our lives in a foreign country, and I was eager to introduce my children to the wonders of our world. Our two-day stop in Singapore was just the beginning of our journey, but it was a significant one, an introduction of what was to come.

While exploring the vibrant city, with its mix of old and new architecture and bustling streets filled with exotic sights, sounds, and smells, I felt a sense of confidence that assured me this experience would infuse Aaron's and Arielle's young minds with a heightened sense of curiosity and diversity and a broader sense of life in a world meant to be explored.

Our one-night stop in Jakarta was, without doubt, the most frightening of the entire journey. We arrived at midnight. We were to travel the Indonesian Island chain to Bali by train. The next train would leave the Jakarta station thirty hours later. I hailed a cab driver to take us to the hotel closest to the train station. He deposited us at the front steps of an old, dilapidated building that served as a hotel. The hallway door opened to a dark, unwelcoming room with paint peeling off the walls, a double bed with the mattress sagging in the middle and looking like it had already been slept in, and a few ceiling tiles ready to fall onto the head of an unsuspecting guest.

With three sets of scared eyes glued to me, I put our luggage down while explaining we wouldn't be in the room long—it was just a layover. By that time, we'd been traveling for four days. The luggage had continued to feel heavier and heavier even though I packed light. I opened the luggage and began making two stacks: one stack to keep, one stack to leave behind.

The kids melted into tears. I was already constantly reassuring them that everything was okay . . . and that we were safe.

Morning light couldn't have come soon enough since sleep didn't come to me. I was filled with thoughts of doubt, second-guessing what I was doing . . . along with monitoring the ceiling tiles hanging by a thread of plaster. With feigned excitement, I ushered Aaron and Arielle out to a waiting taxi for a tour of the city. Keith stayed behind, as he had slept on the floor. He gratefully got in the bed when we got out, placing a pillow over his head to cushion the potential blow from a falling ceiling tile.

I didn't have a particular destination in mind when we got into the taxi. I asked the taxi driver if he could give us a tour of the city, showing us the highlights of what the city was best known for.

Within minutes the previously bright morning sky darkened to a torrential downpour—a tropical monsoon. The rain was so hard you couldn't see past the hood of the car, but I could see that we were leaving the city behind.

The taxi driver didn't answer me when I asked him where we were going as I leaned over the front seat. Suddenly I was filled with bone-chilling terror. Where were we being taken? What was this man's motive with us?

As a primal sense of protection enveloped me, I grabbed a fistful of hair on the back of his head. Between gritted teeth, I whispered into his ear, "You better pull the car over immediately." I pulled his hair harder, the whisper turning to a hushed growl. "I am a Cherokee Indian from the United States. We scalp our enemies, and I'll scalp you right now with the knife I have in my purse, if you don't stop and let us out of this car!"

~ *Reflection*

When my mother remarried, our family relocated from Oklahoma to Southern California, moving to different cities and states every year, sometimes multiple moves in a single year thereafter. New cities meant new schools and new friends. My mischievous little brothers had a penchant for getting into scuffles with the latest neighborhood kids. Invariably one of my brothers would extricate themselves from the brawl, running breathlessly to fetch me, so I could finish it for them. I was very protective of my brothers. Although I didn't like aggression or conflict, I had no problem taking care of business for them, even if it meant fisticuffs. The ace in their pocket when in trouble or fights was, "I'm gonna go get my big sister!"

With a stroke of good fortune, he pulled over, more than likely because he had underestimated this American girl and simply didn't want to deal with me. His slight build also served my tough girl bravado, although I really don't think size would have made a difference to me. As the saying goes, "You never know how strong you are until being strong is the only choice you have."

Aaron and Arielle had their little noses pressed against the back seat window, so captivated by the pounding rain they didn't know what was going on. They were confused when we exited the taxicab and entered an empty parking lot, rain still coming down in solid sheets. They got mad at me for aborting our tour of the city!

After hailing another taxicab, I asked to be taken to the Four Seasons, one of the most luxurious hotels in Jakarta. They forgot all about being mad at me as they swam in the warm waters of the rooftop pool. We were swinging from the seediest to the finest . . . collecting a lifetime's worth of memories and experience.

New Home . . . Bali

The train from Jakarta to Java was packed full of local men, women, and children. We were the only foreigners. Aaron and Arielle quickly made friends with a couple of children, language differences not presenting a barrier. After five days of travel, surrounded by adults, they were happy to be with kids their own age. Watching them create new ways of communicating was exhilarating.

The train moved across the land relatively slowly alongside a water canal. Hanging over the canal, there were enormous webs strung together with spiders the size of a dinner plate in the middle of each web. We were able to take a seat on the platform between two train cars, swinging our legs in the open air and listening to the clacking of the train wheels—an impossible seat back in the States.

From the train station in Java, we boarded a beat-up Greyhound wannabe bus for the final journey to Denpasar, Bali. Trains, planes, automobiles, and buses—we were on them all. So far my idea of a grand adventure had not disappointed!

Once in Bali our accommodation for the planned next few months was a thatched-roof little beach cottage, directly on Kuta Beach. The days were spent frolicking on the beach, having Arielle's and my hair cornrowed by Native women, and traversing the island town on motorcycles, which was thrilling for Aaron and Keith. We were living a carefree, island life.

Aaron's prized possession was a pair of paint-splattered high-top Converse shoes . . . that were three sizes too big. As much as I tried to convince him they didn't fit, his love for them made him insist they were "just right." He proudly strutted around with his feet looking longer than his legs. The only time he took them off was for bed, the swimming pool, or the beach.

One day, while on the beach with all the trinket hawkers flashing their wares, a beautiful, intricately carved small flute was offered to us. Arielle excitedly took it in her hand, thinking the woman was giving it to her. I explained that it was not a gift and I would not be purchasing it right then. I handed the flute back to the woman, turned over, and continued reading my book.

Suddenly, I heard Aaron howling in distress. I turned to see him jumping up and down, with Arielle right in front of him, the beautiful carved flute in her hand. She had traded Aaron's beloved sneakers for the flute.

Although I was impressed by her negotiating skills, I scolded her for not asking her brother if she could trade his shoes. She had watched others on the beach bartering for goods, trading one item for another. She wanted the flute and she knew I didn't like the large shoes. In her mind she had satisfied two issues. Inside, I smiled at how she was already learning valuable life skills on the beaches of Bali.

After a few weeks in the thatched-roof cottage, it was time to begin to settle into normalcy—work for me, school for Aaron and Arielle. All was going well, until that point. They weren't homesick and didn't even talk about home; they were so immersed in making new friends and experiencing island life.

All hell broke loose on the front steps when we went to enroll them at the new school. School meant we were staying. All the way back to our cottage they cried. But these weren't normal cries. They were deep belly cries as Aaron and Arielle were going through a list of people they suddenly missed: best friends, teachers, grandparents, aunts, uncles . . . mostly, their dad. "Momma, we're never going to see them again . . . you didn't tell us this. How can you do this to us?" . . . And the cries continued, finally putting them both to sleep.

Tossing, turning, and sniffling continued throughout the night. My mind was consumed with the consequences of staying. As good as I thought my plan was, I realized it could also have lasting negative effects on their young minds and hearts. I suddenly felt selfish. I wasn't alone to pursue a new life. My desires for my children and their well-being far outweighed my own.

By morning I had decided to return to the States the following week. Keith, for many days, had been looking up at every passing airplane in the sky, saying, "Wonder where he's goin'," signaling his homesickness. A part of me felt accomplished, that I'd been courageous enough to at least try to make a massive change. The other part felt a weary defeat that I was returning to the very thing I had sought to leave.

Although we had been gone only one month, it felt like a lifetime to me. I had believed we would be staying and had relinquished all possessions and furnishings before embarking on the journey to Bali. Still, there was no doubt about where we would go if we did go back to the US. I knew it would be Carmel.

Chapter 3:

Return Stateside

Returning to Carmel meant reestablishing the life I had left behind. I called Preston. I had indeed become the manager of his gallery prior to leaving, so I asked for my job back. I also asked if we could stay at his home until I found a new one. Excited and welcoming, he agreed to both requests.

Within a few days I found our new little one-bedroom nest on a private beach cove in Carmel Highlands. Preston and I resumed our relationship, both personally and professionally.

The travel experience to Bali heightened my ambition and goals significantly. At night, after Aaron and Arielle were tucked in bed, I read the dictionary to increase my vocabulary, committing four words per week to memory and proper use. Classic novels such as M. M. Kaye's brilliant *The Far Pavilions*, Tahir Shah's *In Arabian Nights*, and Benazir Bhutto's *Daughter of Destiny* gave me a greater understanding, connection to, and appreciation of the culture and nuances of the countries I was going to resume traveling to for work.

The autobiography of famed British explorer Sir Richard Francis Burton—who disguised himself as an Islamic pilgrim, with death being the outcome if discovered, and made the trek into the heart of Arabia, visiting the holy cities of Medina and Mecca in 1853—filled my imaginative heart and mind with bravado. I thought . . . if he could do that, then I, an American girl from Oklahoma, with an against-the-grain personality from birth, could be fluent in foreign lands and with the people who inhabited them.

Initially I was looked on as sidearm candy—a cute tagalong companion for amusement—by the foreign nationalists we conducted business with. This changed when I challenged their perception of me with in-depth knowledge of their arts, catching them off guard.

"You know as much about these pieces as I do," said one merchant with a smile, and twinkling approval in his eyes. "It's not usual for an American woman to love and understand this business," said another.

Having soaked up the art of negotiation from the masters, I learned to go toe to toe with some of the most respected in the industry. The once placating, dismissive attitudes and opinions of me gave way to respect and eagerness to work with me as a businesswoman.

Five years and a couple of moves to other little hidden gems on the peninsula later, Preston and I were married, resulting in a *Brady Bunch*-style home with his two sons and Aaron and Arielle.

As a family, we traveled the world, from the beaches and rain forests of Central America to locations throughout Europe and Asia. We entertained people in our home from a multitude of diverse cultures. Our lives were exceptionally rich in every way I had ever imagined.

I, the girl who was initially seen as an inadequate rug washer, defied expectations and helped Preston evolve from operating a modest gallery to successfully expanding into a significantly larger space. We curated an extensive collection, featuring higher-quality art decor, oriental rugs, jewelry, and textiles. We also opened a second gallery. My professional journey was filled with excitement and satisfaction as I learned the art of procuring fine pieces from exotic locales, followed by their sale and installation in various residential and commercial settings.

Preston and I had an extraordinary partnership. It was elevated by my deep love and admiration of his unique nature and his flair for being adept and at ease no matter where we were.

Venerable Messaging

Of all the fabled experiences and priceless memories that period holds for me, there are three that stand out the most: meeting with (and working for two days beside) Mother Teresa at the Kalighat Home for the Dying, in Kolkata, India; joining Leonard Crow Dog, a well-known Lakota Sioux Native American Indian chief, in a ceremonial sweat lodge on the Pine Ridge Reservation, South Dakota; and sitting in meditation with and receiving my personal yogic mantra from a *sadhu* (holy man), the Milk Baba, on the banks of the Bagmati River, at the Pashupatinath Temple, in Bhaktapur, Nepal.

Each of the three extraordinarily revered, idolized individuals conveyed a consistent message—my life would undergo a transformative shift, placing me at the threshold of the momentous undertaking I was destined for. The exact nature of these changes remained a mystery.

I remember Mother Teresa looking deep into my eyes, touching my soul, with my hand in hers, saying, "It's one person, one act of love, one act of kindness at a time, that makes all the difference."

Within the steam-filled, sage-infused ambiance of the sweat lodge, surrounded by resonating rhythms of the drums, I knelt with my forehead against the cool earth beside the esteemed Leonard Crow Dog. In that sacred space, my silent prayer reached out to Tunkashila, Grandfather, the Great Spirit. I asked for guidance to channel my time and existence toward a more significant purpose.

Nestled within the humble abode of the Milk Baba, I sat in reverence beside him. In a tender moment, he leaned in close and whispered a precious gift into my ear—a meditation mantra especially for me. He said to use it to stay in a spiritual connection and keep a sense of purpose for the difficult times that lay ahead.

The words and messaging from these three venerated leaders felt inerrant and hung in my mind like sacred relics; however, I did not have a clue of the exact path or purpose I wished to pursue in order to make better use of myself. And I did not know I would not choose it.

Blended Family

Prior to my marriage with Preston, Aaron had taken on the self-appointed role as the man of the house. With the arrival of two elder stepbrothers, whom I loved like my own, Aaron found himself demoted to little brother, a position he was at odds with. Arielle now had three big brothers. This was a significant adjustment for her since she was used to having only one.

Although our children enjoyed being friends and loved the time we all spent together, living together was different and was made even more complex by the double lives Aaron and Arielle already led.

To my dismay, Aaron's father presented him with a motorcycle, once again, when he was thirteen years old. He then spent every weekend he could over the hill in Salinas, winning races on his motorcycle with his father and friends. His growing collection of trophies lined the floor of his bedroom.

Arielle indulged in her passion for riding horses. The blue ribbons she earned at horse shows decorated her bedroom walls. It was evident that both of them had remarkable skill in their respective sports.

I believe their passions were deepened because they provided an escape from the contrasting lives they led, with the same massive divide of difference that had taken me to Bali. I was committed to doing whatever it took to make it all work. I believed that with time, patience, and love, it would.

Point of No Return

I answered the phone one day at our gallery, the caller identifying himself as the manager of one of our favorite hotels in San Francisco. The hotel had an exquisite collection of handwoven Persian rugs. Preston and I had, for years, been trying to secure their rug account. Preston had gone to the hotel the day before to try, once again, to negotiate a deal for the preservation of the valuable pieces. The manager, assuming I was the secretary, was calling to relay details about the new rug contract he had just finalized with Mr. and Mrs. Carter. He had presumed the woman accompanying Preston was his wife.

I catatonically gave the manager the information he needed. The shock ripped through my body like an arrow. I didn't take time to assimilate the sickening revelation.

As soon as I hung up, I dialed Preston. He answered, the tone in his voice sounding like he was caught with his hand in the cookie jar. My usual loving lilt was replaced with a flattened tone. I matter-of-factly stated that since Mrs. Carter was with him, he should send her back to the gallery, because this Mrs. Carter was leaving.

Every part of me was destroyed. Up to that time, I believed our marriage was sacred, faithful. We had gone through several indiscretions while we dated, but he had promised, on the oath of marriage, that it wouldn't happen again. I believed him . . . fully trusting the promise he gave me.

I'd caught inappropriate flirtatious glances, on occasion, after we married, but I truly had no idea he was having extramarital relationships right under my trusting, unsuspecting nose. I was committed to go through whatever we needed to do as a blended family, but I was absolutely not willing to accept continued infidelity.

Carmel is a very small seaside town and Preston and I were well-known in the community. After we separated, I ran into him escorting other women, which exacerbated my pain. It became clear to me that I needed to leave Carmel . . . if I were to save my soul.

After a decade together, our relationship ended. The devastation of losing my marriage and my stepsons was heightened by the fact that I had invested all my hopes, aspirations, and career in the "Carmel basket."

In January of 1996 I got behind the wheel of a loaded thirty-foot U-Haul truck packed with my collection of treasured memories, furnishings, and belongings. With my cat, JJ, draped around my neck, and his brother, Angus, in my lap, I began driving south to the iconic seaside town of Malibu, the new place we would call home for two blurry, solace-lacking years. Aaron and Arielle followed in equally loaded vehicles.

Carmel was in the rearview mirror, and while my days of residency took a final bow, Carmel would forever remain my soul home.

Malibu

Leaving Carmel with my heart weighed down by sorrow, the journey south felt like a metaphor for my emotional state. The heavens above seemed to mirror my tears as the rain poured relentlessly throughout the entire six-hour drive to Malibu. It was as if the weather itself shared my grief, weeping alongside me as I navigated the winding roads in the long, heavy U-Haul truck.

Our caravan pulled up to the small home, situated on a hill up one of the meandering canyon roads off Pacific Coast Highway, around midnight. The next morning as I stepped outside to begin unloading, I was met with an unexpected, shocking sight. The massive U-Haul truck stood perched at a perilous angle. The right-side tires of the truck had sunken deeply into the unforgiving mud, while the left side hung precariously in the air.

It was a scene that reflected my own heart—one side sinking into despair, while the other struggled to stay afloat. The weight of my sorrow clung to me like the mud to those tires.

The two years spent in the idyllic enclave, a beloved destination for those seeking the quintessential California dream, were anything but beloved for me. It was mired in a heavy haze I have a difficult time remembering, and I do not want to.

One random day, I picked up the phone and called my mother. I asked her to find a ranch I could buy not too far from where she and my father lived.

She didn't believe me. I called again a few days later to ask if she had come across any places I might like. Although she was doubtful I was serious, she located a few possibilities and sent me the photos. I was immediately drawn to a bucolic eighty-acre spread with several ponds, and lush, rolling hills. The long tree-lined driveway led to a beautiful country brick home.

Two weeks after calling the real estate agent, I was the owner of a ranch in Oklahoma. Aaron, Arielle, and I went back to the lands where I was born—the lands I believed would help me recapture my broken spirit. Additionally, Aaron would have acreage for a practice track, and Arielle would be immersed again in her passion for horses. My mother was battling breast cancer, so my plan seemed to serve many needs.

Our familiar caravan was now eastbound.

As fracturing as it was, Preston's influence on me and my life will be held dear forever. Eventually, the exquisite memories and experiences became stronger in my heart than the ones that broke it.

Chapter 4:

The Racer

January 1992

Aaron and his dad had promised me Aaron wouldn't race, that he would ride only in the dirt. Within a month after getting the motorcycle, all I heard about was the natural talent he displayed. Of course, Aaron could hardly contain himself—he wanted to race.

He actually told me he would go live with his father if I didn't agree to it. This was absolutely not an option, but I was cornered and up against his will. At thirteen years old he could have decided to live primarily with his father because we shared joint custody.

I decided to create a contract between Aaron and me. Some of the stipulations were that he maintain a minimum of a B average in school, continue participating in school activities and sports, travel, camp, hiking, and guitar lessons. He agreed to all my terms. With a giant smile and a thankful hug, he signed the contract. He upheld his agreement and, in no time, was winning races.

Even though I didn't approve of his sport of choice, I relished his passion . . . and, yes, natural talent. I enjoyed helping him with physical training, nutrition, goals, and mindset.

~ *Reflection*

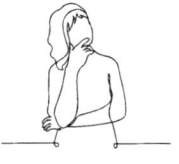

The love of the motorcycle was actually no surprise . . . . At fourteen years old my mother and biological father remarried. Part of my father's courting and means of persuading us to return to him was the promise of buying himself, my mother, my three little brothers and me motorcycles along with a camper for weekend and holiday excursions. We, as a family, were then blazing away aboard Kawasaki dirt bikes on dusty trails in Southern California's deserts. This was pure liberating freedom for me. I could not go fast enough, jump high or far enough, or find a rocky mountainside or sandy river bottom I could not conquer in the quest of satisfying my thrill-seeking heart. I once took my new boyfriend, Danny Baker, on a day trip desert outing. Much to his utter shock and surprise, I outrode the living daylights out of him. Although he wasn't happy about being outridden by a girl, he was affected by the spirit of riding and held the desire to pass that to our son, years later.

My love of the motorcycle did not surpass the fear I felt when my son fell in love with the machine and all of its blood-pumping thrills. My stance seemed contradictory, a double standard of sorts. But in my mind there was a glaring major exception: while the motorcycle was okay for my young self . . . I didn't know any better, at that time. I wanted more for my young son. I wanted him exposed to all the world had to offer, a "salad bar" sense of life, before attaching himself to a single-minded pursuit. Tucked in the far corners of my mind was also the fear of something bad happening to him.

Bedroom Posters

I had encouraged Aaron and Arielle to "Be Your Own Poster" during their formative years, rather than the typical image of an obscure idol. I took their favorite action photo, doing something they loved, and made posters to hang in their rooms.

Aaron made additional posters with sayings like, *I Will Be a National Champion*, and, *I Am a Winner.* My favorite was, *I am a good person. I have a positive outlook on everything. I have a great attitude and kindness toward others. I am mentally and physically strong. I Will Win Win Win.*

He became an Amateur National Champion, winning two national events when he was fifteen years old. After achieving a celebrated amateur career, he was ready for the next phase—a professional career.

He left our ranch in Oklahoma in February 1999 to ride for a race team based in Simi Valley, California. He had received the call every young hopeful rider dreams of and works hard for: a sponsorship offer. Aaron Baker had become a well-known name on the race circuit.

Return to California, April 1999

Right after Aaron left home, Arielle began yearning to return to more familiar grounds in California. Born and raised in idyllic Carmel, along with a couple of years in Malibu on the Southern California coast, rural life in Oklahoma was initially amusing and curious for her but lost her attention. She loved our ranch and our extended family, but the cultural differences were just too great for a budding eighteen-year-old. She also went back to California, not far from her brother.

A few weeks after Arielle left, I flew to LA to see them and to celebrate their respective next chapters. We spent three glorious days together sharing in the excitement of what lay ahead for all of us.

The morning they were taking me to the airport, we stopped at a golf range. I sat behind them as they practiced hitting balls. I marveled at the liquidity of Aaron's body as he swung the golf club. It was lithe, poetic, and in harmony with the club, ball, and his intention.

This image is so easily brought forth in my mind, all these years later. I didn't know this would be the last time I would witness his body in motion in that way—free, unencumbered, proficient, capable of whatever task or movement he wanted.

Three days after returning to Oklahoma I received the phone call that changed our lives forever.

Chapter 5:

Fight to Improve

I took an aggressive, proactive approach to Aaron's care once we had "recovered" from his death experience. This action helped me as much as it obviously helped Aaron. My field of vision shrank to a tiny pinpoint—ensuring Aaron's needs were met.

On the first day of physical therapy while he was in ICU and still in the rotating bed, two therapists appeared unannounced at our room to do range-of-motion exercises with him.

The therapists were lighthearted, talking and laughing between themselves while they were preparing Aaron for movement . . . this took thirty minutes out of the forty-five-minute session. While normally lightheartedness and joking would be welcomed in a hospital room, on this occasion, it was absolutely not.

After watching this, with the minimal amount actually accomplished, I said, "Please tell me what time and what day the next session will be."

"We actually don't have a schedule. We'll just fit Aaron in when we have availability," I was told.

This was unacceptable, and I insisted on a specific time frame for subsequent sessions. I kept a schedule on the whiteboard in the ICU room. I said, "I'll have Aaron ready for the session so all of the time can be spent working with him, *seriously* working with him."

The therapists recognized and responded to the intensity of my energy. The following session was significantly more productive and focused as a result. By collaborating and helping them help us, we created a more supportive, empowering environment.

We unified as a team, with one directed focus: to give Aaron the best possible opportunity for recovery.

We developed a strict regimen suitable for the professional athlete he was rather than the severely injured patient he was rendered. Every hour of every day was documented and accounted for. The moods changed from jovial to serious, matching our intense demeanor and approach. We were now in the business of recovery, with no time to waste.

The next day a standing table was wheeled in—Aaron's first time standing in two weeks. Once he was transferred to the table and strapped down, the table slowly began to incline. The therapist would stop every ten degrees for his blood pressure to stabilize. Aaron kept his eyes closed during the ever-so-slow rise, mouthing the words to the music playing by the Cardigans: "Erase/Rewind." The words and melody floated in the air, perfectly fitting the time and situation he was in. It took about two months of daily work on the tilt table for him to tolerate a full standing position.

Paralysis affects not only the limbs, but every organ in the body. As the tilt table was raised, all the blood would pool into Aaron's lower extremities, causing his blood pressure to drop dangerously low.

Unbelievable changes were taking place at lightning speed, none of them positive. I watched forty-five pounds fall off his body in three short weeks. He was literally a skeleton with a skin covering. His appetite became compromised due to early satiety, a premature feeling of being full, another common complication after spinal cord injury. Additionally, the undeniably strong, unpleasant smell of hospital food turned his stomach upside down upon its placement on the bedside table. I asked Dan to bring in a small refrigerator, which we kept stocked with foods Aaron enjoyed. The hospital meals stayed outside the doorway until they were eventually discontinued.

Even though I was rubbing lotion on him several times a day, his skin became very dry and cracked, a result of lack of circulation. He did develop one decubitus ulcer (bedsore) on his sacrum only eight days post-injury.

It is mind-blowing how quickly the body begins to degenerate without movement, circulation, and proper blood flow.

For months Aaron looked as though he was ready to be refrigerated due to the Saran Wrap-like protective bandages I placed on all the bony landmarks on his body, trying to prevent any further bed sores from developing.

Being There

I chose to live in the hospital room with Aaron, both for his benefit and for my own. Given his inability to press the call button, something as simple as an itch on the nose could cause intense discomfort with no way to relieve it. It didn't make sense to me to leave his care largely in the hands of the nurses. I also didn't want a constantly rotating nursing staff to be in control of his personal needs, and neither did he. The first time a male nurse came in to give Aaron a bed bath, I asked Aaron if he wanted me to step out of the room. He shook his head no and mouthed, "You do it." He needed care as though he was a newborn baby again and I wanted to protect his dignity while trying to keep his spirit strong and alive.

I refused photo-taking. I'd say, "No photos. We're not staying in this condition, there's no need to be reminded of it later." Looking back now, I regret not allowing photos to be taken during those early days because they would serve as a profound record of progress.

New Race Boots

One day I left his room to let Steven, the owner of the race team Aaron was riding for, come in for a visit. Afterward, I walked into Aaron's dad holding up a pair of bright blue boots, exclaiming, "Look, Aaron, your new racing boots!"

I was horrified. I thought Steven had brought them to Aaron for inspiration or as some kind of joke.

For me they were a cruel reminder of why Aaron was in this condition. I was still blaming the motorcycle. As soon as they weren't looking, I took the boots and buried them deep in the closet under some clothing so they wouldn't be found. Soon afterward a nurse came in. She began looking around the room, then asked, "Where are the boots I dropped off just a bit ago? I know I put them right here on the bedside table!"

The nurse went on to explain that they were "contracture boots" specially designed to keep paralyzed feet from dropping. I sheepishly retrieved them from the closet, explaining with an embarrassed laugh. "Oh my, I thought they were actual racing boots!" That was the first laugh I'd had in almost three weeks!

Once Aaron was medically stabilized, the physical therapists began getting a little creative with their approach. One therapist brought in a plastic cup filled with frozen water and rubbed it on the muscles on his arms and legs to try to activate a response.

One of these sessions brought forth a twinge of movement! We all shrieked in hopeful delight. From that day on, tiny returns started happening on an almost daily basis. These tiny flickers didn't have the same impact on the medical staff as they did on us. For us the flickers were monumental, signs of response . . . hope. For them, they were inconsequential. I felt as though the medical staff was just humoring us with their comments of encouragement, because I knew they thought we were in serious denial.

Learning to Reconnect—Painted Toes

Arielle came in one morning with a devilish smirk on her face, carrying a makeup bag. She sat at the end of Aaron's bed, unzipped the bag, and proceeded to line up bottles of nail polish the colors of the rainbow. Aaron's upbeat attitude turned into fury as Arielle began to paint his toenails, each one a different color. He couldn't move a muscle, only his mouth. But his mouth made up for the frozen state of his body. Out of it came profanities like I had not heard before from him, especially toward his sister. Arielle continued on, not fazed at all by his demeanor nor the shout of, "Don't paint my shit." As she painted, she said that she would stop if he could kick her. It truly was a "funny not funny" situation.

Once completed, Arielle stood up, admired her paint job, and boldly told her brother to "do something about that." Once the shock wore off, he did indeed do something about that. He focused on his bright blue big toenail, visualizing the color blue throughout his entire body. The blue toe moved ever so slightly. The three of us saw it move, and we looked at one another with disbelief. As if on cue, Arielle and I said at the same time, "Do it again!"

Aaron closed his eyes, and his bright blue toe quivered again!

This was all we needed to move optimistically into the next hour. Powered by the flicker, I didn't feel quite so off base with my unshakable belief that Aaron would defy the doctor's prognosis.

Monumental Flickers

One finger responded at a time, with flickers so slight they were barely perceptible, but it was movement and tremendous cause for celebration. I would wake him up in the mornings and ask what was waking up today for us. These tiny flickers provided a total perspective shift for me.

Day-to-day life moves through the minutes and hours, turning into days, so fast, without real awareness of the current moment. I know I was generally always looking ahead. At breakfast I would be thinking about dinner. On a Saturday I would be planning Sunday, not realizing how much of *now* I was missing.

I have always been a spiritual seeker. I was naturally drawn to Native American spirituality and sweat lodges, Eastern Buddhism, meditation, great thinkers, and authors of metaphysics. Aaron's injury brought forth a realization of how little I truly understood.

*My greatest teacher became the
infinitesimal flicker of movement.*

~ *Flickers*

Flickers of movement were monumental. The individual flicker, on its own, may seem small and insignificant, but with each flicker stacked upon another, progress emerges, revealing the power of incremental steps. Like the interlocking pieces of a toy building set, an impaired body is rebuilt one flicker at a time, constructing a sturdy foundation while being stimulated by the potent forces of awareness, focus, and deliberate intention.

Unrecognizable

During that period, the passage of time seemed distorted and elongated. Each hour felt like a whole day, and every day felt like an entire week. It was as if we had entered a parallel dimension, where our concept of time aligned with a different rhythm. Our lives became immersed in this altered time zone, where everything was distinct and unfamiliar.

The only thing the same was my clothing. I didn't bring anything with me except a toothbrush and a pair of pajamas. My mother offered, more than once, to send me clothes. Friends offered to buy things and bring them to me . . . all of which I refused.

Frankly, not thinking about what I was going to wear for the day was liberating. I didn't have the mental bandwidth to make any decisions other than what Aaron needed. My daily attire became a T-shirt of Aaron's and a pair of the never-ending supply of crisp, clean, flower-print hospital pants.

I know my choice of clothing frightened all those close to me, especially my daughter. I was always known for my fashion sense. A fun fashionista, with a tendency toward flamboyant, some might say "one-of-a-kind outrageous." I relished getting "dressed" in the mornings, each day a different presentation. I mixed and matched handwoven garments from foreign markets, paired with a classic European piece or the best of Western gear mixed with a little rock 'n' roll leather and layers of silver and turquoise jewelry . . . finished off most of the time with a pair of seriously groovy cowboy boots.

My taste in clothing was a reflection of my eclectic nature, yet I had now been presenting myself in the same uniform every day for six months. Interestingly, my favorite T-shirt had the band name *In Flames* printed across the front, the letters spelled out with fiery imagery. Arielle told me several times that she didn't recognize me, that nothing about me was familiar to her.

Noncompliance

I know my family, friends, and the hospital staff thought I had become lost in denial, lost in the torment and gravity of our situation.

Those were others' opinions, not mine, and those opinions would not penetrate my psyche for very long. I was actually told by several different doctors and therapists that I was doing my son as much harm as his injury because I was shielding him from the reality of his condition by not allowing him to struggle with tasks he needed to learn how to do again. The insinuation was that I was a helicopter mom and hovering way too close.

"Laquita, it is obvious how much you care for your son, but you must understand how important it is for you to back up. Aaron needs to adapt and accept his injury and condition," the doctor said.

I would listen to what they had to say to me, then calmly remind them that Aaron was my son, and the benefit of that was that I could do what I believed was best for him.

Some days found me questioning my sanity, seriously wondering if what they were saying was true. This self-doubt was sheer torture, and my stomach would turn with the thought of any of it being even slightly true . . . and then I'd shake it off, sincerely believing that if I followed what was being suggested, the dire prognosis would be painfully true.

I believed with all my heart that my actions would help ease Aaron's suffering and help him become more capable of whatever he put his mind to, not what the injury dictated. If it took noncompliance, I was just fine with that.

I don't subscribe to the belief that we human beings *deserve* anything in life. This situation, however, dispelled that belief entirely. . . . My son deserved every opportunity possible to improve and I was steadfastly intent on making sure he had them. For me, it was an unequivocal commitment to empowering him and enabling him to chart his own course.

~ *Reflection*

Recovery is a nebulous term, as you never know what type of or how much recovery you may have after catastrophic injury. It is completely true that the pursuit of recovery itself is the best remedy for a hopeful outcome, whatever that may be. Knowing you are doing everything possible, every day, provides satisfaction, willingness to continue, and a sense of peace with what is.

Our process was not about learning to adapt to the injury, as is often facilitated in the rehabilitative system. Instead, we worked for improvement, utilizing every moment in rehabilitation to move forward.

Being proactive assisted tremendously with my ability to cope, knowing, without a doubt, that my actions were vital to his well-being. I passionately believed that if I could alleviate even one of the devastating frustrations from the myriad Aaron was experiencing, it would allow him to conserve his limited energy and channel that energy to his rehabilitation.

"Everything can be taken from a man but one thing: the last of the human freedoms—to choose one's attitude in any given set of circumstances, to choose one's own way."

~ Viktor Frankl

Chapter 6:

Setting Our Foundation

After twenty-one days in the ICU, Aaron was deemed medically stabilized. We were then transferred to a regular hospital room and prepared for the transition to rehabilitation. I called a number of referred rehab hospitals, which I declined because of the accommodations.

They all had patient wards, no private rooms, and this prohibited my staying. The frantic emotions rose again. There was no way I was going to leave Aaron, and neither did he want me to. We had developed a great program. We were in sync, in tune.

The nurses had taught me how to provide all Aaron's personal needs. We were on a good path to recovery—altering it now would be disastrous to us. Northridge Hospital Medical Center came through. I was told that they did have semiprivate rooms, several of which were currently vacant, although that could change at any given moment. That was enough for me, though. I was already witnessing miracles, so perhaps another one would appear, and we would be granted a room.

We left the acute care hospital with soaring spirits. The medical staff was not quite as positive, though, as Aaron was still a malnourished, paralyzed young man. Per the medical textbook, it had been declared, decades previously, that the spinal cord was unmalleable, irreparable, and, therefore, the therapeutic focus was on treating secondary complications, not on the infinitesimal flickers we were so enamored with.

Shockingly, the arrival at the rehab hospital was completely deflating. Wheelchairs, shower-toilet chairs, gurneys, and the odd est-looking equipment for the disabled met us outside the open elevator doors. The reality we'd been refusing was trying its best to set in. I was pulling from the words I repeated constantly: *We can do this. This is part of the process. This is temporary* . . . over and over in my mind. Aaron and I locked eyes; "We can do this," I said, forcing myself—and him, I hope—to believe it.

The semiprivate room we were taken to held a patient who'd had a stroke. He was probably close to eighty years old and not mentally lucid. Although my heart went out to this poor man, this was not a conducive healing environment for a twenty-year-old athlete who just lost all physical function . . . *and* I wouldn't be able to stay.

I was rapidly losing my positivity, yet I needed to remain strong. With Aaron's eyes glued to mine, I assured him all was okay. I would see that our arrangements were changed, even though I was sinking inside.

The admitting nurse came in and informed me that I could stay with "the patient" for twenty-four hours, but then I had to adhere to visiting hours and rules. My reputation of noncompliance had preceded me. She said, "It's in the patient's best interest to learn to be self-sufficient as soon as possible. That is, after all, what rehabilitation is all about."

Here it was again—rehabilitation was being defined as learning to adapt. Right or wrong, I don't believe in rehabilitation being defined as a means of learning skills of adaptation.

Our program, the program we created over the past thirty days, was on the brink of collapse. Somehow, I had to diplomatically convince this nurse that our system was working, that Aaron's continued progress depended on it, in conjunction with what the therapy team provided.

I had pushed and forced my way around the first thirty days. This would require a completely different approach if I was going to be successful in convincing her that I was an integral part of Aaron's process. I determined diplomacy would be the best approach, coupled with intimate knowledge of performing the tasks the nurses would usually do for their patient. I needed to prove I was a tremendous help not only to Aaron—but to them.

During the admittance interview, while reading from the admittance form, the nurse went through the list of daily personal tasks they would be doing for Aaron. I explained that I performed those tasks. I also assisted with turning him in bed every two hours. Once the form was completed, she looked up over her eyeglasses and said, "There's an empty room at the end of the hall, you can stay there with Aaron for a few days."

Aaron and I looked at each other with smiles, silently communicating: *Anything is Possible . . . WE CAN DO THIS.* I was allowed to stay until we were discharged . . . five months later.

> *Wanting something is not enough. You must hunger for it.*
> *Your motivation must be absolutely compelling in order to*
> *overcome the obstacles that will invariably come your way.*

Chapter 7:

Mashed Potatoes and Rehab

The next morning our first day of scheduled "rehab" was posted on the door. On a small square of paper, the day was broken into half hours. Every Monday through Friday, half-hour each of occupational therapy, physical therapy, educational classes, support groups, and recreational therapy. Saturday included two hours of therapy and the occasional outing to socialize for community skills.

His therapy program was based on the initial evaluation by the physical and occupational therapists assigned to work with him:

I entered his room for the first time to evaluate and obtain objective measurements of his physical and functional status. This information would be used to obtain a baseline to compare his progress from week to week. This included a thorough examination of his muscle strength and sensation from head to toe as well as his functional abilities. What I found was a skinny twenty-year-old, lying supine in bed in a rigid neck brace, who could not move himself one millimeter in any direction. I took what seemed like so little, at first glance, as hopeful: the flicker in his toe was accompanied by scattered sensations throughout his body below his injury level. Not many other people, however, saw much that gave them hope, including his doctor. As Aaron's physical therapist, my goal was not to prove anyone right or wrong but to help develop his potential to its fullest.*

My position became even more steadfast the first time the occupational therapist came to our room at lunchtime. Instead of going up to the therapy/exercise floor, the therapy session time was going to be spent helping Aaron with his lunch. The therapist placed a frame on the back of his wheelchair, with elastic bands hanging from the frame. The elastic band had a cuff on the end, strapped to Aaron's left wrist.

The injury had left Aaron's right side far more impacted, with the left side of his body a little stronger. The therapist wrapped a washcloth around the stem of a spoon and inserted this into Aaron's clenched left hand. She lightly held his limp forearm, suspended with the frame, helping direct it to the waiting mound of mashed potatoes.

As an observer, this tedious effort was mind-bending. It brought forth feelings of total incapability, and excruciating rage. I watched, for what seemed like the entire hour, as Aaron tried to move the spoon toward the mound of potatoes. He finally made it to the mound, stuck the spoon in to retrieve a mouthful, and then brought it halfway back to his open mouth. The mashed potatoes dropped from the spoon onto his lap.

I had never felt such defeat . . . and this was me, the observer! I couldn't even imagine how he felt. His body slumped in resignation, which shot me out of my chair, again. I took the spoon from his hand, unstrapped the cuff from his wrist, and announced that I would take it from there.

---

* Roger Rich, PT, Northridge Hospital Medical Center. Excerpt from "The Physiological and Psychosocial Effect of Exercise and Nutrition on a Male Incomplete Quadriplegic," Taylor-Kevin Isaacs, MS, CPT, CSCS, California State University, Northridge.

I told the therapist we would not be using another therapy session in this way again. We wanted the emphasis to be on activating his muscles. I said I would feed him until the day came that he could feed himself. Period. No amount of challenging from the therapist changed my mind.

I felt it cruel to put him through that kind of painstaking humiliation. We wanted to focus on the process of reconnecting and rebuilding his body. The adaptive skills would evolve, over time. Aaron and I instinctively knew this.

I assured him that we would direct his care and therapies according to what we felt best for him—more importantly, to how HE felt he should engage. We needed to be in control of what we could actually control—our approach. It didn't matter to me if it was against the normal procedures or medically based protocols. There was nothing normal about any of this anyway. We were creating our new normal.

Bottom line was I wanted to keep the possibilities open and his spirit lit.

Blank Canvas

Even in those early days neither of us talked about "getting our lives back, getting back to life as we knew it." We knew that life had taken an enormous turn and that it would never be the same. We committed to the re-creation of our lives. Our canvas was blank. It was completely up to us to color the canvas . . . on our terms.

~ Redefining Life

The power to rise above *lies not in the wreckage of what was, but in the choices we make to shape what will be. I have found peace and satisfaction in the company of devastation by committing to repainting life, not looking back . . . looking only straight ahead, viewing our life as a blank canvas that beckoned our brush to illustrate a new future. Every step added new color, dimension, direction. Our new life began to appear one intentional brushstroke at a time.*

We adapted well to the rehab schedule; however, due to Aaron's fragility and weakness, it took a month before he could tolerate a full day of activity. Arielle would often bring a few of her girlfriends for visits. Their loving laughter, joking, and occasional sushi dinner provided welcomed respite.

One of Arielle's best girlfriends lived a short distance from the hospital, giving her a comfortable, familiar home to stay at when she wasn't at the hospital with us.

By that time, it was becoming clearer that our stay in the hospital would be long-term. Arielle offered to fly to Oklahoma with her friend Shelley and drive my motorhome back for us so we'd have a personal space to go to, outside of the hospital room.

She surprised me by bringing my most beloved cat, JJ (aka Jesse James), back with her, in an effort of reconnecting me with the soothing companionship that little boy had always given me. I didn't end up spending any time in the motorhome, so she would stuff him under her jacket and bring him to the rooftop lounging area of the hospital for me to be with him.

Visualization and Touch Assist

To help guide Aaron in reaching a peaceful state of mind for sleeping, his uncle Joe showed me a method called "touch assist." The purpose of touch assist is to reestablish communication with injured—or in Aaron's case, paralyzed—extremities. This is done by repetitively touching the injured body part and putting the person into communication with the injury. Some ancient healers attributed remarkable flows and qualities to the "laying on of hands."

For Aaron, the workable element in this method was simply

heightening and focusing his awareness. I would begin at the top of his head, touching a spot and telling him, "Feel my finger." He would acknowledge with a *yes*. I then would go exactly parallel to the other side and repeat. Back and forth, back and forth, all the way from the head down to the toes, then back up again, traversing the body. When I got below his shoulders, he couldn't feel anything. I'd tell him where I was, and he'd acknowledge with focused intention. This method began assisting him in reconnecting with his disconnected, nonfunctional body.

Visualization was coupled with the technique. Aaron would draw an imaginary, colored line back and forth across his body, connecting with each spot my finger was on.

Arielle, Dan, and Aaron's friend, Adam, learned this method as well so he could engage in the process, no matter who was with him, every night for our six-month hospital stay. We would later continue the practice once we were home, for many years.

"Visualization is seeing, feeling, smelling, sensing, and experiencing something in your mind, exactly as you would in real life. Visualizing triggers the same processes in your brain as real-life experience would—transmitting the same energetic frequency and vibration through and around you. Therefore, you can influence whatever you want to create in life, through visualizing it first."
~ AARON BAKER, *THE REBELLIOUS RECOVERY*

Purple Foot

On the Fourth of July, Dan came to visit. I decided to go meet friends in Malibu for an evening out of the hospital.

In my distorted state of mind, I lost my balance descending a stairway, severely twisting my ankle. I couldn't put my foot down. The pain was searing, and swelling set in immediately. I stayed the night at my friend's home, hoping my ankle would improve overnight.

I woke up to a huge, throbbing, purple foot. I hopped to my car, cursing everything and everyone. Why did this have to happen NOW?

Back at the hospital the nurses urged me to go to the emergency room for treatment. I knew the treatment protocol would be elevation and rest. Dan was leaving so I needed to find a way to deal with it.

It actually ended up serving me. It put me in better communication with Aaron, learning to transcend the pain along with him. Every time I would get up to do something for him, he would apologize. I couldn't stand his need for an apology. I would tell him it didn't hurt. I did eventually succeed, so much so that I honestly couldn't feel the pain. I became used to it.

Aaron and I looked like a fine pair at that time—me hobbling while pushing him in a large high-backed wheelchair. Through this added difficulty, I knew, without a shadow of doubt, that he would get well, that anything was possible with hard work, a burning desire, and an absolute refusal to give in.

We used the enormous stack of odds against us as a ladder.

Determined Spirit

At that time, Aaron took hold of his rehabilitation with focused determination. He wasn't weighed down with regret, remorse, or anger, which so typically hinders one who's been so traumatically injured.

He seemed to transcend his condition. I didn't know that breaking his neck had been his greatest fear; therefore, when it did happen to him, he exhibited a sixth sense. He knew what he had to do. We committed to the phrase "head down with eyes up."

Each and every day, Aaron gave as much effort as possible into therapy. We both bonded with his physical therapist, who was an older man with a Buddha-like energy.

I then allowed the therapy sessions to be filmed. I felt like the intensity Aaron poured into his sessions needed to be captured. I didn't know, at that time, just how important it would become for Aaron's long-term process of recovery to be able to look back, especially on days when it felt as though he wasn't progressing.

~ *Power of Video*

The video becomes the storyteller of recovery, the proof of improvement over time. When one has suffered a debilitating injury, the improvements are very difficult to recognize. By documenting the journey on video, you can capture small victories and track progress. As time unfolds, we find reassurance in revisiting these recorded chapters, for they hold within them the confirmation of progress.

Pool Standing

Three months after the injury, pool therapy began. With water being Aaron's natural element, I saw a force course through him as he was transferred into the pool. His head disappeared underwater, and he emerged standing on his own!

Without the pull of gravity, he was able to stand and lift his leg. He was electrified. Aaron's laughter and energy was contagious and everyone at the pool joined in the celebration.

"Look, Toots! I'm standing on my own!"

One therapist yelled out, "YAY, Aaron! This is so fantastic!"

"I KNEW you would do it," I said as I hugged him tight.

His very first steps were taken between the parallel bars in four feet of water. Within two weeks the parallel bars were placed in three feet of water. Soon afterward it was time to try to stand on solid ground.

Words cannot begin to describe the feeling of watching your child take his first steps, for the second time in his life. Although he was braced from his hips to his feet, accompanied by three therapists and a four-wheeled walker, he took a step. A step that was never to have been possible.

Facilitating Ability

We celebrated my birthday at the end of August. As I transferred Aaron from the wheelchair to the bed, he asked me to help him stand at the bedside for a moment. He lifted his frail arms and embraced me, ever so lightly, for the first time in three months. He told me that although he couldn't get me a birthday card, he could now give me a hug. I couldn't have been given a greater gift. That single embrace held volumes of possibility, hope, and love. A hug, as I had been told, he was never supposed to be able to give again.

I discovered that embracing the term "facilitator" instead of "caregiver" was empowering and encouraging, thus increasing the importance and effect of my ability. By definition, a facilitator is a person that makes an action easier.

Knowing I was the buoy keeping Aaron's head above the water, giving my ability to facilitate his, transcended the feeling of giving myself as a task.

~ *Caregiver's Ode*

The role of a caregiver/facilitator often remains hidden, an invisible thread woven into the tapestry of your life. It's like an unspoken ode to oneself, a quiet symphony of love and selflessness. While it may not always be visible to the world, its impact feeds the heart. It's a labor of love performed in the shadows, where satisfaction doesn't come from applause but from knowing you are making a difference in someone's life. It's the gentle touch, the late nights, the sacrifices that go unnoticed by many but are cherished by those you care for. It's a silent journey that speaks volumes in the language of love, a sacred duty that brings personal gratification in the most profound yet inconspicuous ways.

Chapter 8:

Discharge

Aaron's discharge date was set as October 9, nearly six months after entering hospital living. For months I'd gone outside after Aaron was asleep, for fresh air and reflection under the neon sign of Northridge Hospital Medical Center . . . an otherworldly sight, never becoming familiar in my mind. That was until October 9.

The cocooned existence we had developed was supported by skilled staff who could be called upon at a moment's notice. We hadn't participated in the weekly support group meetings. I hadn't paid close attention to all the potential adaptive equipment Aaron might need at home, because I was so focused on his daily grand improvements, which were, in reality, infinitesimal. I had maintained the belief that he wouldn't need any of those pieces. My denial couldn't serve me now. It was slapping my face. Panic set in.

Part of the panic resulted from the fact that our family home was fifteen hundred miles away, so there was nothing familiar to go home to. Another hard fact was that Aaron's injury wasn't like a broken bone with a cast that could be removed a couple of months later and all would be well—it was becoming clear that this injury would affect him for his lifetime.

Every hour of the last 170 days had been spent fighting this tragedy, never stopping long enough to think about living with it. Although we didn't depend on nursing care for anything other than administering medications, there was tremendous security in knowing they were right outside our door. Leaving the safety of the hospital and stepping into an unknown, frightening world was staggering.

The real wake-up set in as we arrived at our new home for the coming days: Motel 6.

Dan, and Aaron's best friend, Adam, accompanied us from the hospital to the nearby motel. The four of us shared a stark, dank, small room with two double beds and a rollaway. Stale cigarette smoke hung in the air.

Upon entering the room, all of Aaron's so-called functional gains we had celebrated in the hospital seemed inconsequential. Fact was—he was a quadriplegic, every part of his body from the neck down impaired.

Dan scooped him up from the wheelchair, laying him on the bed. Later that night I heard Aaron's muffled sobs. He hadn't cried since right after his accident six months earlier. He was making up for it now. As my heart broke into a million pieces, once again I became enveloped in the repetitive meditation that had pulled me from the depths so many times since his injury: "WE CAN DO THIS . . . we will find our way."

Quite simply, I allowed myself only positive affirmations. I forced myself to carry on. I gave myself no other choice. That was all I had at that point, and . . . I still had my son.

Something Familiar

The following morning, Dan asked us if we would like for him to check for availability at the apartment complex he lived in a few years back. Aaron showed a little interest, as it was a somewhat familiar place.

Dan returned later that day, letting us know that there was a vacant two-bedroom unit. I secured the deposit. I had absolutely nothing to furnish our new home with. We began collecting the essentials over the coming days, with the priority on Aaron's bed and an electric La-Z-Boy chair. When he wasn't in bed, he was in that chair.

He came to detest the sight of the big blue dinosaur that, with the push of a button, could lift him to transfer to his next chair, the wheelchair. It was a huge sense of victory when, years later, we gave that heavy beast away.

We settled into a new schedule, as best we could. Aaron, Arielle, and I were living together again. Arielle was attempting to live life as an eighteen-year-old. Her ability to move around freely and spontaneously was difficult for Aaron, as it was for her. He loved seeing her live her life yet held great conflict with her freedom.

Arielle held a silent guilt in her heart. "Why was Aaron so tragically injured and not me?" she shared with me one night. She would vacillate between devastation and anger that so much had been taken from us, each in different ways.

Not only had she lost her brother as she knew him; she had lost a big part of me too. I wasn't available to her in the way I had been throughout her life. This was a feeling she had never known.

My dreams at night were pure torture. One recurring dream had my face under a body of water, eyes looking up to the surface, trying to see through the watery film, gasping for air, water filling my lungs, a large hand pushing my face down farther into the water. The loud sound of my gasp would awaken me. Lying in the aftermath of the horrible, realistic dream, the same sense I had while sliding down the hospital wall would come over me . . . and I would think, if you fall, Laquita, so does everything else.

The two dynamics of my children were polar opposites. I was in the middle of them, each one pulling my heart, and methods, in different directions. One allowed my involvement—he didn't have a choice. The other did not. One was fighting to live, the other fighting with reality.

~ *Reflection*

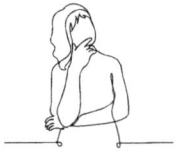

In the pool of life, there is an analogy that resonates deeply with the dynamics of catastrophic injury. Imagine two children at a swimming pool. One child is in the water struggling and appearing to be drowning. The other child stands at the pool's edge, hungry, but not in danger.

In this scenario, it is the child in the water, facing a life-threatening situation, who commands all the attention. The urgency of their predicament rightly calls for immediate intervention and everyone's focus is on rescuing and assisting them.

The impact on the non-injured sibling can be deep and complex. It often leads to a range of emotions including guilt, fear/anxiety, sadness/grief, responsibility/isolation, anger/resentment, and concern about their identity/future. Or, on a more positive side, the impact can foster greater empathy/compassion and more sensitivity to the needs of others.

It is essential for families to provide emotional support and communication for all their children and themselves, the silent casualties, after such trauma. Addressing these complex emotions and experiences can help everyone navigate this challenging journey and find ways to better cope and adapt more effectively.

Nowhere to Go

We now had outpatient therapy three days per week. On off-days I would take Aaron to the apartment gym. These visits were a miserable fail. The equipment wasn't accessible for people with disabilities. Also unhelpful was the stark contrast and intimidation he felt with the he-man next to him, sweating and grunting from the effort of lifting one-hundred-pound dumbbells.

All the enthusiasm Aaron had exhibited while an inpatient was fading fast. The therapy sessions lessened in intensity, and the attitude of the therapists became seemingly complacent. They were working against the insurance clock and knew time with Aaron was soon to end. I heard the words "he's reached his maximum potential." This was perfectly impossible in my mind—and most certainly to Aaron's.

Aaron's body was just beginning to wake up and respond. Stopping therapies at that point was unthinkable.

As I watched the light dim in Aaron's eyes, I was pleading with the therapists for information on what the next step was. I went to the local library to look up anything and everything related to the ongoing rehabilitative process. It was beyond comprehension that I could not come up with anything to help him.

I was painfully reminded of what the medical staff tried to prepare me for back in the beginning. I became filled with a different type of panic. I knew Aaron was silently plotting his own demise. My broken heart gave way to blinding anger . . . toward God and life, for us being in this tragic reality.

Aaron was giving up—no fighting other than fighting me. Fury overtook him. He hated every aspect of his life . . . hated every bath, every bowel program, every spoonful of food . . . because I or someone else was doing it for him. The only comfort he ever reached was in sleep.

He knew what he was capable of and all he wanted to do was work toward rebuilding his body. Therapy held the only hope and possibility of improvement—yet there was nowhere to go to do that.

> *Courage does not always roar. Sometimes courage is the quiet voice at the end of the day saying, "I will try again tomorrow."*

Stand

Possibility

Part 3   Initiate

Reason

Intention

Transform

The miracle is in the work by taking massive, determined action.

Chapter 9:

Moving Forward

One week before my "ditch" ordeal, I'd begun to clear Aaron's room of objects I believed he could use to harm himself. I told him I knew what he was plotting and that I wouldn't allow him to take that action. I knew in my heart he was at his end, and I was petrified. Anger was consuming what little energy he had. This was the one thing I'd been fiercely committed to . . . helping him maintain his spirit. Without spirit, there is nothing left.

In desperation, I called his dearest friends to come be with him, thinking that they could somehow help him move through his darkness. This made him even angrier toward me. He wanted to suffer in silence and not be met with the indignity of his despair being known to everyone.

"Toots, I don't want anyone to come over. I'm over all this. I want you to leave me alone and let me do what I need to do!" he would yell at me.

Arielle had begun to spend less and less time at our apartment. She found diversion in touring with her favorite band, ultimately having a long-term relationship with the lead guitarist. As difficult as it was to not have her there, I was relieved she was going on with her life. She was finding happiness, instead of being surrounded by the misery of our home. Or so I thought. Since she'd been a young teenager she had been experimenting with drugs, but now she started turning to them as a coping mechanism.

This question haunts me to this day: Would she have made the same choices if our family hadn't suffered such tragedy? I can only speculate, as I will never know the answer. I do know I would have been more cognizant of what was happening to her sooner. That brings another question: Would my awareness have made a difference?

All three of us were unable to cope with the wreckage of our lives. Arielle, unwittingly, was heading straight for self-destruction while Aaron and I, simultaneously, hit our respective bottoms.

While I focused on removing things I thought Aaron could use to harm himself, it never occurred to me that his method of self-demise was driving his electric wheelchair into the swimming pool.

While Aaron sat at the pool's edge, contemplating ending his life, I was lying in a Calexico ditch begging for mine to end.

He made the decision to "pull back." I made the decision to "get up."

We never talked about our near self-demise until years later. There were things we just weren't willing to share with each other, or anyone else for that matter. We were well aware of our pain and extreme vulnerability. We spared one another the gruesome details.

Talking about it or commiserating gave our pain more power . . . power we didn't have to give away.

Some aspects of our experiences needed to remain clothed in silence. Exposure takes confidence and security, something neither of us had. I lived on a floor of glass, tiptoeing daily, afraid of the floor breaking underneath me, swallowing me into a deep, blackened abyss that I wouldn't be able to find my way out of.

I found strength in my silence.

After I told Aaron I needed to stay, I walked into my room and called a young man we'd met while in hospital rehabilitation. Andy had been in an accident just two weeks after Aaron's, resulting in paraplegia. We were close to Andy in rehab, but after both our discharges, we lost contact. I called Andy to invite him over for dinner and to reconnect.

I knew Andy had suffered depression and dark days while we were all in the hospital; perhaps now he could now help Aaron. While on the phone with him, I asked him what he was doing with his life. He was enrolled at California State University, Northridge in a program called the Center of Achievement. It was a center with adaptive equipment and a learning lab for students studying kinesiology, the study of human movement. He said the program director, Taylor-Kevin Isaacs, was someone he thought we should connect with.

Andy came over for dinner and the next morning I called Taylor. I scheduled a meeting with him at the Center of Achievement the following day.

"We can do this" . . .

The Door Effect

On a searing-hot Wednesday, after completing our usual morning routine, in my bruised and fragile state of mind, I scooped Aaron up and proceeded to carry him to the car. I told him we were going to see someone I believed could help us. His screams of protest didn't alter my decision or direction. He was slumped over, belted up in the passenger seat. His protests didn't stop for the thirty-minute drive to Northridge.

For weeks, as the insurance coverage for ongoing outpatient therapy was ending, I was researching other therapy opportunities. I called every gym in Southern California, only to be told over and over, "We don't work with disabling conditions."

Yet again, I was reminded of my so-called denial. There were no opportunities for the ongoing process of recovery from spinal cord injury, at that time. I had come across an experimental aquatic therapy program in Boston, but it was cost prohibitive with no real measures of long-term success. All roads were seemingly ending at the same darkened point . . . until the Center of Achievement.

I parked the car in front of the university campus and sat Aaron in his wheelchair. His one look at the campus filled with students his age, running around, laughing, and joking with one another, while he was being pushed in a wheelchair by me, was almost more than his compromised sense of self could tolerate.

Although his screaming stopped, his head dropped down in resignation. Without saying one word, I continued pushing him forward across the campus to a set of glass double doors.

As the doors opened, we were greeted with a sense of vitality, an energy of promise. Upon the bright red carpet sat pieces of equipment unlike anything we had seen before, all adapted for wheelchair users. The space was filled with other people with varying degrees of injury and disabling conditions. I saw Aaron's eyes reluctantly taking this all in, and his head began to lift. I saw life and interest begin to course through his body again, much like pouring water on a sun-soaked, wilted flower. Little by little, Aaron sat up a little straighter, with a slight spark returning to his eyes as we observed the activity in the center.

A tall, imposing man with a black-and-white paisley bandanna tied around his head walked up to us and stretched out his hand to Aaron. With a broad smile and thick South African accent, he introduced himself, "Hi, I'm Taylor Isaacs. Welcome to the Center of Achievement!"

I explained to Aaron that Taylor was the man I had told him about on our drive, even though I knew he wasn't listening to me in the car.

To my utter surprise, and delight, Aaron took Taylor's hand, replying, "I'm Aaron Baker. I hope you're the one who will help me fix my tattered body."

Almost awkwardly, I interjected a premature question of what it would take for him to begin working with Aaron the very next day. What Taylor didn't know at that time was that he was taking on two tattered bodies . . . mine was just not visible.

I hadn't asked Taylor if he worked one-on-one with clients. I had actually been afraid to ask him during our phone conversation the day before, afraid he would tell me no. I know Taylor saw desperation beyond the obvious effects of Aaron's injury. I believe he also saw a fierce desire to work hard, and he saw commitment.

To a therapist, Aaron and I were dream clients—Aaron bringing the heart of a lion, me bringing the support and desire to leave no stone unturned in the pursuit of wellness. Taylor was a bit taken aback by the clumsiness of my request. He did, however, excuse himself to go look at his schedule. He returned to say, "I can see you tomorrow at eleven a.m. Will that work for you?"

With a relieved smile, I said, "Absolutely."

Just outside of the glorious double glass doors, Aaron and I locked eyes, in the similar way we had after he had experienced his death in the ICU. Many of the walls constructed over the past few months fell away in that gaze, for both of us. Anger seemed to know it had found someplace to be released. With a slight smile, I said, "Buddy, let's get busy. We found our place to do work." His returned smile sealed our decision.

The drive home felt victorious. The high noon sun felt brighter. The scenery was richer. We were both filled with a new hope and promise of a better path forward. The destination was unknown, and that was okay. We now had something we could work with, and that was all that mattered. We were standing on the bottom rung of the ladder that was made of all the odds stacked against us, and we were ready to begin the climb.

That afternoon, instead of fighting life and one another, we began to align again. Those glass doors opened to a space that, as Aaron has since described, was like being bathed in angelic light radiating from above. We termed that experience the "Door Effect."

Another seed was sown. That promising center and Taylor's brilliant approach were too limited and too hard to find. The concept of building a center for others like Aaron became the vision that would light our path forward, and was central to our making sense of the tragic reality.

~ *Miracle of the Work*

In the wake of a disabling injury, through deliberate intention, the miracle of the work unfolds. It is a confirmation of the indomitable spirit that resides within us all. Each step, each effort, each small victory becomes a brushstroke on the canvas of redefinition of oneself. It reminds us that our potential has no bounds. In the face of adversity, the miracle of the work shines like a light. It is the extraordinary power that lies within us.

Chapter 10:

The Work

On the first day at the center, Taylor welcomed us and told Aaron, "Let's place an apostrophe between the I and the M of the word *Impossible*, to make it 'I'm Possible,' and then focus on the 'one' and not the million!"

This was music to my ears. It undoubtably fired Aaron up, who wore a hat with the words "On A Mission" written across the front. We had told Taylor about the initial prognosis of Aaron having a one-in-a-million chance to regain function.

We went all-in on our new program.

The shell that had encased Aaron's body began to take on a suppleness. His skin-and-bone frame had added a couple of much-needed pounds within the first two weeks of going to the center. We discovered he could consume additional calories, without the effect of early satiety, by having small snacks, a piece of fruit with nuts, cheese slices, or a protein smoothie, every two to three hours. We were at the center six days per week.

Years later, the personalized method Taylor used with Aaron was named the "System of Function." Taylor designed programming that addressed every component of function—musculoskeletal conditioning (strength, endurance, power, stability), flexibility, cardio, balance, posture, gait mechanics, and performance.

Another bedrock term we coined, which underscored our commitment:

Education + Motivation = Results

The days now revolved around our time spent at the center. Wake up, make a smoothie, prepare Aaron for his morning program, bathe, dress, walk him out to the recliner chair, prepare breakfast. While Aaron had breakfast, I packed a small cooler with our lunch and snacks. I would quickly dress and tidy up the apartment, all the while looking at the clock every five minutes or so. Go to the center for four to five hours, return home. Aaron napped, ate dinner, watched TV or played video games for an hour, then went to bed. Wake up the next morning and repeat.

The intent behind my intense clock-watching was to make sure we were exactly on time for our appointment with Taylor. I didn't want to give up one minute. I felt that time was irretrievable, and Aaron needed every possible minute we could give to repairing his broken body.

My routine was the same as Aaron's with the exception of when we returned home from the center: while he was napping, I was scrounging for odd work for income. Aaron did qualify for monthly disability income, but the meager amount didn't even cover the monthly apartment rental. It was additionally challenging because I couldn't commit to a structured work schedule.

Letting Go

By that time, I had been out of the workforce for seven months. We had been living on my savings, which were quickly being depleted. Up to that point I had held on to my ranch as well. In the beginning it was too much for me to make the decision to sell it. There was a permanency to that decision that I had not been willing or ready to face.

I'd sold my car and Arielle's car early on. It was now time to let go of the ranch. I'd decided it was the right choice to buy it through photos my mother sent me, and then I purchased the ranch over the phone. The first time I physically saw it was when I drove the truck carrying my belongings down the long driveway. I sold the ranch the same way I had purchased it: over the phone.

All my furniture, clothing, and everything else I owned was packed and placed in a storage unit by my mother, brother, and a few family friends, where it remained for the following four years.

~ *Reflection*

Neither did I want to make the time, nor did I find the desire, to retrieve my stored items. Those items were a reminder of a way of life that no longer existed. The reality of our situation necessitated my shedding the trappings of the familiar to make way for reinvention. The storage unit became a metaphorical vault, housing not just my belongings but also a key to unlocking the true richness of the intangible, invaluable aspects of life.

Projecting

Everything but Aaron's care became inconsequential, most of the time.

On days I felt I couldn't lay my personal wants down enough, I would project into the future. I looked ahead at what it might feel like if I had not been there for Aaron's well-being. What kind of state would he be in if I were not? Would I be able to live with the outcome, knowing I had not done everything possible to help him improve his condition?

Those thoughtful projections were extraordinarily powerful. They allowed me to examine the what-could-be's, the what-if's. Fact is,

I wouldn't have been able to live with myself if I had chosen to not be there for him.

~ *Projections/Foresight*

A powerful tool when examined with wisdom and self-awareness. It is the act of envisioning ourselves in the future, looking back on the path of where we have been along with contemplating the impact of our present actions on our future self. It is an invitation to step outside of the immediate circumstances and gain a broader perspective, to view our choices through the lens of hindsight before they actually solidify into missed opportunities. We can find comfort in the knowledge that we will not feel the grip of regret, for we have acted with intention and foresight.

I then began to contemplate the juxtaposed concept of "selflessness being selfishness." In my so-called selflessness, which is what many refer to as the act of caregiving, I was actually being quite selfish. My selflessness had as much of a positive, necessary effect on me as it did Aaron. The realization of using my ability to facilitate his was intensely impactful. These aspects lifted me when I felt I could not lift myself.

At first glance, selflessness may seem to imply an abandonment of one's own needs and desires to be in service to another. But, underneath the surface, a different story unfolds—a tale of interconnectedness, where our individual well-being becomes intertwined with the well-being of another. In the depth of this paradox lies a profound truth: that in selflessly giving, we receive. In lighting the way for others, we illuminate our own path. By embracing this truth, we unlock a path to personal fulfillment, where in the act of uplifting another, we uplift ourselves . . . and Rise Together.

> **"The greatest surprise of human evolution may be that the
> highest form of selfishness is selflessness."**
> ~ ROBERT E. ORNSTEIN

Need for Income

I made an arrangement (with the Persian family I had worked for
prior to moving to my ranch in Oklahoma) to list some of their
oriental rugs on the internet. They sent me photographs of rugs
deemed appropriate for online sales, and I made the listing from
the photos. In theory this was a perfect job opportunity. I could
do the online work when time was available. The problem was that
online sales at that time were few and far between, which meant
inconsistent sales . . . and income.

I also offered cleaning services in our apartment complex. For-
tunately, I had several clients who trusted me with their keys, so
I could go in and out during the scheduled cleaning day. That job
was by all means the most mentally challenging of any job I ever
held. Cleaning the pee off someone else's toilet was a stark contrast
between my past expertise and the humbling nature of unexpected
twists in life. These days were softened by the constant reminder of
my *Why*. It was a grueling schedule with so many ends to juggle.
But I was doing it because it was my choice—and my choice was
much stronger than the circumstance.

~ *Reflection*

*I recognized very early that everything I
thought was important in my life was, in fact,
not. I thought I had known what sacrifice
meant until I was faced with the necessity
to do so. I made choices that supported our
process and were not diverting of my time and attention. I had
once thought of sacrifice as giving up, resigning . . . but when I
truly engaged and embraced the act of sacrifice, I found it to be*

supportive and empowering. By identifying the things in life and separating into categories of wants versus needs, I began to let go of all that was unnecessary. I was amazed at how little I actually need when the needs of someone I loved held more power than anything else in my life.

Chapter 11:

Roommate

My days of financial comfort and security were far behind me, as were my glory days of a career I loved and worked so hard to achieve. Every day I tried to come up with creative ways to earn money and still maintain my focus and schedule with Aaron. Andy had become a weekly visitor, and he and Aaron had developed a special relationship.

One night while Andy was gathering his things to go home, it occurred to me that we should all move in together. Sharing the rent would make financial sense and we could help and support one another.

I explained my idea to Aaron after Andy had left. He lit up and said, "That's great. I would enjoy living with Andy."

I called Andy the next morning and invited him back over that same evening to present the idea to him in person. Andy's response was very much like Aaron's. He was thrilled with the thought of us all living under the same roof.

Trying to find a rental home in 2001, the height of a rental market frenzy in Southern California, was a seemingly impossible task. Every single-story, three-bedroom home, appropriate for wheelchair users, would have thirty people vying to rent it.

My rental application was easy to dismiss and throw in the trash.

A single mother with meager, inconsistent income and two disabled young men. I put myself in the owner's shoes. I knew what it looked like on paper but there had to be a home out there for us—I just needed to keep looking.

Finally, a kitchen interview with a homeowner, who became genuinely interested in my seemingly exaggerated tear-jerking story, yielded a signed rental agreement.

I didn't tell Aaron and Andy just how difficult the process was. I felt in my heart that this kind of information would have a negative impact on Aaron. He had a hard enough time keeping himself in the game. He didn't need additional negative input about things he had no control over. I was aware and protective of the silent guilt I knew he carried—constantly feeling like I wouldn't be going through these challenges if he had not been hurt.

Two weeks later, the three of us moved into our new home, with Arielle coming and going. The home was surprisingly accommodating for the two wheelchairs. We didn't need to do any kind of modifications other than placing a portable metal wheelchair ramp at the front door. The home was also only seven miles from the university.

A Rhythm

Life quickly assumed a steady cadence. Everything revolved around Aaron's rehab. Andy was always home when we returned from our daily sessions at the center. He and Aaron would play video games and watch TV together. Aaron had also begun to experiment with drawing and would become immersed in the creative process. This gave me additional time to put into outside income-earning endeavors.

Taylor taught me how to do proper stretching and a machine-based exercise program with Aaron, becoming what he termed "Motherapist." Soon after, I began to be paid to work with other young men with spinal cord injuries, while Taylor worked with

Aaron. One of them came to the center in the middle of the afternoon, after we'd returned home. I didn't want to take the one car we had. Somehow it made me more comfortable and able to leave Aaron at home with the car parked in the driveway in my absence.

I bought a bright yellow bicycle from a garage sale for thirty dollars. It had rock-solid tires, giving it the feeling of a *Flintstones*-era type of ride. I cycled my way back to the university to work with a client while Aaron either rested or entertained himself with Andy.

The rides to and from the university were extremely beneficial for my mind and spirit. The physical effort kept my mind from wandering and assisted in keeping my attention in the moment.

Not long after we settled into our new home and routine, the day of confronting my DUI came about. For months I was filled with anxiety and fear of the potential sentencing the judge would impose because my blood alcohol level had been so high, plus the additional charge of reckless driving. I wrote the judge an impassioned letter explaining my situation. I didn't know what would happen to Aaron if I had to go away.

Seven months after my arrest, I stood before the judge in Calexico. His shaming admonishments stung but were rightly deserved. He acknowledged my situation, and he explained that if I were in a different circumstance, his sentence would be an automatic sixty days in county jail.

As horrified and remorseful as I was, his ultimate sentence felt like a pardoning gift from an angel. A revoked driver's license, driver safety classes two times per week for one full year, and one year with a Breathalyzer on my car. Upon completion of these requirements, I would be granted a driver's license again.

Chapter 12:

The Classes

I absolutely refused to install the ugly mandated Breathalyzer, to detect even a trace amount of alcohol in my system, on the only car we had. The mere thought of blowing into the device to start the vehicle, while being watched by Aaron or others in the car, was inconceivable.

I rode the yellow bike to my driver safety classes two days per week for one-hour meetings. The meeting room was devoid of any decor, only folding chairs lined up against the wall, U-shaped around the room, with a solid darkened border just above the back of the chairs from greasy heads rubbing the white wall. I was stunned to be a part of this scene.

I attended each meeting, the hood of my sweatshirt covering my head, with a tough-guy kind of countenance, wanting to be invisible, to be left alone, afraid of probing questions piercing my exterior lie.

I began journaling while in the meetings to stay busy while feeling so demoralized. I ended up taking away some incredibly profound life insights once I accepted I was no different from anyone else within those dirty walls.

~ *Thoughts for Myself (to Remember)*

 *Take ownership of your actions and behavior, recognizing that you are solely responsible for where you are now.*

Refrain from using external factors such as heartbreak or life-altering events as excuses for your choices.

Resist the temptation to blame others (they) for your circumstances, as it only diminishes your own power and control.

Embrace personal accountability as a tool for self-empowerment and transformation.

Recognize the impact of your behavior on the people you care about and consider the consequences it may have on your relationships.

Shift from a self-centered mindset to one that embraces the collective well-being of others, aiming for a more balanced and compassionate approach—Me to We.

Choose acceptance over resistance when faced with problems.

Embrace a growth mindset by focusing on finding solutions rather than dwelling on the problems themselves.

View problems as opportunities for growth and personal development, understanding that they shape who we become.

During the course of the classes, I realized how this experience actually informed me on how to move forward with our life. Nothing was clear; it just seemed as though some of the clouds were parting, giving way to better understanding of how to navigate the road we were on and how to better navigate my own.

I began to appreciate the value of that ditch.

Chapter 13:

Auspicious Meeting

I developed a rhythm within a few weeks of moving to our new home—the rehab home. Juggling the home routine, Aaron's therapy at the center, work, bicycling back to the center, dinner, driver safety meetings, and back to the center two evenings per week, soon felt manageable. I felt my grueling schedule was something I could build upon, laying a solid foundation to rebuild our brokenness together, one step at a time.

One evening at the center while I was working with a newly injured client, I noticed a gentle-looking young man assisting another spinal cord injured individual. I went up to him and introduced myself. I told him I was curious about what inspired him to do this type of work. He didn't fit the stereotypical profile of a nonfamily caregiver. He had the air and energy of someone who had just returned from an ashram in India. Yogic in nature with tanned skin, long brown hair, and a genuine, disarming broad smile. His reply to my query was, "Why not?" This left me with even more curiosity.

Over the coming weeks, Jeffrey and I became friends. We looked forward to the end of evening sessions, finding time before leaving the center to talk for a few minutes. I was proud of him for choosing the work he did, as I did not choose the work—it chose me.

One evening we walked out to the parking lot together. He was quite surprised to see me unlock the yellow bike to ride home at nine o'clock in the evening. I didn't accept his invitation to put the bike in his car and drive me home.

As he was walking away, shaking his head, he yelled over his shoulder, "I have a car I'm not using you can borrow." I laughed, thinking he was fooling with me.

The next time I saw Jeffrey I told him why I was riding a bike. After I gave him a summarized version of Calexico, he said he was serious about loaning me a car and that I could use it for whatever I needed, even a Breathalyzer!

Once my disbelief in this most unlikely offer subsided, the received blessing was stunning to me. The mandate didn't have a statute of limitations. Before I was ever to receive my driver's license again, I had to spend one year blowing into the device to prove I was not intoxicated behind the wheel of a car. I'd put the mandate far out of my mind, not having any idea of how or when I would be able to meet that requirement.

A few days later, Jeffrey pulled up in our driveway in an older-model little white convertible Pontiac Sunbird. He handed me the keys and told me to do whatever I needed to do to take care of business. It was my car for as long as I needed it.

Some people appear in your life when you need them most.
They love you. They lift you up, reminding you of the best
even when you are going through the worst. These people are
not just friends—they are Earth Angels.

Chapter 14:

Discovering the Artist

Prior to his injury, Aaron was right-handed but now relied solely on his more functional left hand. Taylor and I had encouraged him to spend time learning to write again with his left hand. The left hand–right brain exercise proved beneficial to building his self-confidence through creativity.

I looked forward to and counted on my occasional visits to see my dearest friends, Lynn and Ed, in Carmel, to help soothe and fill my heart with their tender love and care. They and the magnetism Carmel held for me was pure soul food, my respite, a vital rejuvenation of my spirit.

On one of my visits, when I told Lynn, an accomplished artist, about Aaron's newfound interest in drawing, she took me to her favorite art supply store. She carefully selected the best of art supplies—a set of paints, pencils, brushes, canvases, and sketchbooks—for Aaron.

After returning home from hours of strenuous therapy, he began to lose himself to active meditation and the practice of patience through the paintbrush.

I hung a framed quote in Aaron's bedroom that read, "There is in this world no greater force than the force of a man determined to rise." He read these words every day and etched them into his psyche and heart.

His first painting, entitled *Rise Above*, depicted a man kneeling forward with the globe on top of his back. It symbolized the weight of the world upon his shoulders. In the background a faceless angel stood among rolling green hills, her wings outstretched, her arm pointing him forward. In the center of the canvas, at the bottom of the scene, a long, winding road disappeared into the horizon. The words *Rise Above* were signed in the lower-right-hand corner.

Aaron had, most poignantly, captured the essence of how he felt. That painting was the first of many and was the first step in his creative process of redefining himself from paralysis.

After he completed a series of pieces, I had multiple color copies made of all his artwork and set up a booth at the yearly Abilities Expo at the Los Angeles Conference Center. Listening to myself express the unembellished story of how the paintings were created and the significance of each image made me smile from deep within. Much to Aaron's surprise, I sold every piece.

Chapter 15:

Biking Forward

One day, while at the center, I noticed Aaron eyeballing a tandem bicycle that was hanging on a back-office wall. He asked Taylor if it was rideable. After they talked about it for a few minutes, two of the therapy assistants came over and pulled it down off the wall for further examination. Aaron then encouraged Taylor to take it outside to see if they could actually ride it together. Taylor laughed and said, "Mate, I'm not a bike rider, but I'll give it a go for you!"

Once Taylor was securely straddling the long, double-seated bicycle, I pushed Aaron's wheelchair to the rear side of the bike. An assistant and I hoisted his thin, limp body up and onto the tiny rear seat. We strapped his feet onto the pedals with Ace bandages and taped his hands to the handlebars with white cloth athletic tape. Once Taylor and Aaron were balanced and ready, I gave them a gentle push from behind. They pedaled forward, leaving me standing in awe.

Aaron's feeble arms could barely brace against the handlebars. Because of lack of torso strength, he tilted from side to side. But he was able to remain safely on the back of the bike for about five monumental minutes.

Once stopped, with an excitement similar to taking his first steps in the pool, Aaron declared, "Toots, you're next! Together we can ride this thing!"

"You bet! I'll ride with ya, Buddy!" I confidently said back.

As I unwrapped his feet and hands, we began brainstorming on how we would set the bike and ourselves up to be able to ride it. I had never ridden a tandem, but I wasn't afraid. Once again, my ability was going to enable Aaron to do something he otherwise wouldn't be able to do.

The truth was I was more afraid of standing still and not taking the risk than I was of the enormous undertaking on a tandem bicycle. Yes. I would handle it.

In Tandem

I wrote a proposal for the local bike shop, outlining the benefit of the exposure the shop would receive if they donated a tandem bicycle to a mother and son, who was a recovering quadriplegic. In another show of the grand mystery of the universe and timing, the sales manager of a bike company, KHS, happened to be standing behind me while I was giving my pitch to the owner of the shop. He came around beside me, handed me his card, and said, "Come to our warehouse. I have something for you."

Aaron and I were presented with our first KHS golden-orange-and-black tandem bicycle the very next day.

Fear comes from uncertainty. When we are absolutely certain, we are almost impervious to fear.

Recovery was a daunting, endless endeavor with improvements in tiny, mostly unrecognizable gains. Aaron needed periodic wins to keep him engaged in the long-term process. These wins also helped my engagement and flamed my motivation to tackle whatever I needed to propel us forward. They became a series of meaningful stepping stones on our climb of a seemingly insurmountable mountain.

The tandem bike presented an opportunity to put all the hard work in motion, to take all the gains realized inside the walls of the gym to the great expanse of the outside, with wind in our faces and hair.

A quest that began with a functional electrical stimulation (FES) bike that sparked movement through FES to artificially generate body movements, and progressed to a variety of adaptive cycling modalities, brought us to a pivotal day. Seated in the back of our SUV, with the tailgate up, we found ourselves staring at the long double-seater tandem bicycle. Giddiness soon evaporated as the reality of just getting on the long, heavy beast set in.

Captain and Stoker

In theory, we had painstakingly made our plan. Now was the time for execution. An unexpected surge of self-doubt came over me, casting uncertainty on being able to ride the thing. My hands were cold and wet from nervousness and were visibly shaking. Seeing my body and hands shake caught Aaron off guard, sending him into severe unease. He was completely dependent on me and my ability to maneuver the bike safely. Instead of commiserating, or showing empathy toward me, he began to shout, "Toots, you can ride this thing! Come on! Stop acting like you can't!" He admonished the obvious fear and lack of confidence I couldn't hide. "Now take my arm and help me step over the bike, and knock it the hell off," he growled, as I stood stiffly beside him.

My initial reaction was to fight back, but somehow, in what I was perceiving as cruelty, I knew he was right. Instead of feeling bruised and hurt, I used his harshness to fuel my ability. It was imperative I navigate the bike with strength and confidence. I had to find a way to keep us upright. I demanded it of myself, and I found within me a treasure trove of willpower I wasn't aware of or connected to until then. Again, my *Why* superseded my *cannot*.

"Strength does not come from physical capacity. It comes
from indomitable will."
~ MAHATMA GANDHI

The tandem bicycle was a strict, unforgiving professor who handed out a punishing workload every time we were on it. The process of getting on the bike was tenuous and laborious. Although Aaron continued to experience low blood pressure, needing to wear an abdominal binder and compression stockings, he was able to stand upright with a little assistance and ankle bracing. I would hold his arm, bracing him, as he took a single step over the bike frame, lying on its side. Still holding on to his hand, I circled to the front and pulled the bike upright with the handlebars. Aaron then grabbed his set of handlebars with his stronger (left) hand while I swung my leg over the front seat. The steps had to be taken swiftly and in complete concert with each other.

Starting off was the most precarious. We stood tall and stiffly with our feet flat on the ground, straddling the bike frame. I gave a firm squeeze on the brakes, positioned our right feet into the pedal cage, and then, with a synchronized choreography and one-two-three count, all in one motion, we pushed off to initiate just enough forward momentum to coast for ten to fifteen feet. While coasting, Aaron boosted himself up onto his seat and adjusted his feet in the cages. His necessary actions caused the bike to wobble and sway from side to side, making it extremely difficult to keep it upright. From the moment I took hold of the handlebars until the moment we dismounted, my knuckles were white, my hands and forearms numb and throbbing from the intense gripping and isometric hold.

Our rides initially lasted no more than five minutes as Aaron's weak torso would collapse into my back. After a number of these five-minute sessions, we slowly increased the time. After a while, I felt I had the bike and our effort under control, even when Aaron would collapse into my back.

A Dumb Crash

One day I held the handlebars so tight I lost all sensation in my hands and forearms. As we were approaching our car, I couldn't lift my fingers off the handlebar to pull the brake lever. As we got closer to our car, Aaron began yelling at me to stop, but I couldn't press the brake. I couldn't turn the handlebars . . . and I ran us straight into the back of our car.

My adrenaline was pumping furiously, and I immediately burst into tears, fearing I had hurt Aaron further. He couldn't brace himself against the fall in any way, and he fell like a tree trunk. Lying there, I felt irresponsible and downright foolish for taking such a risk with him. He assured me he was OK, but that we had to get better at communicating. This mishap had nothing to do with communication; it had everything to do with my ability.

Once we realized we weren't hurt, while still under the bike, we burst into laughter, replaying the scene of my steering us directly into the back of the car. That one would have made for a viral video if caught on camera!

I had a lot of riding and training to do to safely navigate the tandem, which felt like steering a semitruck. I was the workhorse—in tandem terms, the captain, and Aaron the stoker. Although he didn't produce much power, his effort was always 100 percent. His background as a motocross racer gave him the authority to direct our effort. I bristled initially at his barking of directions: "Up a gear, brake, turn right, turn left, down a gear!" All these orders were in staccato tones. There were many times when I wanted to jump off the bike and send Aaron and the bike off a cliff.

Did I often despise the efforts and feelings of inadequacy while trying to improve his condition and our tragic circumstances? You better believe I did. It felt like a living hell—purgatory. I can't count the nights I would go to sleep hoping I would not wake up—and be fully pissed off when I did.

But, I loved my son and my demand for a better life more.

Perspective Shift

In those heated, teeth-clenching moments I would also try, as best as I could, to understand how he must have felt behind me. Aaron's body had been able to do anything he asked of it, and do it well. He was masterful with movement, strong, capable, and graceful. It was almost too much for me to process when I thought about how he must have felt in his new body compared to the previous one. I realized that his commands gave him some sort of sense of control that he otherwise didn't have.

I listened, I learned, I executed . . . and I wanted to handle it. I was moving beyond the *me*-oriented world, broadening my sense of *me* into *we*.

These realizations were incredibly powerful and allowed me forgiveness and empathy. I found it imperative to always carry both perspectives.

Over time I became an athlete. I stretched and pushed myself in ways I otherwise wouldn't have. I know how instrumental I was in Aaron's ability and opportunity to recover, but he was equally vital to my personal evolution as well. I believe this equality was part of our becoming more than mother and son. We became a team . . . and began our rise—*together.*

~ *Me to We*

To see life through each other's perspectives is to embark on a quest for deeper understanding, a quest that transcends the confines of our individual stories. It allows you a stronger sense of empathy, compassion, respect, and common ground when faced with differences or disagreements. In this act of seeing and feeling, we bear witness to the joys and sorrows, triumphs and struggles that shape another's path, dismantling the barriers that divide us . . . discovering that together you are stronger than you ever could be alone.

TEAM: together each achieves more.

Just Don't Stop

Rain, wind, or shine, we were on the bike three to four committed days per week. Many days would find us lying in the back of the Ford Explorer, trying to muster the energy to begin and saying to one another, "Let's don't and say we did." We would laugh, then get up; we knew better than that. We were responsible for ourselves, and we would not let ourselves down.

> *It does not matter how slowly you go,*
> *as long as you do not stop.*

After many months of riding, we began to feel we were capable, solid riders. As we were feeling especially pleased with our effort one hot summer day, an elderly, overweight lady riding a creaky old beach cruiser, wearing sweatpants and flip-flops, passed us without effort.

Argggggghhh, hell no! We couldn't believe she passed us! Our heads went down, pushing the pedals even harder, both of us cursing out loud. Our previous moments of self-satisfaction had vanished. The tandem always had a way of showing us we had to stay on it, without reprieve.

Keep your head down and eyes up.

Balboa Park served as our training ground for about two years. We were ready and fit enough to take our riding to new ground. We needed new scenery. Aaron also needed a new goal. Progression was key to continue moving forward. Knowing this still didn't prepare me for what was to come next.

LA Marathon

One day Aaron saw a billboard advertising the Los Angeles

Marathon. He yelled from the back seat, "Hey, Toots, how 'bout we ride the 2003 LA Marathon!"

Just as I was starting to find my footing and confidence in my ability to handle the tandem, Aaron dropped this bombshell! I felt a surge of fear rise in my throat, nearly choking me. My inner mind-talk yelled, "WHAT! That's 26.2 miles! We're just now able to complete ten miles! How in the world am I going to navigate a ride like that, for that many miles, and with thousands of other people!" As though it were an out-of-body experience or someone else's voice, I heard, "Well, okay, why not? Let's do it," come confidently out of my mouth.

Even the thought of this felt darn near impossible. In my commitment to Aaron and whatever challenge he needed, I said yes, and then figured out how to do it later. I knew my outward response concealed my inner feeling, but that was critical to Aaron having confidence in me, and therefore having confidence in himself. But, oh my goodness gracious, 26.2 miles in the LA Marathon!

To prepare for the marathon, we needed new training grounds that provided hills, turns, and technical riding conditions. Aaron researched routes out of a Thomas Guide. Without the safety and certainty of Balboa Park, we pedaled along rural streets, citrus fields, and the undulating Pacific Coast Highway in Malibu. Not having any aid or alternate route served to sharpen our focus even more and thickened our skin. One way in, one way out. Handle it—there is no other option.

I believe when you don't give yourself any options, other than what you've made a decision to do, you're more likely to achieve whatever it is you have intended.

On a dark, cold, mid-March morning, in downtown Los Angeles, we pedaled our tandem bicycle to the starting line, lining up with hundreds of other cyclists. From the outside looking in, Aaron's limitations weren't visible. The only difference between us and the others was our demeanor. There was lighthearted laughing, talking, joking, and poking going on among the other riders that didn't penetrate our silent, determined concentration. We had the outward countenance of Olympic athletes preparing for the most important event of their lives. Nothing or no one could break our focus.

Up until that time, we hadn't ridden with anyone else, and here we were handlebar to handlebar with throngs of other cyclists. A sense of raw power swept over me, replacing the nauseating butterflies and fearful doubt I'd had the days before the race.

> *Courage (kə-rij), noun: a willingness and strength to do*
> *things that frighten us, to be brave in the face of hardship*
> *and harness the drive to keep moving forward and overcome*
> *our fears.*

We counted *one*, *two*, *three*, and pushed off into the frantic scene, dodging other cyclists. My riding position was always a bit hunched over to gain better control of the long, heavy, wobbling tandem. But this time, I went into attack mode, leaning over into the handlebars even more. I grunted and growled with each pedal stroke as Aaron gave the proper cues to shift, turn, and brake. The adrenaline pumping through our veins kept us oscillating between fight and flight.

The time and miles ticked by at a surreal pace. In seemingly no time, we were nearing the finish line as the morning sun came up, shining bright into our scrunched, sweaty faces. Aaron let out a yelp of delight: "We did it, Toots!"

After navigating through the hay bales to a nearby open grass area, we came to a stop, dismounting the bike. My exhaustion was accompanied by heady elation. The words of the neurosurgeon, some years back, were loud in my ears—*Your son has a one-in-a-million chance of ever regaining any type of function . . .*

As we gave one another a grateful hug, he whispered in my ear,

"Thank you, Toots, for your commitment and for never leaving my side." With my voice breaking, I tearfully said back, "I thank you for wanting to work so hard, for giving it everything you've got and for wanting me to do it with you."

Perhaps the greatest test of love is the way we act in times of need. It's the moment of accountability that all relationships seem to arc toward.

The level of success you achieve, in anything you do, will be in direct proportion to the depth of your commitment and actions.

~ *Reflection*

While observing the passing scenery from the passenger seat, my spirit soaring and imagination running rampant on a cherished road trip, trucking with my daddy, he would occasionally ask me if I wanted to continue traveling the interstate highway or take, what my young mind had named, the "Woolly Road." The Woolly Road always, always being my preference. Two-laned, narrow, hilly, winding stretches of blacktop, nary another vehicle in sight, cutting through desolate Indian reservations, rural townships, or barren unforgiving open landscapes, added a sense of mystery to what I deemed an adventure. Unlike the more predictable interstate, you never knew what surprise or peril you might encounter around every new bend. The Woolly Road, the road less traveled, by nature, was where I was most comfortable and alive.

Chapter 16

The Man inside the Helmet

A few weeks after our successful completion of the Los Angeles Marathon, the City of Los Angeles awarded us a plaque of recognition, saluting and recognizing our unique mother-and-son relationship and achievement. This was followed with a lengthy newspaper article that summarized our backstory and our unlikely endeavor aboard the tandem bicycle. Our story began to generate interest.

Taylor told us about a fitness conference where he was invited to speak about his work with disabling conditions. He asked us if we would be willing to be a part of his presentation. He wanted us to share our perspectives on recovery from injury. We ended up creating and rehearsing a unique three-part keynote presentation titled "The Man inside the Helmet."

The three of us had a special dynamic, sharing from a clinician's, client's, and mother's points of view.

Taylor spoke clinically about exercise science and the biomechanics of human movements—and how, given the proper components for healing, the body can be repaired or improved. He also emphasized the importance of his role as an educator while working with Aaron or other clients. A saying he always shared was, "If I give you a fish you will eat for a day. If I teach you how to fish, you will eat for a lifetime. However, if I teach you to think, then you won't have to eat fish every day."

Aaron spoke from his experience as an injured athlete, talking about how he does what he does and what he feels in the process. He brought the audience into better understanding of his condition while speaking of his analogy on walking:

"Would you like to know what it is like for me to relearn how to walk? It's like walking on your hands. Imagine the concentration, strength, endurance, balance, and coordination it takes to walk upside down on your hands. Now, imagine walking down the hall, across the grass, and up and then down the stairs . . . on your hands. That's what I feel now, standing here, trying to make that happen."

I shared my vital role as a facilitator—and how, without this type of full support, any functional gains or improvements would likely be compromised. I explained: "It truly does not matter how hot an inner fire might burn after one has suffered a debilitating injury. Without support and assistance their desires or hopes may not be realized."

Speaking invitations began coming on a regular basis and were often given to audiences filled with doctors, scientists, researchers, and therapists during a time when improving from a spinal cord injury like Aaron's was rare and not understood. Our story flew in the face of accepted norms; we shared a process and a commitment to healing that the antiquated textbooks did not speak about. Invariably, someone from the audience would say, "Aaron is a miracle!"

I would reply, "The actual miracle is found in the work."

Guinea Pig

I pushed for Aaron to be used as a subject in every pertinent research study California State University, Northridge, had to offer. The most notable was a twelve-month study on the effects of therapeutic exercise on spinal cord injury:

> A midtest and posttest revealed a marked improvement in cardiovascular endurance, muscular strength and endurance, range of motion, balance, gait mechanics, flexibility, posture, total body weight, fat-free mass, and motivation toward exercise. Furthermore, the client demonstrated an improvement in functional ability, independence, and self-efficacy. Aaron has not experienced any of the degenerative changes and secondary complications that typically accompany incomplete quadriplegia since he started his formal exercise and nutrition program. Thus, exercise therapy may positively affect individuals with incomplete quadriplegia. However, adherence to exercise without the aid of a fitness specialist needs to be further investigated, in order to determine the continued benefits of a therapeutic exercise program.[*]

Our involvement in these studies helped shape our feeling of participation in something much greater than ourselves, making the journey we were on feel important and necessary.

These studies, funded by the university, also gave me a reassuring sense of not leaving a stone unturned in Aaron's recovery process, giving him every opportunity for improvements and better management, something I was constantly up against with so little financial means.

Taylor submitted his work with Aaron to a contest run by MET-Rx, an international nutritional supplement company. One year later, on a main stage in San Diego, California, the three of us accepted the MET-Rx World's Best Trainer and Client Award for Outstanding Transformation.

---

[*] Taylor-Kevin Isaacs, MS, CPT, CSCS, California State University, Northridge. Summary of "The Physiological and Psychosocial Effect of Exercise and Nutrition on a Male Incomplete Quadriplegic."

Sharing the Journey

Aaron and I then began to share our story on our own, speaking with newly injured patients, family members, doctors, and therapists. We spoke about "the power of possibility" and the necessity of a prognosis that planted seeds of hope rather than the dire one I was given. We encouraged the medical professionals to talk about the long, critical list of secondary complications that occur if one doesn't engage in an aggressive therapeutic program.

Aaron was brilliant at helping one feel the effects of paralysis with an outstanding demonstration, which he would invite the audience to perform:

"Place your hand on a flat surface, tuck all your fingers except the ring finger, and then try to lift the ring finger. . . . You simply cannot lift it, no matter how hard you try. This is what trying to move a paralyzed body or limb feels like," Aaron explained.

We were careful to not share our message in a way that it could be misconstrued with false hope, as every injury is unique, every injured body responds differently, and every family dynamic is unlike any other. Our undeviating message was that by challenging the patient's condition with a positive mindset, and a consistent, dedicated approach to recovery, you open the doors to your own unlimited possibilities, therefore enhancing and improving the quality of life.

> **"On stage we found a purpose as the spotlight exposed our greatest vulnerabilities; our story was a reflection for so many others. The authentic connections we made by sharing our struggles gave us further meaning to an otherwise ambiguous cycle of pain and suffering. My process of recovery began to give me a whole new level of identity, and I became emboldened in my abilities."**
> **~ AARON BAKER, *THE REBELLIOUS RECOVERY***

While talking during a presentation on stage about our tandem cycling success, Aaron turned to me and blurted out, "Hey, Toots, if we can ride in marathons and all-over Southern California's coastal and back roads, how 'bout we just keep riding, Forrest Gump–style, and ride across the country!"

I stared blankly into the crowded, hushed audience . . . yet fully aware of what my response would be. My boy had a way of pushing me out of my comfort zones like no one else could! One side of me knowing if I did not, then he could not, the other contrasting side thrilled with the notion of being on the open road, living on the edge of ability and purpose.

Suddenly a cross-country ride seemed very doable. My exact words, echoing my initial response to the first marathon announcement, after a few awkward moments of contemplation were: "Heck yeah, Aaron! Of course! Let's do it!" I punctuated my excitement with a fist pump in the air.

At that precise moment a cross-country bicycle tour idea was born.

~ *Reflection*

Between the ages of eleven and thirteen, I lived for summer vacation. For two weeks each of those three summers, I was reunited with my daddy, on the road, traversing states, cross-country, in a big-rig semitruck. In those days handwritten logbooks served as the accounting for drive time, and they could be manipulated as needed. Dad was known in the industry and among his driving cronies to be one of the fastest on the road and the first to deliver the goods. One early two a.m. morning, me sitting shotgun, fighting sleep, thinking I was helping him stay awake by staying awake myself, I heard him calling out on the CB radio to a couple of buddies on the road with us. Up ahead was a highway scale that he wanted to run through, as losing time at the scale would keep him from being first on the

dock the following day. I was filled with nervous excitement along with teeth-clenching fear as I realized what was being set up. Three seventy-foot big-rig trucks, one in front, one behind, with Dad driving just on the outside of them, in the middle, so close together that the running lights lining the sides of the long trailers appeared to be sparks of fire, from my view in the rear mirror. The wickedly roaring steel-and-chrome beasts rolled on. One tiny miscalculation would result in a fiery, tangled pile of metal and rubber carnage. As we all approached the scale, like a parting of the waters, the front and back trucks pulled in as Dad hammered down even harder, gaining with accelerated speed, daringly flying past the unsuspecting scale attendant. With both hands full of steering wheel, Dad, throwing back his handsome head, his infectious laugh coming from deep within and out through his wide-open mouth, looked over at me and said, "That's how it's done." I was consumed with blood-pumping exhilaration, giving a fist pump in the air back, breathlessly exclaiming, "When do we get to do it again!"

This gutsy, audacious, wildly thrilling, seemingly death-defying maneuver introduced and connected me to another aspect of myself: a deep love of adventure with an outlaw spirit, fearlessly living on the edge.

Chapter 17:

Torn in the Middle

Between working and being entertained by her musician boyfriend, Arielle was mostly away from our home as time went on. Our isolation and daily grind were in complete opposition to her high-profile life filled with music and touring. I knew she still couldn't accept the hard facts and limitations of Aaron's injury.

She missed her brother and me, but at the same time, she couldn't leave soon enough. I wasn't the fun-loving, adventurous mom and friend I had been. I didn't allow myself diversions. Diversions, I believed, would weaken my focus or allow longing for a different life to set in. It felt like window-shopping: If you can't buy, then why even bother? I had self-imposed blinders affixed to my mind. Perhaps this mindset fostered denial and kept me from being fully aware of just how deep Arielle's drug problem was getting.

Denial is the protector, the security blanket and shock
absorber for the soul until the time comes when you are able
to handle reality.

Normally I talked to her every day or every other day to check in. Our "Hi, how are you, I love you" provided some comfort for a little while. After four days of no communication, fear set in. I called her, but she didn't answer. I then drove to the apartment she shared with her boyfriend. She opened the door and quickly came out, shutting the door behind her. I didn't recognize the person standing in front of me. Disheveled and wild-eyed, her typically exquisite, dewy skin broken out with bumps, she growled, "Mom, I'm an addict. Yes, Mom, I'm a drug addict." She implored me to accept it. In sickened disbelief, I moved backward, giving a barely audible, "I'll be back."

Another Rehab

I went back about an hour later with Aaron and their father, who happened to be, auspiciously, visiting again. I told them that Arielle was in serious trouble; we needed to move her out of the apartment and get her into treatment that day. Somehow I felt I could bulldoze my way into making her see she needed help and that we were there to help her. This wasn't how to successfully navigate a path to sobriety. Logic escaped me, replaced with a primordial force dictating my emotions and informing my decisions. These were my decisions, not hers.

We did in fact pack up the apartment and Arielle that very day, leaving her shocked but silent boyfriend behind. We removed her from the apartment as she screamed, "What are you doing! I hate you! I'm not going with you! You really think you can just come in and take over my life!"

She continued to resist, refusing to go. We had to literally manhandle her, roll her up in a rug, and carry her out to our awaiting car. A forced intervention. We rushed to the nearest hospital. A nurse in the hospital emergency room sternly reminded me that our method of intervention would not work on someone with addiction issues.

> *The worst part about anything that's self-destructive is that it's so intimate. You become so close with your addictions and*

*illnesses that leaving them behind is like killing the part of
yourself that taught you how to survive.*

I know from my own experience with alcoholism that changes are
made when you are ready. No one can alter the course of addiction but
the addict. I knew this, but my heart refused to listen or cooperate.

Once Arielle was stabilized, we brought her to our house. While
she was sleeping, Aaron, Dan, and I decided it would be best if we
took her to a treatment program in Sacramento, where Dan lived.
She would be away from Los Angeles and all her known influences,
but near family.

We all drove to Sacramento. After identifying what we believed
was the best program for Arielle, we informed her of what her
next step was. "Sis, I want you back. I miss you," Aaron said while
holding her hands.

"This program will help you understand why you feel the need
to medicate your feelings. It'll provide you with new tools to help
you manage your problems better," a hopeful me explained.

"You'll see. After just a few days you are going to start feeling
better about everything," Dan added.

After three days we had exhausted her fight. I know she gave in
to escape our continuous barrage of encouragement and explanations
of why she should go.

To give in does not mean you have given up.

Every Saturday the treatment center held a family day. On Fri-
days I would finish the day with Aaron, get him set up for a night
and day alone with Andy, then leave at 7:00 p.m. for the five-hour
drive to Sacramento.

On my first family day I found Arielle distant and removed.
It felt as though she and I were strangers. She was still protesting

being there, using her limited calling ability to talk to her boyfriend in Los Angeles.

After spending the afternoon with her, I felt I had lost my daughter. Though I was filled with thoughts about what I could have done differently, I knew in my heart there was no other way for me to have handled the situation.

~ *Hindsight*

 *Hindsight offers us a vantage point from which we can survey our journey, armed with the knowledge that comes only from the intersection of time and reflection. Hindsight is always twenty-twenty, crystal-clear vision. Remember, you did the best you could with the knowledge you had at that time. It's so easy to look back at an event and see a better choice or pathway, because we've already learned from our experience. Hindsight happens after the lesson, so we cannot condemn ourselves for not knowing the lesson before we learned it.*

My drive back home was filled with sorrow, guilt, doubt, and helplessness. The thirsty fiend always perched on my shoulder was screaming in my ear, exerting its influence. "C'mon, Laquita, one drink and everything will feel better, you know it will!" The voice of my alcoholism wanted to exploit my weakness and provide a solution to cope with my anguish.

I pulled over to the side of the freeway to gain control over the duel going on in my head. I acknowledged that this was not my thought, but rather a manifestation of addiction. I questioned the rationale it presented and countered it with objective thoughts and the bitter consequences. The voice's influence over me slowly diminished. I brushed my hair back, took a deep breath, smiled inside at my achievement, and got back on the freeway.

Through my purposed decisions I assert authority over the fiend's seducing whispers. It fluctuates in volume, but never fully disappears.

Breakthrough

The following Saturday during our family meeting at the treatment center, Arielle had written me a letter that she read out loud to the group of visitors and residents. She expressed her pain that resulted from her childhood. She expressed her feelings of being shut out, forgotten by me after her brother was hurt. Logically she understood why I was absent, but to her inner self the reasons were irrelevant. Her words stung me to the depths of my soul, but I knew she needed to release these suppressed feelings.

The letter allowed her to expose her vulnerability, giving her a safe stage to share what she held inside. It then gave us the opportunity to talk to one another in an open and honest way.

> *If we could look into each other's hearts and understand the unique challenges each of us face, I think we could treat each other much more gently, with more love, patience, tolerance, and care.*

Previously impenetrable walls began crumbling as we stood in the driveway, holding one another in an embrace that caused my knees to weaken. I didn't want to let her go. She didn't want to let me go.

As I drove off, the reflection in my rearview mirror was my daughter standing a little straighter, seeming a little more accessible, more loving, blowing me a kiss. We were going to make it. We were going to be alright. She was going to be alright. Relief and hope began replacing despair and hopelessness.

I began to see the similarities of recovery from spinal cord injury and recovery from alcoholism and addiction: take one baby step at a time, one day at a time, keep yourself on course, hold very true to each one.

> **"God, grant me the serenity to accept the things I cannot change, the courage to change the things I can, and the wisdom to know the difference."**
>
> ~ SERENITY PRAYER

Chapter 18:

Crossroads

Aaron had worked himself into serious exhaustion. We had spent years with blinders on, operating in a self-imposed bubble. Our life revolved around his rehab, cycling schedule, and occasional presentations. He needed a break—a break from rehab, a break from the daily grind, a break from me. I needed one as well, but this was the very thing that uprooted me and filled me with fear. As long as I was with Aaron, I felt like everything was under control. When I wasn't with him, I felt the injury had control over him and our tenuous life.

The task is not to control the wind, but to direct the movements of the ship so that it stays on course.

He began questioning where all the work he was doing was leading him, as nothing solid or concrete was forming yet. Our vision of a gym center, born on our first day at the Center of Achievement, was still just a dream that wasn't manifesting or even seeming possible. The cross-country bicycle idea was an outlandish undertaking that also felt delusional.

We trained for and spoke about both endeavors as though they were happening, causing us to doubt our mental stability. Aaron questioned his life with me, his pursuits, and his goals.

At that point he could have chosen to move out with a friend. Although it would have been possible, it would have hampered his ongoing improvement drastically, potentially sending him into functional regression. Our visions would have to be given up as well if he headed off in another direction.

I was torn about how to support his needs for independence.

~ *The Dance*

In the delicate dance of facilitating, there exists a fine line between nurturing and suffocating, providing support and being overpowering. It is a thought-provoking tightrope walk to find the perfect balance of attentiveness. It is in the art of attunement that we discover the delicate harmony between offering assistance and respecting autonomy. In this equilibrium, both the facilitator and the recipient find comfort, a sanctuary where independence and support can coexist and where healing can truly thrive.

One day, searching for inspiration, I suggested we take a drive to visit the Olympic Training Center in Chula Vista, California. I thought that looking at images of accomplished athletes and feeling the energy of the grounds they trained on would lift his exhausted, waning spirit. We sat, relatively silent, while we toured the grounds in a golf cart. At the time, our being there did not make any sense, but some years later it would.

Shortly thereafter, he decided to visit his dear friend, Brian, who lived in Las Vegas. Brian had also suffered a spinal cord injury as a young teenager. Brian was a self-made, successful businessman and an immense inspiration to Aaron. After only a few days of being with Brian, Aaron called me to say he and Brian were going to Hawaii. Excitement and fear all rolled up into a confusing mess . . . for me. Aaron hadn't been on a solo trip since before his injury many years prior. I was filled with all the what-ifs that could happen to him. We had been working all this time on his reclaiming his independence. The time had come for him to take those vital steps forward, but it was me that wasn't ready.

While Aaron was away, I received the dreaded phone call I knew could come at any time. The home we were renting had sold, just as the previous one had. This meant I had thirty days to find another. The degree of difficulty in finding a homeowner to say yes to me felt like more than I could manage, especially when coupled with Aaron being away and on the precipice of a potential major change in direction.

The LIFT

As I was lying in bed with the covers over my head, the phone rang. I feigned happiness, answering the phone in a manner that I didn't think revealed my distress. My aunt, however, immediately picked up on my facade. She was keeping in closer contact with me after she and her husband from Phoenix, Arizona, had come to watch us ride in the LA Marathon.

Up to that point I had been alone in managing our life after injury. All my family lived in Oklahoma. My mother had passed away not long after Aaron's injury. My best friend was in Carmel, and I had not been in the state of mind to make new friends in Southern California.

I didn't share the specifics of our hardships or the mind-bending difficulties Aaron, Arielle, and I faced. I tried to paint a brighter picture when I talked to anyone on the phone, sometimes even telling fibs about my personal life to make it seem better than it was. The fibs were also a tactic for diversion from the obvious. I absolutely did not want to hear myself talking about the realities out loud nor did I want to answer the inevitable questions. I felt like I was protecting us by keeping it to myself.

During the phone call, my aunt lovingly broke through my

barriers a little. I disclosed vague details about Aaron's current crossroads and the unexpected news of our home being sold, forcing me to find a new place to live, once again.

She proposed an invitation: if she arranged an airline ticket, would I spend the weekend with her in Phoenix. I accepted.

Our visit was cathartic, filled with understanding and care. As we sat on the floor in her walk-in closet, engaged in more transparent conversation about my circumstances, Aunt Neta urged me to find a townhome suitable for our needs. She and Uncle Rick wanted to help me with the purchase so we could have the security of a home.

My aunt and uncle were pillars of support with their love and ongoing assistance, filling my steps forward with more confidence. They eased our financial pressures, illustrating the power of compassion and unity—exemplifying how, together, we can overcome any adversity.

I came to realize that the most meaningful way to express my gratitude for the magnitude of their involvement was to demonstrate the indelible impact they had on our lives through the success of our ongoing efforts.

"Thousands of candles can be lighted from a single candle,
and the life of the candle will not be shortened."

~ BUDDHA

Chapter 19

Stay the Course

Aaron returned from Hawaii with renewed vigor and sense of direction. It was liberating and critically important for him to realize he did have options, giving his self-confidence a hefty boost. He was no longer bound by the sense of needing assistance. If he chose to do so, he could live on his own, but he chose not to. He chose to stay the course we had planned out.

With the backing from my aunt and uncle, I found a lovely, accessible, small townhome just north of the university, where we continued the daily therapy. It was surrounded by bicycling paths, which made our time allotted to the bike more efficient. Many days we would ride right out of our garage.

The fresh environment and a home to call our own invigorated both of us. We began to find laughter again. Our endeavors began to make sense to us without feeling quite so unreachable.

Aaron mocked up a gym center with the name "Center of Rehabilitative Exercise" across the top of the building. He also mocked up a tour bus with flames emblazoned across the sides of a forty-foot bus that would see us across the country on the bicycle tour we had earlier declared.

A few years back, Aaron, Taylor, and I sat at our kitchen table designing what would become the cornerstone imagery of our logo,

a phoenix rising from the ashes and forming the *o* in the word "of."
We hadn't landed on a name for the tour at that point, but we knew
the phoenix logo would be a prominent part of the name.

I made enlarged color copies of the two images and displayed
them in our office where they served as a visual reminder. The chosen
departure date, June 10, 2005, was written in bold black letters on
a white dry-erase board that hung on the wall.

In a which-came-first-the-chicken-or-the-egg contemplation, we
decided to launch the bicycle tour first. We believed that the tour
would be a high-profile event and serve as a marketing campaign
for the gym.

The tour was to showcase the "power of possibility," and the gym
to provide the critically necessary services for improving quality of
life. In theory the goals were brilliant. The problem was we didn't
have the funds to do either. Big dreams, big ambitions, big valid rea-
sons for necessity . . . but no money. And that was a BIG stop block.

Chapter 20:

Pedaling with Purpose

The demands of pedaling became easier for us to tolerate when we began thinking of our pedaling as pedaling for those who could not. Each pedal stroke took on a greater sense of importance. The future on the bike wasn't clear, but somehow we knew it was leading us to something of great significance.

Aaron drew from his racing days. He created a proposal for the tour, similar to his racing proposals for sponsorship. I set about selling the proposed tour to potential sponsors. We envisioned company logos newspapering the sides and back of our bus, providing great exposure for the company and showcasing their human-interest-driven support.

I convinced myself that the sheer novelty of our endeavor would be of interest to everyone, especially with the components of a mother with her son who was a recovering quadriplegic.

I quickly discovered that was not the case. People would listen, captivated, and offer enthusiastic praise, but had no interest in financial contribution. Our proposed undertaking seemed too precarious, perilous, and downright reckless to most, with a slim-to-none likelihood of being able to actually complete it.

The first date we declared for the tour came and went. The second date, a year later, did as well. We were disappointed, but not disillusioned . . . no, no, this was far too important to let go of. Our vision helped us make sense of all that had happened . . . giving it purpose. Purpose gave us fortitude stronger than what we had been through.

We continued on with dogged persistence, using the naysayers as motivation.

The Tour

Finally, we did it! Through the success of our fundraising efforts and securing a few sponsors, our tour was ready to commence, three years after declaring our intention. I was confident in my ability to ride the distance, but I also needed to manage the tour; secure fundraising events and speaking engagements at hospitals, rehab centers, and universities; and arrange sponsorship appearances and media coverage.

We decided we needed to assemble a team that would include two riders who could manage the captain's seat—my seat. This was a tall order to fill, as Aaron had to have complete faith in their ability to handle him and the bike . . . while I had to accept stepping back.

Aaron called on several of his best childhood friends. They all enthusiastically wanted to join him for the proposed three-month adventure. Two weeks before departure we decided the name we'd been calling the tour didn't appropriately capture the magnitude or spirit of it.

Aaron used the phrase "Rise Above" often in the gym and while riding the bike. He wrote "Rise Above" in the bottom corner of his first art piece. It soon became clear the most fitting name was the Rise Above Tour. The name encapsulated the very essence of our journey up and out of the ashes. The phoenix logo created the *o* in *Above*, becoming the prominent focal point.

At midnight, several days before departure, I drove to the tour bus, freshly wrapped, sitting underneath the bright lights that lit up the industrial complex. The red, orange, and yellow flames on the mocked-up version of the bus that had hung in our office for three years had become letters spelling "Rise Above Tour." The letters danced in blazing hues, giving the entire bus a raw energy that suggested power and hope. As I stood in awe, gazing through tear-filled eyes, I was stunned by the juxtaposition of the image. I remembered the fiery scene of the distant farmhouse I'd come upon the night I received the phone call informing me of Aaron's accident. We had come so far. A sense of victory swept over me—built with the fire of our adversities.

Stand

Possibility

Initiate

Part 4   **Reason**

Intention

Transform

"The mystery of human existence lies not in just
staying alive, but in finding something
to live for."

~ FYODOR DOSTOEVSKY

Chapter 21:

Go Time: The Rise Above Tour

Rise Above Tour—Credo, Our Purpose for Pedaling:

> They ride for those who can't . . . they ride for those who suffer, to create a force of spirit that finds its way into the hearts and minds of our fellow man. The Rise Above Tour aspires to inspire all individuals to the limitless power of what is humanly obtainable through dedication, commitment, perseverance, and most importantly . . . LOVE!

June 10, 2007

Arielle and I drove south alongside the Rise Above Tour bus, heading to Dog Beach in San Diego. Aaron had purchased maps specific to cycling the route he chose. The southern route across the US was the flattest, having the least amount of elevated terrain of all coast-to-coast routes. The ride entailed 3,182 miles, passing through California, Arizona, New Mexico, Texas, Louisiana, Mississippi, and Alabama before ending in the sand in Saint Augustine, Florida.

As we drove into the park at Dog Beach, we were greeted by a large crowd of friends, and friends of friends, plus our beloved friends from Carmel, Lynn and Ed. Aunt Sonja from Oklahoma was there with a friend of hers . . . along with some curious bystanders. The energy was electric, with smiles, high fives, and hugs filling the sunny atmosphere.

I found Aaron lying in the back bedroom of the bus, tears filling his eyes, his mouth twisting as I sat down to join him. He was reflecting on how far he'd come. Eight years earlier he'd been bound to a hospital bed, paralyzed from the chin down. Today he was about to set off on an epic three-month bicycle journey. Tears streamed down his cheeks as he recalled a memory of a morphine-induced dream he'd had while in the ICU. His dream was about having long, wild hair and smoothly shaven legs, wearing tight spandex shorts, pedaling a bicycle around the world. Other than the long hair, he was now living that dream. With a hoarse, cracking voice, Aaron told me once again, "Thank you for never leaving my side, Toots."

Smiling, I said back to him, "Buddy, thank you for giving me a reason to stay."

The tour team, Taylor, Arielle, Dan, Aaron, and I, all gathered around the table in the front of the bus. Taylor gave an impassioned pep talk about our path of recovery over the past eight years. We talked about road perils and potential personal breakdowns due to intense physical effort, drawing on our experiences that had brought us to this point. Just carry on, one pedal stroke at a time, one mile, one day at a time. The nervousness gave way to sheer unbridled excitement as we ended the roundtable discussion, stood up, placed our hands together, and chanted, "One . . . two . . . three . . . Rise Above!"

It was go time.

Stepping Back

I watched Adam hold Aaron's hand as Aaron carefully stepped over the tandem bicycle frame. Aaron and I caught one another's eyes.

Our familiar gaze articulated a depth of understanding beyond words. We both squinted, nodded, and raised fists in the air as he and Adam pedaled off.

Standing back was an unfamiliar role for me. I had been in front, on the bike and otherwise. I drew from my unwavering belief in Aaron and in our chosen path while watching him pedal away. Every step we had taken, every mile we had ridden, was in pursuit of progress—and this was progress.

I stood there until they disappeared from my sight. Arielle came up and put her arms around me. She said, "Let's go, Mom," and drove us home.

I managed the tour from home, intent on making every mile count. Speaking engagements were scheduled in every major city across the route. In Phoenix, Arizona, the bus rolled up to a news station like it contained rock stars, to an awaiting news anchorman. Each team member gave a live interview and invited locals to a restaurant in Scottsdale, where a gracious restaurateur opened her restaurant for an evening of celebration and fundraising.

Newspaper reporters met Aaron at camping sites along the way to document the story. I flew into various cities, traveling with the guys for one to two weeks at a time and joining Aaron during scheduled presentations. We would talk about our backstory, the purpose of the tour, and our mission to provide ongoing rehabilitative exercise for those who suffered disabling injury. The message back to us was always, "Are you going to build a C.O.R.E. (Center of Restorative Exercise) here? We need it too!" These validations fueled our reason and commitment.

Cross-Country Completion

The team experienced every level of difficulty one would expect on an undertaking such as the tour. Their spirits prevailed, though, seeing the tour safely to the shores of Saint Augustine, Florida, three months later. I flew to Saint Augustine to join them on that monumental final day. With arms interlocked, we walked barefoot to the country's easternmost edge, hugging and high-fiving. The air was filled with an energy of accomplishment and possibility. We had risen far beyond all that had been once thought impossible.

We celebrated in a parking lot with a small group of friends and family members who had flown in to support the team. Aaron was handed a bottle of champagne. He popped the cork and shook it, just as he had all those years before at his national championships aboard a motorcycle.

Aaron felt a new level of ability in both body and mind at the conclusion of the tour. He was more motivated than ever for his next phase of life.

We both shared hopeful enthusiasm . . . for a little while.

Sacred Acknowledgment

Somewhere along the desolate stretches of the Texas plains, Aaron had secretly submitted our story to a health organization looking for people who had dealt with adversity with a loved one in a positive way:

To Whom It May Concern,

My name is Aaron Baker, and I am writing on behalf of my fifty-one-year-old single mother, Laquita Dian. I believe Laquita should be recognized with this honor for her selfless acts of compassion and fortitude through adverse times. Looking back on her colorful collage of travel, work, and motherhood astounds the most common of strangers. It is the compassionate drive in her heart that steers her through dark days, overcoming personal loss, addiction, and physical adversity. Eight years ago, I broke my neck racing motorcycles, rendering me quadriplegic, having only a "one in a million" chance of ever moving my body again. At the time, my family was enjoying the fruits of independent success in our respective professions . . . until my accident threw everything off. My mother, Laquita, completely dropped her future dreams and career to aid me in my recovery, vowing to one day see me walk again. "Whatever and however long it takes" were her words to me. Through our journey together, I have witnessed my mother experience great pain from the loss of love, alcoholism, suffering the death of her mother due to breast cancer only two years after my catastrophic accident, and the reflection in her eyes as she helps me unconditionally as I claw my way toward recovery.

Today, we are an unbreakable team. We work, train, and ride together! I am again walking! Because of her selfless commitment to me and my recovery, a purpose was born. We now ride a tandem bicycle together as a progression of my therapy program, an amazing feat for a once paralyzed man and his mother. We ride with a purpose, to show the endless possibilities of love, commitment, and human determination. We are currently on a 3,182-mile cross-country bike ride to further promote our work. We hope that through our adversity we may light the way for so many who suffer. I want to emphasize the fact that none of this would be possible without her.

Sincerely with honor,
Aaron Baker*

Upon finding this letter, my gratitude for my son expanded exponentially. Our journey together was by far the greatest honor I could have ever received. I have read and reread this letter over the years whenever my spirit needed lifting, or my commitment reconfirmed.

---

* The inclusion of this intimate letter came with deliberation and hesitation. As I further explored the meaning behind the words and their effect on my intentions, I felt it important to share. Truths from the heart, from another, are water for the soul, the life force from which our efforts are fueled.

Chapter 22:

Off Course

Two months after the completion of the tour, Aaron fell into restlessness and depression as the "Now What" set in. He felt lost, despite the achievement of the Rise Above Tour. We were both up against the reality that the tour didn't raise the expected funds that were intended to help finance the gym. Our concept remained on paper.

I was also having a harder time staying in our game. Two steps forward and three steps back was wearing on me. In my constant pursuit to generate income without compromising my commitment to Aaron's recovery and our goals, I had been building a network marketing business. This venture allowed me the flexibility to work when time was available. During one early morning network meeting, when it came my turn to deliver my introduction of myself and business, my brain froze. I stood in front of the crowd of three hundred people, speechless, some of whom were laughing at my awkward predicament. I left the meeting embarrassed, knowing something had to give.

BUT—we had to keep moving forward . . . somehow, someway.

Seed of Possibility

Aaron had pedaled thousands of miles on a small seat, directly in the backside of someone else the whole time. He needed a change.

He was ready to ride on his own, but doing it safely was a problem. He felt as though he had plateaued.

Progression and goals for him were as vital as oxygen. Without them, he succumbed to the weight of paralysis and the never-ending battle of the secondary complications he continuously faced. Like the flick of a switch, his body could go dark and unresponsive to his commands. Muscle atrophy, rigid stiffness, spasticity, body on fire from nerve pain, lack of appetite, increased bowel and bladder difficulty all set in with lightning speed. Constant stimulation through action was the only anecdote for managing it all.

These were the times I hated the most. Hate is an ugly word with an even uglier meaning but hate I did. I hated his suffering, the debilitating effects of paralysis, the limitations it imposed, and the relentless absence of reprieve. I hated when I could not help him. I hated feeling desperate. Most of all, I hated seeing the light leave his eyes.

Standing in the garage one day, Aaron shared his feelings of frustration with me. "I need to keep going. I must keep going," he affirmed. He described an ambiguous idea of a three-wheeled trike he thought he might be able to handle; he thought it doubtful but possible.

Aha . . . there it was, the answer to his frustrations. I told him if he could figure out how to safely build a trike to ride on his own, we would do it again. We would ride across the country once more.

My declaration was all he needed—a seed of possibility was planted. Both of our spirits lifted. He walked in from the garage straight to the kitchen table, opened his laptop, and began researching.

Love is an energy.

Chapter 23:

Under His Own Power

On a cold, dreary day at our old training grounds, Balboa Park, Aaron sat looking at the newly assembled trike. For months he had visualized how he would ride and the methods he would use to truly be safe, efficient, independent, and, more importantly, physically able. A small black folding stool he could sit on, placed next to the trike, replaced the helping hand he had needed to throw his leg over.

The tides turned, quite symbolically. Aaron now rode ahead of me on the trike while I rode a bike of my own, behind him. We made slow, steady progress.

Although this was progress, in many ways Aaron was taken back to our early days on the tandem, when five minutes was all his body could tolerate. While riding the tandem he'd been a passenger, responsible only for balance and power. Now he not only pushed the pedals but had to shift the gears, slow and stop with the brake lever, and steer with full control, all while keeping his torso upright on a tiny triangular seat.

Riding behind him, I marveled at the majesty of his pedaling legs—legs that were once motionless, paralyzed. I watched him train, again turning five minutes into ten minutes, then into twenty minutes and so on. While it was liberating for him, it was difficult and, at times, outright dangerous to ride the trike. It wasn't pleasurable for either of us. I had a true love/hate relationship with that trike. I loved the independence it gave Aaron. I loved watching him progress in strength, ability, and function. I abhorred what he went through to achieve those things. He wrestled with his condition every day. The harder he pushed his body, the better it worked for him. Sometimes the push was more than I could bear, and I was often torn apart, screaming inside, cursing, my fists waving in fury over what he had to deal with to live—but herein lies the point—he does it because it helps him feel alive.

I was in constant acute awareness of his body language, watching for the tell-tale signs of pushing himself into a perilous zone of his blood pressure being either too high or too low from the intensity of the effort.

Many times, I would ride in front of him, forcing him to stop, before he fell off the bike from exhaustion or, worse, autonomic dysreflexia, an abnormal overreaction of the involuntary nervous system to stimulation, causing rapid change in heart rate, dangerously high or low blood pressure, and excessive sweating.

Autonomic dysreflexia is a common secondary complication due to quadriplegia. I became very proficient, like an EMT, at peeling him off the bike and laying him down with his legs upright to regulate his swinging blood pressure.

I carried packets of energy gels, a combination of simple and complex carbohydrates, for an immediate energy source. At times, Aaron would just part his lips, with his eyes closed, while lying on the ground, for me to squeeze a packet of the thick, sweet goo into his parched mouth. Once his body had somewhat normalized, we would saddle up and resume the ride.

Self-Induced Suffering

These scenes have been safely tucked away in my memory bank; the act of writing this book has drawn them out. I am stunned by the masochistic nature of our process. At the time, the demanding efforts didn't feel that way at all. To the contrary, they were necessary in our respective rebuilding and redefinition of ourselves.

> **"In the process I have become a student of my own
> suffering and have honed a method for a grateful heart,
> a resilient mind, an emboldened body, and a gracious
> lifestyle. I used my fear as fuel and anger for amplitude."**
> ~AARON BAKER, *THE REBELLIOUS RECOVERY*

Who my son has become is a product of the fires he (we) put himself (ourselves) through. I would do it all over again, and again, and again. I honor every heartache, every tear, every sleepless night, every step, every pedal stroke, every mile, every breathless effort . . . because it all led us to who and where we are today.

Chapter 24:

Marathon Round Four

The seed that was planted three months earlier was declared. June 10, 2008, the departure date of the second Rise Above Tour, was written in bold black letters on the calendar.

The advantage was that the infrastructure was already in place from the tour the year before. Sponsorships were more easily obtained due to the near flawless execution of the first one. All we needed was to publicly announce the mission, go back to the beginning, and set a short-term goal—the LA Marathon once again.

Unlike the previous three marathons we'd participated in, this time we had an entourage of thirty-five friends, all of us wearing black shirts with the name C.O.R.E. (Center of Restorative Exercise) printed in fiery colors on the front. Although the center didn't yet exist, we promoted it like it did.

The most remarkable difference was Aaron on his trike with Arielle and me on the tandem, riding beside him.

While we all wove through the streets of downtown Los Angeles, the trike was a source of inquiry. Most had never seen a trike such as Aaron's. He couldn't maintain focus and answer questions at the same time. I tried to stay as close to him as possible to run interference.

Around the seventeen-mile marker I noticed Aaron's torso beginning to sway, his back curving into a smaller ball. Arielle began calling for him to stop, but I knew the only way he'd stop was if he literally fell off. His head went down even farther, eyes fixed forward, carrying on with the dogged stamina I had witnessed so many times before. He'd never ridden that many miles before on the trike, making the effort all the more perilous. He dismissed all the warning signs his body was signaling to him, because he was so committed to completing the 26.2 miles.

Arielle cried, pleading with him to pull over. She'd never seen him going all out as he was. I tried to console her while keeping up with Aaron, ready to catch him if he did indeed fall off, willing him energy and stamina to finish safely. He passed out and collapsed off the trike at the finish line. The paramedics whisked him up, rushed him to the nearby medical tent, and nursed him back to consciousness.

In the early days after his injury, while he was learning to walk again, I would collapse once back in the hospital room, emotionally and mentally exhausted from my WILLING his ability. Reminiscent of those days, once he was carried back to our awaiting tour bus, I fell onto the bedroom bed . . . spent, just as I had been years before.

I opened my eyes with Aaron nudging me, lying on the bed beside me. He had the most genuinely pleased look on his exhausted face. He whispered, with a grin, "I can ride this thing." I knew then he had proven to himself he had what it was going to take to ride across the country again.

"Only those who risk going too far can possibly find out
how far one can go."
~ T.S. Eliot

Chapter 25:

Rise Above Tour 2.0

Our send-off party all gathered around the Rise Above Tour bus, parked on the sand at the Santa Monica Pier, two days before the actual departure date (June 10, 2008) from San Francisco. This was a dress rehearsal of sorts, a way for us to acknowledge and thank all our Southern California friends and sponsors.

We didn't assemble a riding team this time—it was only Aaron and me. Family members and a friend all rotated duties as support hand and driver. Dan took the wheel the first two weeks as driver, Arielle and her little dog, Micky, taking the following month and a half.

There were three specific bicycling routes traversing the US: the Southern Tier, which we had done already; the Northern Tier, beginning in Washington State and ending on the coast of Maine; and the Trans-America Trail, beginning in Oregon and ending in Virginia. Aaron chose a modified version of the latter, adding the Western Express Route, which began in San Francisco and ended in Washington, DC, totaling 4,202 miles across the middle of America.

Past memories and emotions flooded across my mind and heart as we were driving north, through the central part of California that had been our home for so many years. The term "a lifetime ago" took on a new meaning for me, as it truly felt like a couple of lifetimes ago when I fell in love with the Monterey Peninsula and made the life-altering decision to move there.

My life had changed radically again, just as it had when I made the peninsula my home. My three lives were distinctly different, as though led by three separate individuals. With these differences so great, I couldn't yet unite the past with the present.

While I gazed out the bus window onto the bucolic Steinbeck hills, dotted with wise, old oak trees, I realized I had brought the most important aspects of that time with me—I had stepped out again, against the odds, into the unknown, facing the winds with an open heart, my eyes turned upward toward the sun, on the ever-present Woolly Road.

As the Golden Gate came into view, a memory of our going to San Francisco to obtain Aaron's and Arielle's passports before leaving on our international journey, years before, wafted through my mind. As we were walking to the federal building, they noticed a homeless man wearing a dirty, torn, wool overcoat sitting on a bench. They asked if we could give him something. We decided on a cappuccino and croissant. They lovingly carried the items to him. The man's demeanor shifted as he accepted the gifts with genuine gratitude, closing his eyes to savor the aroma of the hot coffee. With elegance, he delicately dipped a piece of croissant into it, hinting of a past life of abundance before harsh circumstances led him to his current one.

Scenes from the Calexico ditch intermingled in the replay with a piercing realization: without my *Why*, this could have been me.

Send-Off

Our family from Carmel had joined us for the official send-off ride, adding an extra touch of unity and encouragement. My most poignant moment of the day was looking at Aaron pedaling his own bike, while I rode alongside him, taking in the breathtaking view of the iconic Golden Gate Bridge. Its majestic red towers stood tall, connecting the bustling city of San Francisco to the picturesque Marin County, reminding me of the beauty and resilience that can be found in both nature and human endeavors.

We ended the day at the base of the Mahatma Gandhi statue, on Pier One. Gandhi, a great visionary and empathic humanitarian, had led the world by example. While standing at his feet I thought about how appropriate and important it was for us to carry his likeness in our hearts.

> **"The best way to find yourself is to lose yourself in the service of others."**
> ~ Mahatma Gandhi

Chapter 26:

Roads of Togetherness

The first few days of the tour were spent with a friend of Aaron's, Mike Hughes, who is a filmmaker, and his crew. Mike had been captivated by Aaron's extraordinary story, the first Rise Above Tour, and the audaciousness of doing it again—this time with Aaron pedaling under his own power. The crew followed us with cameras as we pedaled through the Sierra Nevada, capturing some of our favorite photos and videos from that time.

June 22 (Day 12)

 *With all equipment issues finally addressed, we headed east on Sunday, June 22. It's funny how the road beckons you as soon as you become aligned with it and the life it presents. Once we had started eastward, I thought about how much I had missed the road, memories of my youth and the year before flooding my mind. It's a very different existence, bringing you directly into appreciation of the smallest things, like washing your face and hands with clean water after a long, hot, dusty ride down remote, winding roads. Water is treasured. In day-to-day life, we forget all the simple pleasures handed to us by the turn of a faucet, flick of a switch, or push of a knob. The road reminds you of these things, minute by minute, removing the*

possibility of forgetting things or taking them for granted. Life is, after all, a series of minutes strung together. It is the dash between the dates of your existence.

We picked up Mike and his film crew in Reno on Monday. Mike was taking us back to the beginning, encouraging memories to flow freely, guiding those memories into today and our purpose. We'd been in and around the Lake Tahoe area all week, immersed in documenting everything, detailing the reality of Aaron's condition, our past, our present, or our future. I was once again in emotional overload and awe—awe at how the path continued to unfold, and in appreciation of others taking interest and participating in the continued development of C.O.R.E. and our efforts.

The Rise Above Tour bus was so very accommodating. We had up to ten people on board, and yet there was comfort. We referred to the bus as "Big Bird." Perhaps it was the energy of flight that sustained us all in such a small space. In the mornings, with bodies fast asleep covering the floor, I made my way to the coffee pot by tiptoeing over the human maze. Instead of feeling cramped or claustrophobic, I felt exhilarated. The collective spirit, all gathered in unity of purpose, was a rare experience, and I intended to immerse my mind, heart, and soul deep into the pool of its uniqueness.

In~Spirit

On the final night with the crew, we sat around an open fire pit in a wooden campsite near Lake Tahoe. The flames of the campfire's reflection on the Rise Above Tour bus seemed to coddle me, allowing me to share aspects of my journey to the camera Mike held in front of me.

"Sure, I missed my former life," I admitted. "I missed the spontaneity and my work. But then I would look at my son and wonder what his life would be like if I weren't there for him, and suddenly it didn't matter. What I missed truly did not matter."

Aaron shared some of his difficulties with paralysis and depression. "In that moment, I saw nothing, no future for myself, no purpose, and no reason to continue," Aaron revealed, talking about when he had contemplated suicide. "I would look at my old race helmet and wonder if it saved my life or ended it." As he recalled his darkest times, he said, "I'd always believed that if I were ever hurt on the motorcycle, like I am now, I wouldn't want to live."

It was a raw and cathartic moment of vulnerability and exposure. Somehow, in those moments, we both knew that the only way to reconcile the pain of our experience was to set it free, share it all . . . the good, the bad, and the ugly.

We were learning that the only way we could endure our suffering and adversity was to transform it into adventure.

~ June 30 (Day 20)

 *Leaving Carson City and energized from the excitement of the past few days, we became a crew of three . . . Aaron, Arielle, and I—the three of us again embarking on another cherished grand adventure. The five-hundred-mile stretch ahead is known as "the loneliest road in America"—the barren Highway 50, crossing the Sawtooth Mountains of Nevada.*

These are unforgiving lands with ghosts of fortune seekers headed west, their visions of finding golden treasures bringing them the only comfort to be found. It's no wonder so many perished here in the impotent, scorched vastness of the American West. Strewn about the landscapes are twisted metal structures, abandoned wagon wheels, windmills, water tanks, the occasional decrepit half-standing barn, speckled with a few boney cattle. You can almost smell the decay in the air. This land stole dreams of the long-ago

prospectors, hungry and eager for a new way of life. It stole . . . just like spinal cord injury steals.

Spinal cord injury is a stealthy thief of the worst kind. It strikes suddenly, without warning. It operates in silence; its grip tightens relentlessly, ensnaring its victims in a web of pain, suffering, and uncertainty. The insidious thief remains ever present, lurking in the shadows, affecting everyone in the family. Life becomes very black and white with two choices: suffocate in the ever-tightening hold OR break the strands of the web one by one, emerging more powerful and determined than ever thought possible.

It took a while for my family to embrace the positive choice. The fire of loss encompassed each one of us in our own way, each of us needing to learn how to manage our fragile existence, redefining ourselves and our relationship with one another . . . to discover who we are now, while dusting the ashes from our hearts.

This harsh land will serve as a backdrop while the three of us take on this part of the journey, with a few of the effects of the thief slowly fading on the road behind us.

~ *July 2 (Day 22)*

With uncharacteristic hospitality, the lands granted us a reprieve today. It turned out to be a spectacular day of riding, a tail wind and occasional drops of rain providing a bit of relief from the scorching heat, allowing us to put down 29.1 miles before stopping! This was a milestone for Aaron as well as several firsts: number of miles completed on the new trike, speeds of up to 34 mph, and the fact that he enjoyed his efforts in light of the fact that his body mostly doesn't want to do what he demands it to do.

He pushes to physical and mental territories unknown to the majority of us. Movement seems a simple thing: we reach, stand, walk, run, jump, with no thought whatsoever . . . for most of us. Aaron can no longer relish in the simplicity of the task. He wrestles his condition every day, wrestling it into his desired state of mental satisfaction.

So here we are, in the middle of no-man's-land Nevada . . . pushing, sweating, hurting, cursing, smiling and living. Why? Because We Can. The memory of Aaron not being able to move a muscle is far too clear. When I am at my own brink of tolerance, capabilities, I find myself thinking that each pedal stroke represents Aaron's and someone else's need . . . and so, I continue to pedal.

~ July 3 (Day 23)

Yesterday's enjoyment melted into today's misery. Aaron was tight, spastic, heavy, low-energy, and he definitely felt the effects of having ridden twenty-nine difficult miles the day before. It was all he could do to get out of the chair and onto his trike. I had to lift his heavy, spastic foot to help him clip into the pedal. I had no idea how he was going to ride—of course he did, but not without a lot of cursing, pain, and sheer iron will. We rode for about seven miles, stopped to snack, stretch, and rest for a bit, on the side of the road, then go for more. We were laughing at what folks passing us must have thought! We did this three times before completing a total of twenty miles. Twenty hard miles. There are days when ten miles feels like one hundred. This . . . was one of those days.

We could not be riding with such security on these desolate roads without Arielle. She manhandles the bus with capable ease, pulling off to the side in perfect timing to tend to our rest-and-refuel needs. She goes into full gear, pulling out chairs, cold waters, orange slices, and whatever else we need to recharge. It takes a lot to have Aaron's full faith and confidence out on the road . . . he has complete faith in her. Her little dog, Micky, is with us as well, bringing so much joy, love, licks, and tail wags.

We rode through the Salt Flats of Central Nevada, which collided into the base of a hill ridge. The topography was beginning its drastic shift. The first ridge opened into a valley and what we expected to be the town of Middlegate, where we planned on staying for the night. A sign with worn paint, hanging by one side, off the side of the road said, "Welcome to Middlegate Station"— this being an open dirt lot, a saloon-style structure from the late eighteen hundreds where burgers were flipped and cold beers served, a few mobile trailers out back, with peeling aluminum siding, a number of broken-down cars with their hoods up, and a toothless welcoming smile from the proprietor, saying, "C'mon in. We's family style here. Ain't got no electricity, but yer welcome to park anywheres yer wants!"

Set against the harshness of the Nevada landscape, I couldn't decide if this was a genuine respite or a scene from a Rob Zombie horror film.

Arielle is a well-traveled, experienced young woman. However, this was challenging her comfort level like no other. The setting brought forth a fear and exposed her sense of vulnerability, due to it being only the three of us aboard the very visible Big Bird. We'd been on plenty of adventures before. I was known for whisking them up and taking off to foreign lands or backwoods, but we'd never had to contend with a serious physical condition, or large equipment, as we do now. It didn't help that we had absolutely no cellular connection, completely out of touch with our known world. But . . . it was already nightfall, and we are riding these roads, not just driving, so packing up and driving to a more suitable area wasn't an option.

We discussed our plan of action in case anything became suspicious and started laughing hysterically at Aaron's rendition of protecting us with his cane! He can be the funniest person I've ever known, with a sense of humor that can deescalate the most trying of situations. We came to the conclusion that the only fear we had was what we'd created in our minds. We settled into our favorite road game, Quiddler, and continued laughing, telling stories, enjoying one another and the symphony being played by the night birds.

The evening proved that any discomfort we had was strictly from our imaginations running amok—the night and Middlegate Station embraced us, safeguarded us, and brought us safely into another day.

~ July 5 (Day 25)

 *We pedaled out of Middlegate Station into the mining town of Austin. It's a historic little place, built into the hills, reminiscent of days long gone. Signs of the Pony Express still hang proudly. All along our route of US Highway 50 across Nevada we climb and descend alongside the spirits of those young skinny, wiry fellas who rode for the short-lived Pony Express. Nowhere can you earn a feel for the way things were back then . . . than here. A* Life Magazine *photographer dubbed this stretch of highway the "Loneliest Road in America" and I think he was right on the mark. The landscape, one of desiccated basins, alternating with relatively verdant mountains, is nearly as void of humans today as it was in 1860.*

With the many days of riding catching up with us, fatigue set in, refusing us even one more mile. We spent yesterday in and out

of sleep. This was quite restorative, though, as it helped propel us up three summits today. Austin Summit, 7,893 feet, Bob Scott Summit, 7,450 feet, and Hitchison Summit, 7,340 feet, which emptied into Eureka. We have never ridden these altitudes before; our altitude training was done on the Grapevine, in Southern California, which is 4,000 feet. It created unknown, unexpected challenges. Basin, summit, range, basin, summit, range . . . a mile of relief between basin and range before summiting again. This mantra began yesterday and will continue for the next several days as we rollercoaster our way over the various spikes of the aptly named Saw Tooth Mountains, the route into Utah. The silence here is almost deafening . . . save for the whistle of the wind, the cry of a raptor flying overhead, the sound of our gears and tires purring against the hot sticky asphalt, or Aaron's occasional rant, summoning all powers within himself to complete the next pedal revolution.

We found an outlook area, at the base of Pinto Summit, behind a long, tall mound of gravel waiting to become a part of that lonely road. Tucking Big Bird behind it gave us a sense of being hidden, like a child, when playing hide-and-seek, covering their face to feel invisible. We were always face to face with vulnerability, seeking any means possible to keep it at bay.

In the still of the twilight air, we lifted weights for a nice upper body routine along with sit-ups and stretching to prepare for the grueling miles ahead. Aaron wouldn't be able to tolerate these conditions or the degree of difficulty if not for the modalities we brought along. He has his stationary trainer on the bus, the NuStep inside the van we're towing, along with various weights and resistance bands for a complete roadside workout. Although we are riding so much and don't have much energy or desire to do any exercise, it's vital we do consistent workouts to counter the chronic holding patterns associated with long-distance cycling.

With Pinto Summit at our back, Aaron had to stop and get on the bus just as the ascent for Pancake Summit was beginning. With a piercing knife sensation in his shoulders and neck, he couldn't continue. I went on to climb Pancake, all out, just to see how fast I could climb it. As I was descending, panting, satisfied with my effort, I reflected on what it means for me, personally, to represent "The Power of Possibility." Through my intention of helping my son regain his function, I never dreamed it would also result in getting in the best shape of my life, at fifty-two years old. In my quest to give him the opportunity of reclaiming movement, I discovered my own "power of possibility"—something I never would have on my own accord.

Cathartic Moment

Pedaling the unforgiving pitches of the Sawtooth Mountain roads gave a new meaning to punishing effort. The days were stifling hot, the air still and thick, silent, except for Aaron's outbursts of anger toward his body, his injury, his pain. He was sunburned and had a saddle rash, adding to all the other issues he faced from moment to moment. I was drawing deep in my reserves as his harangue continued. Finally, I snapped. I could no longer take it.

The mental and physical effort became more than I could push through. The many years of pent-up emotional distress took over, clouding my vision, and all the reasons I was doing what I was doing.

Worn out, I lashed out at Aaron. "I'm not doing this anymore! You can figure this shit out on your own. I'm done!"

I rode off away from him, into the darkening evening, alone. My water bottle was empty. I had no money in my pocket, no way to communicate . . . but I did not care. I did not care if I got run over in the darkness. I did not care if a wild animal swept me up. I felt picked clean to the bone, with nothing left to give, except to give up.

I don't know how much time had gone by when I heard the bus approaching me from behind. I waved my arm, directing the bus to pass me. It continued, at a crawl, behind me. After several more miles, the bus gently pulled up beside me as I continued pedaling. Aaron leaned out the window, apologizing, "Please stop and get on the bus with us, Toots. I'm so sorry."

Reluctantly, I stopped. I put the bike away, in silence. I boarded the bus with Aaron standing right at the entry steps, his arms outstretched. He acknowledged his behavior, and I said, "Aaron, I understand as much as I possibly can, but you need to look at what is written on the side of this bus and find a way to make peace with your suffering. Otherwise, you are an absolute contradiction to everything we work for." We both acknowledged the precarious situation we were in. The embrace we shared somehow reconnected us both to our purpose . . . and to our survival.

From that day forward we never had another breakdown of that nature again.

> "As a whole our survival is due, in large part, to the cohabitation and cooperation between us. It is when humility, benevolence, and altruism come together that magic happens. Our highest virtues arise . . . love, compassion, and empathy transmute life's inevitable struggle into solutions for better lives. In the end, we all live together, and if we embrace each other and temper our egos, we won't just survive . . . We Will Thrive!"
> ~ AARON BAKER, *THE REBELLIOUS RECOVERY*

~ July 8 (Day 28)

Whew . . . we crossed into Utah early yesterday morning. Nevada posed difficulties we weren't aware of. Reason is, and this may sound ridiculous or even reckless, but we don't look at the map until we are in the area the map is detailing. Why? If we knew exactly what we were facing, we may very well not have the mental fortitude to tackle it out of preconceived fear. Without that knowledge, we rely completely on survival instinct. I'm not suggesting this as a mode of operation . . . it's how we operate best. Perhaps it's this method that has kept us pushing forward, in spite of the odds, for so long . . . sometimes no knowledge is the best knowledge. If I had known, before taking on the mountains of Nevada, the degree of difficulty they held, I may have discouraged our taking this route, therefore eliminating the sense of accomplishment we now own.

I draw a comparison between this experience in Nevada and how one takes on the challenge of managing and optimizing one's potential after suffering a disabling condition. If you knew ahead of time what challenges, difficulties, time frame, sacrifices, etc., etc., etc., you would be faced with, you may very well never give yourself the opportunity to fight, due to the sheer enormity of the process ahead of you. In my opinion, absolutes have no place or meaning within this world of managing a chronic condition. One never knows what is possible unless you try, one minute, one hour, one day at a time.

The journey of a thousand miles begins with a single step . . .

~Concept of Time

By releasing our attachment to time, we free ourselves from the constraints of expectation, comparison, and self-judgement.

We understand that healing follows its own cadence, unique to each individual and circumstance. It is not bound by calendars or schedules; it unfolds in its own mysterious and unpredictable way. Healing is not linear; setbacks and detours are part of the journey. It is in the release of time's grip that we find the freedom to heal, to celebrate each small victory, finding solace in the process itself.

Chapter 27:

A Rare Collective

After successfully completing the first tour, two of Aaron's friends with similar injuries expressed their desire to join us for the second one. Aaron explained the demanding nature and the dangers of cross-country touring. Their confidence and pre-tour training convinced us that they could handle it and would benefit by spending time on the road.

With excitement, we greeted each other at the Salt Lake City airport and loaded their adaptive equipment into our van.

After spending the day giving a presentation at a rehabilitation institute, visiting a TV station for an interview, and then a community bike ride around the downtown park, we left on an enormous high. A perfect introduction of the tour's purpose for our new teammates.

July 15 (Day 35)

 *We set out from Salt Lake City to rejoin the bike route in Cedar City, Utah. On the way, the right front tire of the bus blew out! The powers are definitely with us, as, magically, there was a gas station with a tire center right off the upcoming exit!*

The following day was the single greatest riding day I have ever

*experienced. Aaron echoes the same sentiment. I will admit, I
was more than a little apprehensive about our new teammates'
inexperience on the road—I had the utmost faith in their desire,
but we hadn't ridden together before so I didn't know their
capacity. I was taken aback by their ability, quick adaptation, and
determination to call the road their own.*

*Here we are in Southern Utah—Highway 12, which is auspiciously
named the "Journey of Dreams." The rolling summits, with
elevations of up to eleven thousand feet, posed no threat to any of
us. We would shout, while grinding out another pedal revolution
as we passed one another, "Every uphill climb has a downside," and
down we would go, freshly satisfied with the effort, surrounded by
a dizzying universe of pinnacles, castles, fins, spires, cathedrals,
towers, all carved from wind and water, unrivaled by man's most
crowning architectural achievements. The sandstone is an exquisite
ever-changing kaleidoscope of breathtaking colors and shapes, while
piercing thorny cactus and scorching hardened sand lie at its base,
nature's visual of life's contrasts: beautiful/ugly, resilient/fragile.*

*These roads and landscapes remind us that our most profound
experiences and personal growth most often arise from challenging
circumstances, that we find the true essence of our journey in the
cyclical contrasting nature of life's ups and downs.*

~ July 22 (Day 42)

*We've been out of communication again for
the past five days. I now have the immense
task of making sense of and unpacking all the events that have
occurred since we were last in contact with anyone. To quote myself,
"With every upside there is a downside" . . . the past three days
have been solely uphill. To say we've been going through extremes*

in no way does it justice. The road and all its perils almost—I'll reiterate, almost—did us in.

Three days ago, in sweltering heat of 115 degrees, calamity struck in gale force, literally. Our morning ride was abruptly interrupted by two flat tires on Brianna's bike. Everyone's patience was a little thin, but we completed the roadside repair and continued on. The bus had gone on ahead, along with Jordan sitting shotgun. Aaron, Brianna, and I were riding together. The rain clouds out here are in abundance—in every direction you can see a downpour happening. To our left I was watching an ominous-looking cloud formation continuing to gain in size and darkening in color, with an occasional lightning bolt ground strike. We suddenly began to feel warm air turn cool and back again, shifting all the while in every direction. Coming from the Midwest, I'm familiar with thunderstorm patterns and tornadoes. Winds began to pick up to dangerous levels, forcing us to take cover. There was no way we could outrun the approaching storm on our bikes.

Cattle are free-range in these parts, so there are cattle guards every few miles on the highway. Fortunately we came upon one just in time to take refuge. The three of us tucked down in the bar ditch alongside the guard, tornado tails forming and dancing over our heads. It was obvious we could take a direct hit. The next chaotic forty-five minutes were actually spent in calm, knowing there was nothing we could do. We simply held on to each other until the storm passed, leaving us physically unscathed but emotionally a little shaken.

We got back on our bikes, caught up to the bus, and rested our minds until we thought the storms had passed. Brianna needed a break, so I told Aaron and Jordan to go ahead and start riding. I would catch up to them. This wasn't what I would normally do. I usually stayed right behind them, but my instinct was to follow the bus for a bit this time. The bus went ahead of me just a little ways and stopped. A gale force wind had hit the side with such power it completely lifted the awning out of the brackets. Arielle was on the side of the road, holding on to the awning strap with all her might.

I jumped off my bike, the winds battering us at 60 to 80 miles per hour. I quickly grabbed bungee cords and went to the top of the bus to attempt to anchor it down, in an effort to save it. All the while my heart was in my throat with the thought of Aaron and Jordan being on the road with the newly formed storm coming out of nowhere. As well as I secured the awning with bungee cords, they were no match to the wicked winds, set on wreaking havoc.

I ditched the idea of trying to save the awning, because at that point driving to the guys was the main priority. We drove ahead a few hundred yards when the twenty-foot awning holder flew over the top of the bus, dragging on the opposite side of the road. Luckily it didn't take out an oncoming car, but we couldn't go any farther. Arielle and I went again onto the top of the bus, looking at each other in sheer desperation. We had no idea how to handle the situation.

The winds continued their pounding, and the twenty-by-thirty-foot vinyl awning was flapping with abandon, the bracket threatening to break windows, thrash the side of the bus, or smash oncoming vehicles. Adrenaline rushed through me and brought forth a guttural, primal, gorilla chest-pounding howl, which rendered Arielle into hysterical laughter. This shifted our seemingly inadequate mind frames into "Let's tear this bitch apart and get-r-done!" With a kitchen knife, I sliced the beautiful new phoenix-branded awning off the brackets and ripped the metal bracket off its holder, leaving it in a heap of carnage on the side of the road.

A Native American Indian family drove up as I was catching my breath to ask if we needed help. I told them we were okay but asked if they could drive ahead and look for the guys. They returned a while later, assuring me of Aaron and Jordan's safety. They were up ahead at a roadside rest area, safe and unharmed.

We have consistently ridden these summiting roads now for seven to eight hours a day, humbly, respectfully, but in no way backing down to their power. We, the rare collective, are, as the side of the bus states . . . the Rise Above Tour.

~ July 29 (Day 49)

 *We were completely out of water, with the bus running on fumes as we descended the final stretch of Sandstone Mountain into something I've never been so excited to see . . . a Sinclair gas station, the first one we'd encountered in five days, on the outskirts of a little border town called Blanding, Utah. The next day we crossed the state line into Colorado. Another state and bike map behind us. We drove on into Denver, as we had presentations scheduled, along with our teammates departing.*

One of the most difficult parts of the tour was bidding farewell to those who have spent time with us. A different sort of bond was discovered out here. Perhaps the bond of survival and the emotional extremes experienced. The sharing of limited space, disconnecting from attachments (both personal and cellular!), developing new personal capabilities, and meeting and connecting with new friends creates a real sense of brotherhood that makes a goodbye so difficult.

Jordan and Brianna left today. I want to thank them both for giving me yet another perspective on pushing through limitations.

Each day brought yet another hard-earned personal victory for each one of us. They both have the endless well of the indomitable spirit. I will never forget the day Jordan connected with the moment—not reaching too far out in front of himself to bring all his power into a single focused point, which allowed him a perfect pedal revolution. These seemingly inconsequential things become monumental victories after a catastrophic injury. This was a personal victory for Jordan, and I am the lucky one who was right beside him when he discovered it! Brianna told me before she came on board that she was exhilarated and terrified at the same time. She discovered new strengths and abilities she may never have known if not for being on the tour for the past two weeks.

And . . . it is time for Arielle to go back to her life. Oh my, this is the hardest one of all. The injury took so much from our family in drastically different ways. The tour gave us back a little of what was lost. Arielle added an element that cannot be replaced . . . a sense of security. I knew I could handle anything that came up with Arielle there to help me. But the most important gift the tour gave us was time. Time just being together. Time laughing, loving, and appreciating one another.

One of the many magic moments we shared occurred the day after the "breakdown"—still reeling from emotional upheaval, I came upon the bus, where she was standing roadside, Bob Marley's "Redemption Song" echoing in the sandstone amphitheater surrounding us, her arms outstretched . . . I fell into them. My heart expanded and melted into hers.

As we know, there is a flip side to everything.

Dave, my dear friend since high school, who has recently become a part of my life, is now with us. He believes in what we do. He delights in taking over all the details of keeping the tour on the road, which allows us to perform our work.

For all the tour represents, when broken down into the individual effects pushing through perceived limitations is the most important for me. Turning "I Can't" into "I Can," "Impossible" into "I'm Possible."

Chapter 28:

Riding with Crazy Horse

Without the big spirits and energy of Jordan, Brianna, and Arielle, our bus felt empty again. Aaron and I were the lone riders, Dave captaining the bus behind us.

I had scheduled a presentation at a medical facility in Loveland, Colorado, the day after dropping the three off at Denver International Airport. During the Q&A segment of our presentation, a newly injured motorcycle rider encouraged Aaron to go north to the Sturgis Motorcycle Rally that was starting the following week.

"Why not, Toots?" exclaimed a very excited Aaron, in front of the audience. Laughing, I said, "Yeah, why not? Let's ride our bicycles right alongside the Harley hogs at the Sturgis Rally!"

What really excited me about the rally was the fundraising potential. I immediately began brainstorming ways to share our story with the other motorcycle enthusiasts. Motorcyclists are a brotherhood, and I believed they would take us into their fold, with Aaron having been a former motorcycle racer.

Once again, we declared our intentions publicly, giving ourselves no way out. We had to follow through.

~ *August 12 (Day 62)*

 True to the multitude of extremes we live with, we shifted gears entirely as we headed north from Denver to Sturgis, South Dakota. The world-famous Sturgis Motorcycle Rally was in full swing. I've never seen so much chrome, leather, and bandannas gathered in one small area before. Now, I'm not too sure the Harley-Davidson culture had ever witnessed their main drag being drug by bicyclists wearing spandex instead of leather and denim. We did indeed cause more than a few wrenched necks and raised a lot of eyebrows due to the sheer absurdity of our cruising with the boss hogs. We were stopped by a number of curious old salts, whose scorn quickly turned to praise, high fives, and well wishes upon finding out what we were doing and why. Keep a spot on your couch for us, Jay Leno. You're sure to get a kick out of this story!

After posting our flyers all over town, we pedaled south, leaving all the Sturgis enthusiasts with the two-fingers-down wave (traditional biker peace sign). Mount Rushmore was alive with visitors from all over the world—everyone smiling, waving, shouting "hell yeahs," and wishing us luck as we pedaled by.

Birth, Expansion, Development, Preservation, depicted by carved figures of four great leaders in American history, charge the air surrounding the granite monument, making it seem all the more important to do something indelible in our world.

Crazy Horse Memorial was next on our travels back south. The spirits in the Black Hills are ever so present—at one point it felt as though someone was riding right beside me. So much so I actually looked to my left to see who it was. Maybe it was Crazy Horse himself—I choose to think so, anyway. I am strongly connected to the Cherokee Indian genetics I was given by my maternal grandfather.

"As long as rivers run and grass grows and trees bear leaves, Paha Sapa [the Black Hills of Dakota] will forever be the sacred land of the Sioux Indians," Crazy Horse is quoted as stating.

Traveling at the slow pedaling speed, I could most certainly feel their ever-present spirits, encircling me, whispering encouragements, infusing me with their strength and courage. The spirits permeate the land, wind, and air . . . I am in such honor to feel their spirits, alive and well within my own.

The Black Hills roll into expansive grass prairies, replete once again with roaming buffalo. Just as Aaron and I were talking about how cool it would be to see a herd up close, we came around a bend to a sleeping giant just off the side of the road—fortunately, the opposite side. As I stopped to snap a photo, Aaron called out that I better hurry, as the buffalo's tail was flipping side to side, which indicated his displeasure in my actions. With a shot of adrenaline shooting through me, I got my photo and quickly pedaled away, the hair standing up on the back of my neck, hoping the beast would remain in repose and not come after me! I looked over my shoulder to see him lay his head back down . . . thank goodness.

I'm really looking forward to getting to Oklahoma. All our extended family live there. They will get to see firsthand how Aaron is progressing and what we are doing. We have a number of presentations scheduled as well. For now, we have some time to make up, so we are riding as many miles per day as possible, pushing even harder than we have been, adhering strictly to the four Rs: Ride, Refuel, Rest . . . Repeat. With the flat plains of Nebraska and Kansas separating us from Oklahoma, there will *be many days ahead of just that—Ride, Refuel, Rest, Repeat. Exhausted but exhilarated, we continue to do what we do . . . Rise Together.*

Chapter 29:

Parade of Family

The relentless prairie winds sometimes assisted and sometimes hampered our push south from the Black Hills of South Dakota to Oklahoma. Those gosh darn winds swirled in all directions, continuously changing the intensity of our effort. The spirit of Crazy Horse inspired our bravery as we pedaled alongside the speeding Harleys, big rigs, and cars. Only a small swath of blacktop marked off with a solid white line separated us from droves of vehicles whizzing by. No bicycle lanes on the prairie!

Surprise! Just outside of Woodward, Oklahoma, hometown to many of our family members on my mother's side, my aunt Sonja had organized a group of family and friends to greet and lead us directly to my grandmother's home. We literally crested a hill to a parade of cars eagerly awaiting us on the opposite side of the road. Leaning out of their windows, aunts, uncles, cousins, and friends hooted and hollered *hey*s and *how-ya-doin*s as we continued pedaling into town.

With tears clouding my eyes and staining my road-dusted face, I couldn't see the last few miles. I had no idea they would all meet us on the road like that! Aaron in front and me behind him, we led the horn-honking parade of cars . . . the Rise Above Tour bus behind, ushering us into town.

As my grandmother's first grandchild from her first daughter, I held an incredibly special place in her heart, just as she did in mine. With emphasis on the *graa* in *Graamaw*, as I called her, she was cut from the old country cloth. Norwegian in origin but raised during the Dust Bowl and Great Depression era in Oklahoma, she knew how to make a tray of biscuits from a teaspoon of flour. Somehow a delicious hot meal was placed on the table no matter how empty the cupboards were. Tough as boot leather, witty, beautiful, open-hearted, unbent from the harshness of her life, she was an example of pure resilience.

My mother was the same type of woman. They held their head high no matter what life threw at them, rarely showing or caving to the hard times they faced. "Laquita Dian, wish in one hand and shhhit in the other, then see which one fills up faster," my mother would often say to me when I was young and yearning for something I didn't have or for things in life to be different than they were. Another one was, "You don't have a right to the cards you believe you should be holding; you just play the dickens out of the ones you've been dealt!"

Once at the doorstep, we dismounted our bikes, hugged necks, then walked in to surround my Graamaw, lying in bed propped up with pillows, her eyes giving me the tight, warm embrace that she could not. She'd had a massive stroke several years before. Unable to care for herself or communicate verbally, her gaze gave voice to her silence, saying everything I could possibly want to hear. I could feel and see the pride and love as her eyes went back and forth between Aaron's and mine. She knew exactly what my commitment to Aaron was all about. She had gone through a major illness with her youngest son many, many years previously, never leaving his side until he was well enough to leave hers.

The Torch

Later that evening, I crawled beneath the warm, sweet-smelling sheets of my Aunt Sonja's sumptuous feather bed. It seemed to caress and embrace every fiber of my tired, spent being. I was filled with an overwhelming sense of gratitude for the simple comfort the bed offered me, an exquisite reprieve from the road. I thought about the women whose fabric I was woven from and their mettle I had inherited. It powered me through the long, extreme days. The thoughts made me proud of who I am and where I came from.

It's a torch I am most honored and grateful to carry . . . and to pass on to my son, daughter, grandsons, and granddaughter.

The next day, my grandmother squeezed my hand with a "you can do it" firmness that conveyed both strength and belief. This would be the last time my hand would be in hers.

We mounted our bikes and pedaled eastward.

The women who preceded me, like branches on a tree, all grow in different directions, but our roots remain as one.

Chapter 30:

The Unsuspecting Ozarks

We left Oklahoma with a new passenger, my brother, Kenny, riding shotgun. He provided welcomed support, bringing us chilled fruits, cold water, and wet cloths to wrap around our sweltering heads and necks when we stopped for a break. I would often stretch Aaron's stiff body right on the roadside.

By that time we had become quite road savvy, undaunted by speeding cars, buses, semitrucks, motorcycles, and farm equipment we shared the asphalt with.

With two thousand miles of our country's most savage roads behind us, the Ozarks, surprisingly, proved to be the most difficult stretch of the entire tour. It was mostly due to our dismissive attitude toward what seemed, on the map, as easy elevation.

Once there, the elevation pitches were uncommonly steep, unforgiving ribbons of blacktop, the stagnant air filled with bugs so dense they stuck to our skin, teeth, and helmets. The recumbent bike was the only way Aaron could manage to climb the steep, seemingly endless waves of sweltering pavement.

All along the way, our presence on the road and our brightly colored motor bus inspired attention from onlookers. "Are y'all a band or something like that on tour?" many would ask.

We would answer back with, "No, we're riding our bicycles across the country."

"Why would y'all do that?" was a common question. Our answer, "There are a lot of folks who can't, and we ride for them," created a lot of head-scratching . . . but we did get their attention. Many times, the inquiry warranted our taking time to explain what we were doing in detail. I left hundreds of people with our brochures, promotional material, and shared contact information, with high hopes of a contribution toward our goal of opening our gym.

Attention we did receive; financial contributions we did not.

~ *August 18 (Day 68?)*

 *At this point I have no idea what day it is. We've been out of communication for many days. I am relying on my Native instinct for time of day, as I gave up watches many years ago. Time is posted everywhere in daily living—the clock in your car, on building walls, the one standing next to you generally boasts a timepiece. I became very proficient at observing the sun's position in the sky or simply feeling the day for a quick determination of the general hour. I now get to put that instinct into practice, as the sun is all I have to follow. There are no building walls or even people in these very desolate parts. It is discombobulating to relinquish the familiar.*

Living with a chronic debilitating condition forces you to relinquish so much of what was familiar. Depending on the severity of the condition, everything you once knew to be true can suddenly be no longer, including how you define yourself as a person. The redefinition of self is daunting and filled with uncertainty— uncertainty of that person looking back at you in the mirror and how you operate and fit into the world. I find this to be true to not

*only the injured but also those closest to them. I am a mere fragment
of who I was prior to Aaron's injury. Some days I present with
a list of contradictions . . . more aware / less open, more grateful
/ more fearful, more confident / more confused, more accepting /
more heartbroken. I am finding that the differences between each
of these emotions is what is making its way to real clarity. Clarity
becomes the fuel necessary to focus on what you "can do" to make
sense of the causal why . . . why your son, why your daughter, why
you, your family. We all know there is no answer to why . . . there
is only the question of "how." How can I make the most of what
has happened, whether it be a life-altering injury, a diagnosis of
illness, addiction, a fire or natural disaster, divorce, death? Any one
of these experiences that upends your known world can bring you to
your ultimate power and purpose . . . if you muster up the courage
to embrace and welcome the changes it brings . . . it's your choice.*

*It is through this process that you can find the true meaning and
purpose of who you are, how you relate and contribute to the world.
For me, I attached almost immediately after Aaron's injury to a
belief in purpose. At the time I had no idea what that purpose was.
The hazy vision pulled me out of bed on many mornings, helping
me face the day, face the reality of Aaron's condition and all that
had been sacrificed. I adopted the motto of Bill Wilson, cofounder
of Alcoholics Anonymous: one day at a time, making it my personal
goal to use each day as though it were our last, retiring at night
satisfied, without regrets. Over time a subtle sense of acceptance
replaced fear, because I knew we/I/he were doing all we could.*

*With this mindset, we are now on the open road . . . nine years
ago Aaron was completely frozen, with the only movement
coming from his eyes, which darted side to side. Without complete
belief, willingness, fierce determination, he would still be in that
bed . . . or would he? My guess is that he would be flying free*

from the confines of his impaired physical body, free, but not in this world. He is here today because he is committed to sharing his bounty. Together, my son and I will continue to play the hell out of the cards we were dealt.

We've got a lot of pedaling to do.

Top Fuel Fury

Once we had conquered the Ozarks, we desperately needed a break, and not just a day or two, but a solid week. Aaron's good friend had arranged for us to park our bus right in the pit area with all the race teams at the National Hot Rod Association's yearly national event at the Lucas Oil Raceway in Indianapolis, Indiana.

Aaron had long been a fan of the sport, oftentimes fancying himself in the cockpit of the fire-breathing, nitromethane-fueled beasts. As a young teenager, I had also been a speed junkie. I had a huge poster of the famed Blue Max funny car plastered on the wall of my bedroom with dreams of commanding it myself.

I also remembered my father and Forrest Lucas, the titan behind the legendary oil giant, had been friends, as young men, in their respective cross-country truck-driving days. Aaron was lost on fumes and speed. I was lost on the idea of getting our proposal for the specialized gym center to Forrest Lucas.

Some of my father's attributes that had the most impact on me were the reinvention of self, boldness, and confident audacity. I called Dad to ask him if he would make the initial connection for me, fully aware of the absurdity of my request. Without hesitation he said, "Sure I will." Although he hadn't been in contact with Forrest for several decades, he picked up his phone and called Forrest at the main office of Lucas Oil. Forrest took his call, recognizing my father's name. After their hellos, *what-in-all-heck*s, and the sharing of a few old truckin'-days stories, Dad explained why he was calling.

While I was walking around on the first day of the race event, I saw Forrest ahead of me, driving a golf cart through the pit area. I had my proposal in hand, carrying it with me everywhere I went, ready at all times to lay down my pitch. I waved down the golf cart with a gleeful, "Hey, Forrest, I'm Laquita, Kennie Stovall's daughter!"

He stopped the cart, smiling broadly, patted the seat beside him, and said, "C'mon on, girl, come sit down with me."

Forrest listened intently to my story, my proposed endeavor with the gym, the purpose of the tour. He responded with sincere appreciation for what we were doing and for Aaron's remarkable journey of recovery. With a deep sigh, he said he didn't believe he would be of any benefit to the overall business plan and idea. I left his golf cart with my proposal still securely tucked under my arm.

Although disappointed, I was undeterred and still smiling due to having had the opportunity of sharing my information with him. With each and every share we were one step closer to seeing our vision into reality.

Trust the process.

Chapter 31:

Role Reversal

On a high, fresh and well rested, we parted ways with all our new friends from the racetrack. We had our own racetrack, so to speak, to get back to—the long lanes of open road heading east into Ohio.

Energized and inspired by all the racing greats, Aaron pedaled with renewed vigor. I marveled as I watched his body pedal in harmony, reminiscent of how captivated I had been watching him on the golf course, all those years before the injury.

We rode along the cornfields of Ohio, laughing, fist-pumping, with power in our legs and songs in our hearts. In all our years of riding we had never had fun while riding. It was work, hard work, that did end with satisfaction, but it was never fun. On a flat road, the wind at our back, accelerating our speed, we found fun!

Sailing along, finding yet another gear with each pedal stroke, I heard the distant bark of dogs. Right at that point a large, lumbering dog approached my wheels. I was so confident in my ability I didn't even wince when I saw the dog approaching. I simply shooed him away, never missing a beat in my effort to keep up with Aaron.

That Damn Dog

Just ahead I saw four snarling varmints on the opposite side of the road. One of them darted across, narrowly missing being hit by a passing car. Aaron swerved a bit, dodging the open-mouthed dog. I was right on Aaron's back wheel, clocking twenty-five miles per hour, and had no way of preventing the hound from going directly under my front tire. The impact was immediate, sending me straight up in the air. Before I even knew what had happened, with the feeling of being shot out of a cannon, I hit the pavement, hard, on my left side.

Ahead of me, Aaron was screaming at the dogs. I quickly stood up, adrenaline masking the pain of the impact. I tried to grab the handlebars, insisting I was okay, but my left arm collapsed. I felt blood rolling down my cheek into my mouth. I was so angry that I couldn't make sense of any of it. Aaron pleaded with me to sit down and stay put while he rode ahead to flag down Dave and Kenny in the bus.

I didn't want to be taken to the emergency room. I told Aaron and the guys that I would be fine after an hour or so. Aaron insisted on taking me to the hospital. I grumbled all the way to the ER, just to pacify what I believed was his protective overreaction. I was sure that an ice pack and some rest was all I needed.

A Wired Elbow

A nurse came into the room to tell me that a surgeon was being called in after my x-ray had revealed a displaced, fractured ulna that forms the elbow joint and connects to the humerus bone. She further stated that she had already processed the request for the imminent surgical procedure.

I could not believe what I was being told. All I could think about was finishing the tour. "We will finish this tour" was the first thing I said to Aaron, Kenny, and Dave after the nurse delivered the news. It was going to take a lot more than a wild dog to keep that from happening. No sir, no way, uh-uh.

One week later, with my wired and heavily bandaged left arm held securely in a sling, I stepped over the frame of Aaron's recumbent bike. The pedals were too far for my shorter legs to reach, so Dave stuffed pillows behind my back to bring me closer. Kenny secured my helmet as I took the handlebars with my right hand.

As I adjusted myself on the unfamiliar reclining seat to begin pedaling, Aaron took his position behind me, becoming my guardian, my support, my rock to lean on. I had been this for him for so many years. To have him in my position was another example of the interchangeability of our experience together. There were times I pulled him . . . and there were times he pulled me. We shared the supporting roles with loving responsibility and empathy.

We rode in this fashion through the Appalachian Mountains, Quaker settlements, and old coal-mining towns. I could touch the ground with my hand on my low-slung chariot, giving me a sense of pedaling in the footsteps of the generations before me. I felt at one with our path, with love and belief leading the way and my son at my back.

Reflecting Pool

Despite the cold, sunless September day, our spirits were lifted, and our hearts warmed with the satisfaction of achieving our shared goal. While standing at the base of the Lincoln Memorial, gazing at the Reflecting Pool, four months after we began our tour, I couldn't help but feel in awe. Completing the arduous journey of pedaling across the country with my son, whose chances of regaining function were so bleak, had at times felt delusional and impossible. Yet, here we were, standing at the heart of our nation's capital, having completed the improbable.

As we stood side by side basking in our shared accomplishment, it was evident that with a steadfast refusal to settle for anything less than our belief, there was no limit to what we could achieve.

~ *Reflection*

For four months we had lived one pedal stroke at a time, one mile, one road, one handshake, one purpose . . . the desire to create opportunities for those who suffer. Although the Rise Above Tour 2008 was completed, Aaron and I both knew it was just the beginning. All that had been experienced on the road would continue to unwind and reveal itself as time went on.

The power of the tour will evolve, as will "The Power of Possibilities." We look optimistically into the future . . .

In~Spirit,
~ Aaron & Laquita

Chapter 32:

White Flag Moment

Once we had returned home, I organized a Rise Above Tour Day of Celebration for all our community friends, previous tour teammates, crew, and sponsors. Aaron made a beautiful video of our four-month journey to share with the audience. It was a highly spirited day, full of enthusiasm and hope that our endeavor would bring us closer to our dream center.

Arielle joined us, driving from northern California where she had relocated after successfully completing the rehab program in Sacramento. I believed that she had been effectively managing her substance abuse.

Upon her arrival for the celebration day, I could immediately see that this was not the truth. Confrontation yielded nothing but denial and accusations of my insulting her with my distrust. I was thrown into the dark pit of sickening fear and hopelessness, again.

I feigned positivity while sharing details of the tour, masking the nausea, fear, and anger I felt. With her denial firm, I stood helplessly as I watched her drive away, desperately fending off the unthinkable question of, "Will this be the last time I see her?" I was enveloped with blinding rage as her car disappeared. I wanted to tear trees out of the ground by their roots, turn cars over, rip everything around me apart.

I was scared out of my mind.

~ *Reflection*

*Watching someone you love, who has fought
so hard to beat addiction, throw everything
away and sink back into a life that will most
likely lead to a calamitous ending is one of the
hardest things you will ever do. All you want
is to help them back to a clean and sober life, but you realize by
doing this, as you have before, you will just enable them, because
it will show them that you will always be there to bail them out.
You want to grab and shake them and say, "What are you doing?"
But at some point you realize that it wouldn't make a difference. So
you sit back and watch the tragedy unfold, as if you are watching
a movie. Feeling helpless to stop it, feeling like you haven't done
enough to help . . . even though you know only the addict can help
themselves. Battling alcoholism or drug addiction is a beast for the
person held captive and the ones who love them.*

*Addiction destroys everything in its path. Getting out of the way is
the most loving form of detachment you can practice.*

Arielle called me while driving, trying to assure me of her
well-being, actually saying she was doing better than ever. She may
have convinced herself of all she was saying, but she certainly did
not convince me. I knew she wasn't yet ready to battle her personal
demons. Before ending our conversation, she told me she would be
back for Christmas, three months away.

> *Addiction is the only prison where
> the locks are on the inside.*

I found some consolation and better understanding from doing
something I hadn't done before. I opened up to other mothers going
through similar situations with their children—strangers in an

Al-Anon group. My own experience with alcoholism didn't inform me in any way of how to deal with my daughter's addiction. I finally accepted that if I were to be effective for her and for myself, I had to step back, which was the single most difficult thing for me to do. My nature to stand up against and never back down from anything increased tenfold when it involved my son or daughter. Yet that very approach was the exact opposite of what was needed.

~ *Detachment*

In the depths of challenges like addiction, detachment becomes a paradoxical act of love. It is a journey of relinquishing control, a conscious release of the desire to fix, rescue, or save. Detachment whispers a profound truth: sometimes, to truly help, we must step back and allow the unfolding of another's path, even when it feels unbearable. Within this surrender lies a flame of hope—a realization that by detaching, we create space for growth and trust in the strength of those we love.

In a Target parking lot, three months later, Arielle and I sat in the car, never making it into the store for our intended Christmas shopping. She told me she was tired—tired of the heavy lifting of lies, betrayal, and destruction that held her hostage to feed the ravenous addiction. She said the single most important thing to her, and her future, was to be a mother.

When Arielle was a young teenager, as I was driving one day to pick her up, a song came on the radio that compelled me to turn the car around and head straight to the nearest record store. As she climbed into the car, I turned up the volume, the lyrics "you gotta be bold, wise, strong" communicating what I wanted to convey to her.

Years later, after hours of difficult conversation, as we sat in the car, the song played, once again filling the air with its powerful message. Through tears and laughter, we sang together, the words penetrating her heart and intentions. She knew if she did not commit to herself and wellness, she would never have the sacred chance of motherhood. I believed her and the white flag she was waving.

With my forehead leaning heavily on the steering wheel, I was filled with grateful relief and admiration for her courage. She was now willing to face her inner struggles and work toward overcoming them.

I sincerely believe love and directed desire . . . can redeem. They could transform the brutality of Arielle's life into something beautiful, just as they had for her brother's and mine. I felt Arielle on the precipice of her own unfolding, like a butterfly within the chrysalis, morphing into her power and self-worth.

It takes what it takes.

Stand

Possibility

Initiate

Reason

Part 5 **Intention**

Transform

The level of success you achieve, in anything you do, will be in direct proportion to the depth of your commitment.

Chapter 33:

Fully Vested

Arielle closed the chapter on her time up north. As she walked through our townhome front door, I could see the strength in her posture and a new light in her eyes. She had turned the page and was writing a completely new script. I could not have been prouder of her.

Around the same time, Aaron received an auspicious invitation.

Having attained some notoriety because of our cycling tours, he had been selected to join a weeklong Paralympic athlete discovery camp at the Olympic Training Center in Chula Vista, California, the center we had visited some years earlier.

His performance was slow, but he had given it his all, which was the Olympic Creed the coaches looked for in an emerging athlete. He was chosen to begin official Paralympic training in pursuit of joining the USA Cycling Team.

His training rides underwent a significant change. Instead of covering long distances at a slower pace with me riding alongside, the focus shifted to shorter distances that demanded maximum effort from the first pedal stroke.

Aaron chose a two-lane farm road as the designated training course. This road, known for hosting time trial events, was the perfect setting for his intense sessions. I followed closely behind in our van for support.

His life was evolving again, progressing from rehab riding to race cycling.

The whiteboard that hung in our office now had national and international cycling event dates boldly written in black letters. *Paralympic Games London 2012* was written in red.

We were fully invested in both Aaron's performance cycling and our vision for the center. We made the decision to do both simultaneously, as one supported the other. We saw the potential in using the pursuit of Paralympics as a unique and outstanding marketing campaign for the center.

Aaron's progress and accomplishments would serve as the forward-facing representation of what the center stood for.

The Need

Every company or individual I proposed our plan to concluded with sincere overtures of appreciation for the concept of the center and acknowledged the great need for all who could benefit from the services, but I was told time and again that from a financial perspective, it would not work.

The reasoning was valid: the one-on-one services were expensive. The process of onboarding qualified staff was too complicated and labor-intensive. The costs couldn't be offset with general memberships due to the assistance our clients required.

My business mind understood this; my heart refused to accept it.

I had seen the devastating effects of the lack of opportunity for improvement and the management of disabling conditions. Tragically, several of our friends had died due to complications of their injury; these losses could have been prevented with specialized care. Aaron's initial prognosis would have been entirely accurate if we had not pursued the process we did. . . . Without it, he would have ended up like our friends.

We were not just dreaming up a noble idea; the center we aimed to build was an absolute necessity and a critical component for quality of life.

Auspicious Twist of Events

Neither of the two tours were successful in fundraising. On paper, my presentation fell short, lacking the strength required to secure a loan or even a credit card. My absence of a business degree and any experience in gym ownership added to the complexity.

Sometimes, gifts from the universe come wrapped in the most surprising packages. The encounter with the wicked dog turned into being the catalyst for our dream. I unexpectedly received a small settlement for the repair and recovery of my arm, which I used instead to open the doors of our beloved center.

The search for funding was over.

Reconciliation

Armed with what we had always referred to as the "Door Effect," the energetic shift we felt upon entering the doors of the Center of Achievement years earlier, we began our search for a suitable space.

Our plan was to be close to the university in Northridge as both a nod to our humble beginnings and to benefit from the network of students, training staff, clients and friends we had formed. Despite finding many potential locations that could have worked, the management firms repeatedly turned us down.

One day we came upon an empty space that had been a Wells Fargo loan office. A chill went through my body as we peered through the large plate glass window. The space was small yet seemed perfectly suited for a center of our type.

Aaron and I were accompanied that morning by the daughter of one of my former work associates. She excitedly said, "I have a friend who works at the Wells Fargo headquarters! I'll call him to see if he can give me the name of the building owner!"

My ears perked up with the thought of being connected to the owner, who might possibly be someone I'd known or friends with someone I'd known. Despite my persistence, the management firms had always refused to give me the property owner's name, insisting: "I will give it to you, after you sign the lease!"

In my previous life, before Aaron's injury, I had worked in the Persian rug business. Many of the rug merchants I knew in Los Angeles were also commercial real estate owners. Though I may have fallen short on a written application, within the tight-knit Persian community, the value of a positive character reference was as valuable as a substantial bank account.

I sensed the possibility of my two different worlds merging—I smiled inside at the chance to draw upon my past to assist my present.

A few weeks later Aaron and I put a key in the front door, unlocking our future and soon-to-be specialized gym center.

Manifesting Our Vision

We set about creating our center in the same way we had the entire recovery process. We threw ourselves into the dirty work, maximizing every minute, every penny, and all of our resources.

Dan generously offered his expertise and creativity to assist us in the renovation. He and Aaron meticulously thought out every aspect of the design and floor plan.

Arielle jumped in, taking up a paint brush with enthusiasm. She loved the process and participated in turning the vision into something tangible. It was strikingly similar to what she was doing in her own life.

She had committed to sobriety and had reconnected with her love and unique gift of horseback riding. Along the way, she met Jimmy, a kindred spirit whose path mirrored her own. Their love for one another came with mutual understanding and goals for their future. I was overjoyed for them. I welcomed Jimmy into our family with open arms and a grateful heart.

The Foundation

We had thought the renovation process would be relatively simple. Strip the carpet, paint the walls, hang the mirrors, and place the specialized equipment we had carefully selected.

We were mistaken.

The floor was much more of a problem than what we'd anticipated. Dirty carpet covered decades of layers of old linoleum, glue, and the stories of different visions for the place. Several contractors insisted it would be too labor-intensive and expensive to achieve our desired outcome of exposed concrete. Their recommendation was to install new carpeting.

Nope.

"Well, guys, it'll surely be a slow, dirty grind, if that's what you're set on doing," Dan said with a shrug.

"C'mon, Toots, we can do it!" Aaron replied, with a familiar, convincing grin.

For five days I was on my hands and knees with a vacuum, beside Aaron operating a grinding machine, turning the layers into clouds of talcum dust. That stuff covered every inch and filled every orifice on my body. I thought I would never get rid of it all!

We ground and polished that concrete floor to our satisfaction. After the last coat of polish had dried, we affixed a large decal to the floor near the entrance—fiery phoenix wings that were symbolic of our intention and the spirit to Rise Above.

In that small humble space, belief infused the walls and possibility permeated the air. It was the foundation for our future and the base for others like Aaron.

Luminous Symbol

Two months after receiving the key, Aaron and I stood outside one late evening, watching the large sign being placed on the front of our building.

The same spellbinding effect I had at the Reflecting Pool washed over me as I looked at our magnificent phoenix logo illuminating the night sky. "We've really done it, Buddy," I whispered, with a tearful tone. "I have no words, Toots," Aaron said, barely containing himself.

All the work, hopes, dreams, setbacks, and comebacks were within the glowing lights of that sign set against the moonlit sky.

The following day, Aaron and I proudly walked into the Gold's Gym center where Taylor worked and handed him a key to the front door of C.O.R.E. With broad smiles and hugs . . . a handshake sealed our partnership agreement.

Chapter 34:

From Page to Play

On New Year's Day, eleven years after we had discovered Taylor and the Center of Achievement, our doors indeed opened to the vision we had held. Despite it being a national holiday, we deemed the date 1/1/11 exceptionally auspicious. The perfectly aligned sequence of ones held great significance for us.

We enthusiastically welcomed community friends and clients as they strolled in throughout the day, delighting in the celebratory nature of our long-anticipated opening.

The days were super-charged with an electric energy of possibility for all those who came through our doors. Taylor dubbed our space "a personal war room." We fostered a family-like atmosphere, a sense of belonging, where everyone was greeted with smiles and hugs.

Adding a personal touch, I would casually ask clients who their favorite musician or band was, and I would have that music playing as they came through the doors. It was a small but impactful way of showing we cared and valued their experience with us. Watching our clients work toward their goals, together with others in similar circumstances, was deeply gratifying.

The experience of being surrounded by stories of tragedy offered me a unique perspective that somewhat buffered the challenges of being a grass roots business. We were building much more than a business; we were helping others rebuild their lives.

The Hustle

We had many goals and objectives for C.O.R.E., the big picture being a center in every major city nationwide. This was our business plan, our vision, our future.

We rolled up our sleeves and got to work.

We drew a thirty-mile radius around our location. Aaron and I personally delivered our printed materials to every hospital, therapy center, massage center, and chiropractic office in that radius.

With a skeleton staff, I wore a multitude of hats. As CEO, I was responsible for all aspects of the business. In addition, I assisted clients on the gym floor with transfers to and from their wheelchairs, in and out of their cars, provided janitorial duties, and did anything and everything else that came up over the course of a day.

I also guided clients through their exercise program if their specialist was out. If my action was challenged by staff because I was not a qualified specialist, I would counter with, "A session with me is better than canceling the client!" In my mind I was qualified by the decade of hands-on experience I had with Aaron and others.

I believed that canceling appointments was not an option. It was unacceptable for both the health of our clients and the health of the business.

An Unexpected Setback

After we had finally gotten into a good rhythm of operation and steady growth, Taylor was stricken with a serious illness that completely sidelined him for a long while.

Without Taylor and his clinical expertise with our staff and clients, I was terrified, with no idea how we were going to handle the business from a clinical perspective.

The answer to our problem came by way of another individual, similar to Taylor in demeanor and professionalism. He, too, possessed brilliance and a unique love of working with injury and illness. With him, our business could continue, without compromise. Our confidence was restored.

The new mode of operation was short-lived. The new hire wanted my chair. It was clear to me I was not wanted in the business. Nothing I did was right in his eyes. No matter what happened, who did or didn't do something, what system was in or was not in place, it was always communicated as "poor management" . . . and I was management.

Daily accusations of incompetence filled my ears.

I kept the troubles I was having to myself. Aaron had a packed plate with his responsibilities at C.O.R.E., training for the Paralympics and dealing with the mountainous challenges of his injury. I didn't want to burden him with more worries or distractions.

Wearing Down

C.O.R.E. was so much more than a business idea. It was our purpose, passion, and mission. Providing essential care to those who needed it was central to our pursuits and was the reconciliation of our lives having been reduced to ashes.

For months, that truth was the only thing that gave me the strength to step out of my car, after sitting in the parking lot on many mornings, contemplating my efforts. It's what gave me the stamina to put the key in the door to face another day of complaints, problems, and alleged management failures.

But . . . my sense of self began a slow erosion.

Chapter 35:

Season of Change

Two and a half years and a national championship later, Aaron discovered his absolute physical limits aboard a bicycle when his body refused his unrelenting demands. A rushed emergency room visit took the place of the World Cup Finals in Rome, Italy, thereby eliminating his Paralympic bid for the London games.

Although the Paralympic bid didn't turn out as Aaron and I had intended, I felt deep relief. I had witnessed a slow degeneration in his function, the very thing we had worked so hard for. He was sacrificing his hard-earned function for better performance on the bike.

No amount of pleading could alter his choice to grind himself into the ground. I know he felt a duality between sorrow and solace at the end of his cycling era. I believed, however, he found something much greater than a gold medal. He found his limit, in his quest to see just how far he could physically and mentally go in his pursuit of recovery from a spinal cord injury.

One evening, after returning home from a dinner with his girl-friend, Aaron leaned up against the kitchen counter, rubbed his hands together, with a look of tender contemplation, and asked me, "Toots, what am I going to do with this Katie girl?"

Up to that point, Aaron had been happy and satisfied with

how his life was evolving and didn't feel the need for a committed relationship.

A few months earlier Aaron had invited Katie to our home to meet me. I opened the door and was instantly struck by Katie's presence—a beautiful, chestnut-haired young woman with a broad smile and outstretched arms, and in her hands a lovely blue-and-white pottery bowl filled with a colorful salad. Her countenance spoke of confident grace. I knew Aaron would be reconsidering his previous view of his life.

As I observed Katie's gaze at Aaron, I sensed the deep love and respect she held for him. I saw her seeing beyond his injury—seeing only the fire in his heart. I was filled with grateful satisfaction for the new future of possibility that lay ahead for them.

An exquisite season of change was happening for our family. Arielle had entered her sacred journey of motherhood, welcoming her baby boy, James Michael Aaron, into the world, and Aaron had become engaged to the love of his life.

Arielle's tiny miracle connected her to the power of unconditional love. She and I now shared the privilege and appreciation of the joys and challenges of raising a child.

Amidst these milestones, Arielle and I reached back into our previous life, before Aaron's injury, and purchased a horse together, rekindling a bond that once united us. The horse and baby James created a new connection, becoming a source of mutual understanding and deeper love. Our relationship and our hearts began to heal, mending the Woolly Road behind us.

Stand

Possibility

Initiate

Reason

Intention

Part 6   Transform

Behind every story of success lies adaptation, revision, reinvention, and change—transforming adversity into opportunity.

Chapter 36:

The Abyss

I woke up one morning, just after it was decided that Katie was going to share our townhome with us, to a realization: I needed to find another place to live.

The three of us had discussed living together, not changing anything other than Katie moving in. This was an agreeable situation for each of us. As I continued thinking about this arrangement, a sense of the need for change took over. I knew Aaron and Katie needed the opportunity to allow their partnership to grow without the mother in the wings.

When they first met, Katie was completely unfamiliar with a living situation such as ours. She very graciously came to understand and respect how we operated. Neither she nor Aaron wanted to be the reason I felt I needed to relocate, nor were they.

The smallness of our townhome was a perfect nest for Aaron and me for many years, but it wasn't conducive to our growing family.

Initially I was going to take only my clothes and a few small items. I wanted to leave our townhome the way it was, mainly so it didn't feel like I was really moving. I was just going to spend nights somewhere else.

Once it was understood that I was moving and why, Aaron came to me and said he wanted to take my room, the master bedroom, causing me to rethink my strategy. I was trying to tiptoe out and tiptoe into a new space. This approach was so counter to how I had always taken on new challenges. I went either all-in or not at all. I was not all-in with this move, but I wasn't clear on why I was maneuvering in that way. I was a mess of contradicting emotions that clouded my ability to understand my personal dynamics.

I am certain I annoyed and confused Katie when I would leave with an art piece, book, or other item every time I came over to see them. Taking one item at a time was my only way of transitioning out.

Aaron and I still saw one another every day at C.O.R.E., but driving off at the end of the day in different directions brought forth an ache I was forced to face after suffering a complete emotional breakdown within a year of living alone for the first time in my life.

The Abyss

The constructs I'd held with such a tight fist since Aaron's injury had shattered, exposing my fears and vulnerabilities in ways I didn't know how to manage or even understand. The problem was me, and I had no idea what to do with *me*. I didn't resort to alcohol to escape, separating me from my pain, as I had in the past. But because of it, I hadn't embraced the nuances of grief necessary to surrender, accept the changes, and find understanding with them.

I hadn't allowed myself to grieve losses that began with leaving Carmel, divorcing Preston, Aaron's injury, Arielle's addiction, or the death of my mother. I'd forced myself to get up from the hospital floor and the ditch in Calexico without acknowledging and working through the emotional fractures.

My mind had done everything possible to avoid a reckoning. It confused and contradicted itself until I could no longer distinguish what was real from what was not. It had convinced me I was fine, when in fact I couldn't have been further from it.

Complicating my senses was the contradiction of all I had become through the process of recovery. I questioned why I was feeling so lost, alone, and suffocated by fear, while I had benefited in all the ways I knew I had.

The series of emotional traumas, the incessant probing, and self-eroding days at C.O.R.E., peppered with the drastic hormonal changes of menopause, fell on me like an avalanche, finally cracking the glass floor to the dark abyss I had run from for so many years. The walls crashed down without sound. I was rendered still, silent, catatonic.

A psychiatric ward provided the necessary shock to my system. I had watched my mother experience the very same thing when I was eleven years old. I had thrown open the curtains, letting light in for the first time when I went to see her while she lay in a darkened hospital room. For her, the sound of the closing barred metal doors at the mental institution she was transferred to was enough to snap her into courageous action.

An overwhelming sense of her presence enveloped me while I was in the hospital, the anniversary of her death date being on the second day of a three-day stay. I remembered how she summoned her inner strength to stand higher than the hole she was in. While walking back and forth in the sterile, institutional hallways, I was deep in heart conversation with her voice again in my ear: "You CAN do it, do you hear me!" She and her fierce spirit were with me, within me, reminding me of my long lineage of fortitude.

I now needed to open my own curtains, just as I had many years ago for my mother and for Larry.

The beautiful, sometimes necessary, aspect of hitting bottom is that there is something to push from. Once I had uncovered and accepted the source of my fall, I engaged in the process of gradually reconstructing my innermost self—with love and my *Why* guiding me. I began to release what was and embrace what is, without the anesthetizing effects of the former crutch of alcohol I had leaned so heavily upon during times of emotional duress.

I learned there is always a day of reckoning; issues of life events and the emotional tolls that come as a result will continue to surface and seek resolution, no matter how long they have been shoved into dark corners or stored on the shelves of your unconscious mind.

I began to start each day by making a list of all the things I was grateful for. As simple as this exercise may seem, it helped me in my release of past emotional traumas I had been holding on to and were holding me back. I made lists of each life-shifting event, beginning with leaving Carmel. I wrote the aspects I loved and cherished alongside the painful ones. A pros-and-cons kind of approach. Using logic rather than emotions, I slowly found clarity in my past and the necessity of each traumatic event.

Falling is the greatest thing that can happen to you—the key is to fall forward.

~ *Reflection*

My personal belongings and furnishings were all packed up and stored in a rural storage unit not far from my ranch in Oklahoma after Aaron's injury. Four years later, I waited outside as a pickup truck hauling a horse trailer rounded the corner, the head of one of my valuable Indian statues sticking out between the rungs of the trailer, pulling up to my door for delivery. As I was unloading the trailer that carried my priceless memories and cherished treasures, the stack of broken items continued to mount, while the stack of intact, unharmed pieces did not.

So many beautiful pieces of pottery and items from exotic locales, each a story in my life and of its own, were in hundreds of broken pieces. I simply could not find it in me to discard them—somehow that act would be discarding the time and memories themselves. So, I set out to put them all back together again, one piece at a time, a loving hand, a little glue, a lot of patience, and a sharp keen eye for detail. One by one I saved most of my precious art pieces, just as I saved my family and now myself . . . making whole what had been in ruins. The remaining seams and cracks of the broken pieces, painstakingly glued back together, provide me with the visual reminder today, lending yet another story in every art piece and my once broken life.

Chapter 37:

The Release

Our business grew, Taylor returned, and I had recaptured my energy and drive. Every story of trauma touched the easily accessible mind/ heart space that drew me to the work we did.

Seven years after opening our center, we moved into a location that was three times larger.

From the very beginning, the vision we had always shared with Taylor was to build a C.O.R.E. in every major city nationwide. Although we were committed to our goals, our plans and methods to see it through became vastly different. Our business partnership began to deteriorate due to these irreconcilable differences. The beautiful dream center we had raised out of the ashes of our personal ruin was in dire need of a change of direction.

Aaron, Katie, and I contemplated every possible scenario. We consulted with business confidants and sought legal counsel. Of all the difficult decisions I have had to make in my life, this was by far the most challenging. Our lives had been reconstructed with the glue of our vision, and yet we were at insurmountable odds with the future of our partnership with Taylor. Aaron and I are the best versions of ourselves when we are growing and evolving. The very best times, and working together with Taylor, were behind us—it was time to release them.

With the stroke of a pen, we sold our majority share of the business to Taylor. A blank canvas, a world of new possibilities, awaited right outside the office doors. The course of our lives had just changed, again.

Awaken your spirit to adventure, hold nothing back, learn to find ease and courage in risk; soon you will discover a new rhythm. Your new canvas is awaiting you.

Of all that C.O.R.E. purported to become, what it meant to me is inextinguishable. The idea itself propelled me and my efforts when I grew tired and weary or had lost the ability to navigate myself. The "Door Effect" provided light when my way ahead darkened. Giving it up felt like the death of a sacred part of me, but knowing Taylor would be at that location for the rest of his days was comforting.

Although we didn't realize our vision of multiple locations of C.O.R.E., our influence by example is far reaching. Today there are similar gyms all over the world. The opportunities for quality-of-life improvement after a disabling injury or illness continue to flourish. Stories of individuals coming back from injury, and achieving the most remarkable feats, are more commonplace. None of this existed when Aaron was first injured. Similar to Hands Across America, each story of triumph joins another, creating a force of hope and possibility that inspires all.

Chapter 38:

The Golden Thread

A few months before I resigned from my position at C.O.R.E., I was introduced to a man I would never have met if not for many divine synchronicities, too many to describe. He, like we, had suffered a life-altering accident some months prior.

Up to that point I was fully committed to my life alone, with no desire to have anyone try to step into the sacred cocoon I shared with my children and their families. I had no interest in what I perceived as another responsibility, or worse, another heartbreak. I enjoyed the superficial pleasures of coming and going that dating offered, here and there.

Much to my surprise, Hans and our soulful connection changed my mind. Our shared experiences brought us together in poignant ways that only those who have experienced similar events can truly understand.

Two months into our relationship I saw Hans's heart when he demonstrated a depth of understanding and love that transcended the short period of time he had known me. I told him about Aaron being invited to the Red Bull headquarters in Vienna, Austria, on behalf of his position as Ambassador for their Wings for Life Foundation. This was an enormously special invitation for Aaron. Hans immediately declared that I had to be there to meet Aaron. He knew my love of travel and that this would be my first trip abroad since Aaron's accident.

On a rainy morning in Vienna, Aaron, Katie, Hans, and I marked a new chapter in our lives. Remarkably, it coincided with the twentieth anniversary of Aaron's injury as we stood hugging, laughing, with tears of happiness flowing, on a street corner in the richly storied city.

Together, Hans and I have created a life of love, family, travel, and adventure, with mutual understanding and deep respect. He says I helped him get his life back—and I discovered safety and security in the loving heart he offered me.

After having life cave in on me several times, I had no structural stability. I had become accustomed to living on the fault lines. These fault lines have slowly solidified, giving me a strong, sturdy foundation from which to enjoy this stage of my life. Instead of looking over my shoulder and expecting the next hard hit, I now look ahead with a sense of confidence and pride.

Each person in my family has been positively impacted in unique ways by Hans's steady hand. What I treasure most about Hans's generous spirit and kind heart is the way he embraces us as his own.

Contemplation

As I sit in reflection, I marvel at *How* Aaron, Arielle, and I have endured all these years. What I recognize is that there has been a golden thread woven through our adversity, the same thread that weaves throughout my different life phases—my *Why*.

Aaron

Aaron has become the master weaver of the work he wholeheartedly embraces and continues to cultivate. Through his adversity, he has discovered a profound purpose and deep passion for helping empower others to live the highest version of themselves. He shares, teaches, and exemplifies his optimistic truth: even on the darkest days, we hold the power in our mind to overcome anything.

Aaron and Katie live intentionally and have created together their most beloved masterpiece, their daughter, Cayla Mae. After her birth, he confided in me, "Now I get it, Toots. I now understand the power of unconditional love. I will move mountains for her sake."

I remember the first time Aaron told me, many years ago, "Toots, I am okay with this injury, and I wouldn't change one thing. I need you to be okay too." I was stunned by his truth. My truth is that I will never be fully okay with it. While I treasure, with awed respect, who he is and all that he has become, I abhor the suffering he bears, every day. I've come to believe that the real victory is his willingness to persist despite the spinal cord injury and its wicked grip.

Arielle

Arielle found her purpose in motherhood—her two sons, James and Mason, are guiding lights in her once dark world. She nurtures them with the same fierce love and strength she inherited. She and Jimmy have manifested the life she always dreamed of—a family and a thriving business born from her passion for horses.

A full-circle validation comes by way of a review written by the mother of one her young clients, "Of all the things I love about Arielle, my favorites are her ability to get my son to see the value in hard work and believing in himself."

She utilizes her experience with addiction to mentor and guide others that struggle with its potent grasp, all while holding herself accountable to her commitment.

James, Mason, and Cayla Mae

With the arrival of my grandchildren, I feel like I am experiencing the joys of parenthood all over again. It's like a time machine that transports me back to those treasured years as a young mother, offering a broadened perspective to relive the magic of childhood with wisdom and patience that come with age.

I love seeing the resemblances and the differences between my children and theirs. As much as I cherish my invaluable alone time with each grandchild, I truly get as much pleasure watching Aaron being a daddy and Arielle being a momma. I suppose it will forever be a little surreal to me in the most grateful and beloved ways.

They all remind me just how fleeting life is, the importance of savoring the time we have and how today's actions will have a lasting impact on their future.

While this story is a culmination of what my family and I have done, striving to apply all the knowledge, wisdom, and learned approaches to better navigate the fluctuations of life's ebb and flow . . . is what we do.

As is well-known—the only constant in life is change.

Epilogue

We all know that the journey of life is not an easy one. It requires self-inquiry, introspection, and a willingness to persevere beyond our preconceived limits. It is the power of love and our *Why* that propels us forward. The spirit within will guide and show you how.

My family, my *Why*, has been my anchor, the powerful force that stood me up from the hospital floor and pulled me upright from the ditch. It is the pavement on the road behind me and it paves my road ahead.

It is only through fire and pressure that a gemstone is created. I've come to make friends with the fires of life, knowing they are serving me and those I love. Everything happens for you, not to you. I honor the teachings and strive to keep the knowledge alive and well during times of ease. Time does have its way of diminishing the perspectives gained by the life fire once it has been reduced to smoke and ashes. As in anything worthwhile in life, it takes daily attention, care, and commitment. I have a deepened belief now that purpose, strategy, and action can help you climb out of any ditch you may find yourself in.

The act of lifting another, especially in times of need, can inspire us to become better versions of ourselves. The idea of our actions positively affecting another is a reminder that our actions matter—by lifting others, we lift ourselves.

I offer my story with the hope that you recognize yourself reflected in it. When we look into the mirror of another person, we see not only ourselves but a shared humanity that connects us all.

There are two ways of spreading light: to be the candle or the mirror that reflects it.

Love is the candle.

As Frankl writes: "There is nothing in the world, I venture to say, that would so effectively help one to survive even the worst conditions as the knowledge that there is meaning in one's life."

I did not find meaning in the material realm. Meaning found me in what was left when everything else was stripped away. For my family, our love and the soul-stirring impact we have on each other was *How* we did and will forever—*Rise Together.*

In~Spirit,

Laquita Rian

Closing Note

Despite all the unlikely and remarkable victories that I shared with my son, the fact remains, he lives with a spinal cord injury that never releases its wicked grip.

I pray to the powers that be, every day, that the minds and funding behind science WILL develop treatments to relieve some of the suffering he, the hundreds of thousands of others, and those who love them endure.

That is when I will truly have satisfaction and peace in my heart.

Scan the QR code and head to
laquitadian.com/photo-gallery for this book's
complementary photo gallery!

Acknowledgments

I dedicate this book to my children and their families ~ Who I am today has been shaped by the life experiences we've shared. Aaron and Arielle, we have scaled our mountains, individually and together, each of us becoming more than we ever thought possible. Words fall short of my gratitude and love for you. I am mostly proud of the immense contributions to humanity you both give today. Both of you catalyzed your adversities into a purposeful existence that would have otherwise remained undiscovered. I know, through your demonstrated efforts, that I have done something really right in my life by bringing you into the world. We not only rise together . . . we rise above.

Aaron ~ Walt Whitman's classic quote says it best: "Allons! Whoever you are, come travel with me! Traveling with me you find what never tires!" For your entire life, you have paved your own road, your way. Yes, son, traveling with you, one never tires. Your luminous soul and resilient champion spirit serve as a guiding lighthouse, illuminating paths for others, most notably for your daughter. Thank you with all my heart for wanting me to stay with you during the most tragic years of your life, sharing in the setbacks and the comebacks. You say you are here today because of me; I say I am here today because of you.

Arielle ~ Sharing the messy stuff in life is a sign of profound personal growth and reflects the true depth of an individual. Your willingness to do so in our story exemplifies this. I am in awe and so proud of your strength. You are, without a doubt, one of the strongest women I have ever known. You achieve everything you put your mind to while carrying the family torch for your sons with fierce power and grace. Your book is next! The world needs to hear your wisdom because, angel cake, you are full of jewels.

Katelyn ~ I honor the woman, wife, and mother you are. My son gained a wife, and I gained another daughter. You are everything, and more, that I ever wanted and wished for Aaron and for me. You have my sincerest gratitude and respect.

Jimmy ~ I have always admired how you set your mind on something and do it, wholeheartedly. Thank you for being that example for James and Mason. I honor and love the family unit you and Arielle have built.

My grandchildren ~ You are kind, you are smart, and you are important. You three are extremely fortunate to have your parents as examples of resilience and fortitude to tackle all the life challenges you are sure to face. When you're a little older, may the stories in this book remind you that when life gets hard, you can find ways to handle it and benefit from it, when you reach inside. As Uncle AA/Daddy says, "The only difference between you and the happiest person in the world is the six inches between your ears . . . it's all in your mind and up to you."

James ~ You introduced me to my next-level love! I love seeing the world through your eyes, ducking with you, reading, hiking, exploring, and enjoying our kitchen time. You are exhilarating and will do anything and everything you want in life.

Mason ~ You are one of the kindest, smartest little guys around and a chef in the making! I treasure our shared love of the kitchen and all the planning and shopping we do together to present a quality meal. You are wise beyond your years, and I know you will do amazing things in your life.

Cayla Mae ~ You come from long lines of strong women, baby girl. I can see you already know that by the fire and light in your eyes. I love your fierce little spirit and your boundless curiosity. The world is yours, sweet angel, and I know you will make an important, distinct mark on it.

I hope the three of you never stop running to me when we see one another! You fill my heart with sunshine and all that's magical in life. Thank you for loving me like you do and letting me love you like crazy!

To my mother, Barbara Ann aka Bobbie ~ You were and are a light-house beacon of strength and spunk for me. I'll never forget when we first moved from Oklahoma to California. I was eight years old. Just days after moving into our new house, the girl next door, a few years older, pushed me into the street in front of an oncoming car. I, of course, was scared to death and crying Instead of consoling me, you took me into the house and proceeded to teach me how to fight! You then said, "Now get out there and tell that girl to never push you around again!" Mother, that example of not backing down served me well. I'll see you again one day; for now, your love and sparkling spirit live on within me.

To my father, Kenneth Roger aka Kennie ~ You inspired all the reflections I shared in these pages for the sake of describing my nature and where it came from. You were my first hero: at times I even thought you were bigger than Elvis himself! I am grateful for inheriting some of your qualities I admire the most. I always get tickled when I think of the first words of wisdom you said to me years and years

ago: "Sugar, if ya ain't the lead dog, the scenery never changes."
Well, Dad, that dog has led me down some wild Woolly Roads,
and your influence gave me the courage to not let go of the reins.

To my brothers, Kenny, Keith, and Kevin ~ Being the oldest of all of
us, I learned how to mother and protect my family through you.
Kenny, you are our rock of love and encouragement. I will always
have your back, brother. Keith and Kevin, you both are flying free
from all that shackled you. I'll see you again one day, and we'll have
even more fun than we used to.

My sister, Julia Anna ~ With fifteen years between us, you were my
first baby. The woman and mother you are is remarkable. Out of
five of us, you are the only one with a college degree—and now a
PhD in the making! I think you learned what to do and what not to
do really well being the youngest of our bunch. Our mother would
always say, "She was so proud she couldn't see straight," when we
garnered her approval—darling, we are all so proud of you we can't
see straight! I love you all to pieces.

Gratitude flows to my diverse and vibrant extended family ~ Embrac-
ing the essence of America, with roots reaching from Norwegian,
German, and English immigrants to Native Americans, ranchers,
farmers, cowboys, roughnecks, consummate professionals, along
with a sprinkling of wild seeds for good measure! Y'all's teachings,
memories, and spirits are alive and well within me. I love and thank
each one of you for your unique mark on my life.

To my Earth Angels ~ As a single mother, I was mostly alone after
Aaron's injury, but with what I refer to as my Earth Angels, I did
not feel alone. They shared their love, support, and encouragement
during times when I needed it the most. Each one helped keep me

lifted in their special ways. Without them, I don't think I could have successfully navigated the immense challenges life gave me.

Aunt Neta Irwin and Uncle Rick LaGuardia ~ You are forever held in a sacred space in my heart. A mere thank-you does not convey the depth of feeling I have for your immense contributions to the quality of our lives.

Taylor-Kevin Isaacs ~ In our early days there was God and there was you, and there was no difference between the two for me. Our best days together are unmatched, and your time, expertise, and care are ineradicable.

Lynn Lupetti and Edward Lohmann ~ Your encouragement has been the symphony that lifted my spirits, and your friendship is a most cherished verse. I'll always hold the memory of your taking me to see Andrea Bocelli in concert deep in my heart. Once in the concert hall, we walked down to the third row, center seat, and you handed me my ticket. You then went to your seats much farther back. Thank you for your special way of loving me.

Jeffrey Fergeson ~ Wherever you are, I'm sure you are throwing glitter in the air. Thank you for sprinkling a little of it on me. And to Dave Crook, your big, generous heart will be felt forever. Your impact on me and my family's lives is as big as your heart.

To all the clients and friends I had the privilege of working with and getting to know during some of their most heartbreaking and difficult times ~ I will never forget you. A piece of my heart is embedded within the walls of C.O.R.E.

To my publishing team ~ We did in fact rise it together! Without all of you and your expertise, this book would not have come to be. The number of pages I wrote and then threw away could fill several trash cans. I am indebted to a select group of artists and scribes, whose collective brilliance has illuminated these pages.

Aaron Baker ~ You led the way with *The Rebellious Recovery*, taking our life and shaping it into cohesion, making my task much easier. Your impressive array of talents includes the artistry of being a gifted wordsmith. You are not only a main player in the story, but also a major part of how it's told. I cherish our time across the table from each other, scheming, planning, and then doing.

Katelyn Baker ~ Condensing the layers of my experiences into a compelling front-cover subtitle eluded me. When we were talking about it one day and you offered up "the art of climbing out of the ditch," shivers went down my spine. Those words are the perfect summation and what I aim to convey. Thank you for your immense contribution.

Kory Kirby ~ You are a maestro, a word alchemist, and a skilled craftsman. You "got me," guided me, helped develop the story, and put up with all the changing drafts—fifteen in total! You went over and beyond, wearing more hats than you usually do, to help craft this book of my heart in words. You made a cathartic, sometimes really hard process, enjoyable. I am so grateful Aaron found you in his search for the perfect publishing partner—we have a bright future ahead of us together. I thank you entirely. Salute.

To dedicated copyeditors James Gallagher and Adeline Hull ~ Your meticulous attention to detail and linguistic finesse transformed my manuscript into a polished piece of work I am very proud of. Your commitment to excellence has left a permanent mark on this book.

Melanie Manson ~ The creative genius behind the camera. Your husband and my dear friend, Christopher Voelker, shared his gifts with you well. Your photograph captured my spirit and set the tone just right.

To all my beta readers ~ Whose time, heart, and feedback were critical in shaping this story. Thank you for being a part of its realization and for believing in it! Arielle Baker, Katelyn Baker, Julia Monroe, Debra Eve, Lynn Lupetti, Carmen Hagevort, Stephanie Kish Packebush, Carol Noble, Lori Irwin Untalan, Michelle Marsh, Michelle Gruber, Debbie Spector, Deborah Flynn, Ron and Alexandra Seigel, Shelley Kelly, Shelley Carlson, Emi Pastor, and Dr. Kathleen Slijepcevic.

And to my last-life-chapter love ~ Hans-Juergen Stangl, from the moment I first saw you in a photograph, several years before meeting you, I was drawn to you. Fate and angels brought us together. With you, I feel secure enough to finally write and share this story. *Ich liebe dich fur immer, mein liebling. Danke von ganzem Herzen.*

About the Author

Laquita Dian is a dynamic woman. Native to Oklahoma, she moved to Carmel on the Monterey Peninsula of California in the early eighties. Here she raised her two children while working as an executive buyer, sales manager, and lead designer curating an extensive collection of antiquities, fine art, oriental rugs, and treasures from around the world for a high-end antique gallery. Laquita is well traveled; fluent in foreign lands, arts, and the people who inhabit them; and respected by foreign nationalists she has conducted business with. In the late nineties, Laquita's world was reshaped when her son suffered a catastrophic, disabling spinal cord injury. Simultaneously, her daughter fell into the grip of self-destruction. She embraced the role as a caregiver and earned decades of hands-on experience with trauma recovery. She managed a cross-country tandem bike tour for her disabled son and rode part-time while also securing fundraising events, speaking engagements, sponsorship appearances, and media coverage. The following year, she managed a second cross-country bike tour, but rode full-time beside her son the four thousand miles across America. Laquita co-founded and served as CEO of the Center of Restorative Exercise (C.O.R.E.), a specialized gym focused on helping improve the quality of life for those who suffer a disabling condition. She sold C.O.R.E in 2019. Now a mentor, public speaker, and author residing in Los Angeles, she enjoys time with her two children, three grandchildren, and her partner, Hans.